Kiri Te Kanawa
with
Conrad Wilson

R *LOVERS*

Roeder Publications Pte. Ltd,
179 River Valley Road #02-08
Singapore 179033

Colour separation by Daiichi Process Pte. Ltd.
Printed in Singapore by Craft Print Pte. Ltd.

ISBN : 981-00-7833-1

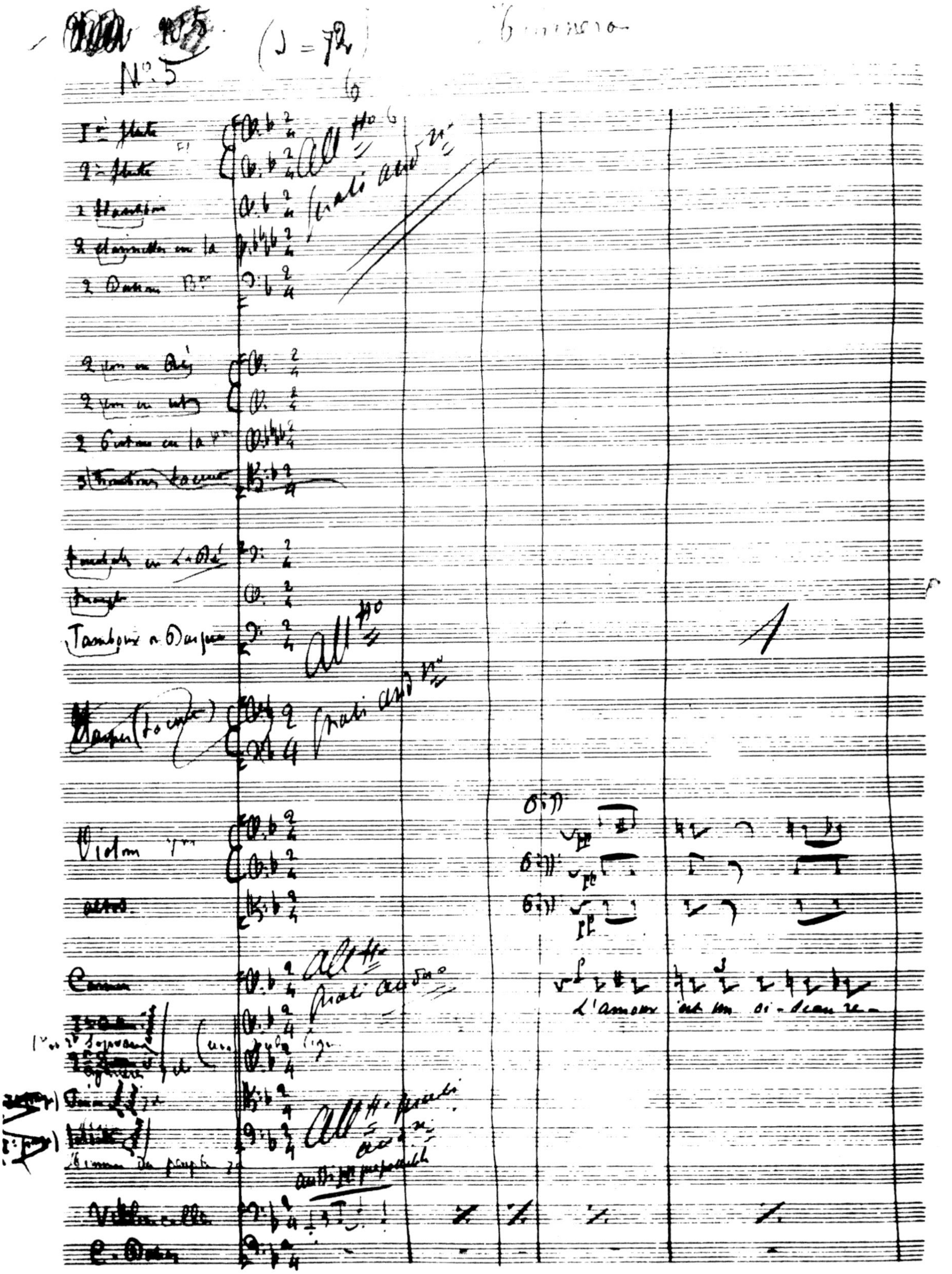
N° 5
L'amour est un oi-seau re

Contents

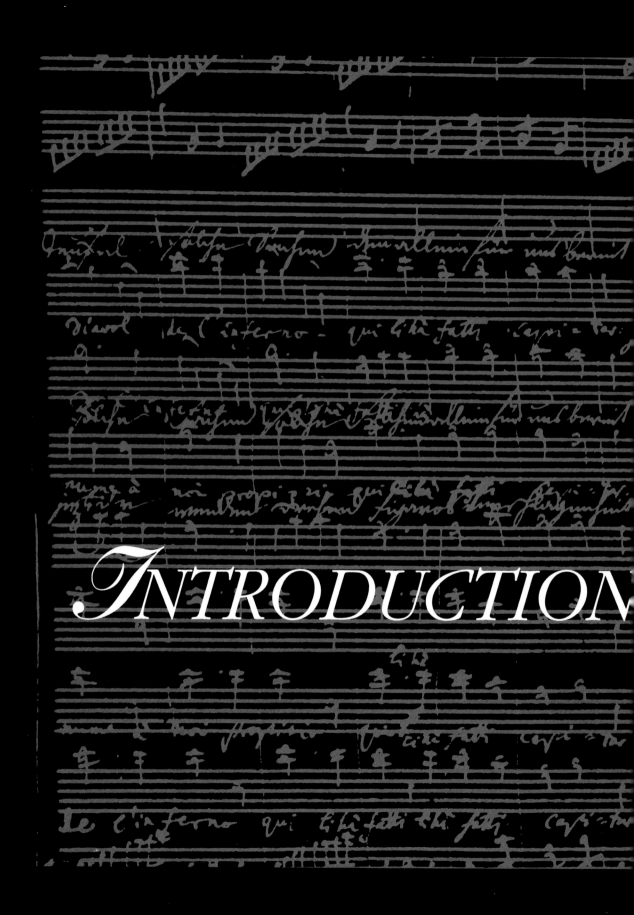

INTRODUCTION

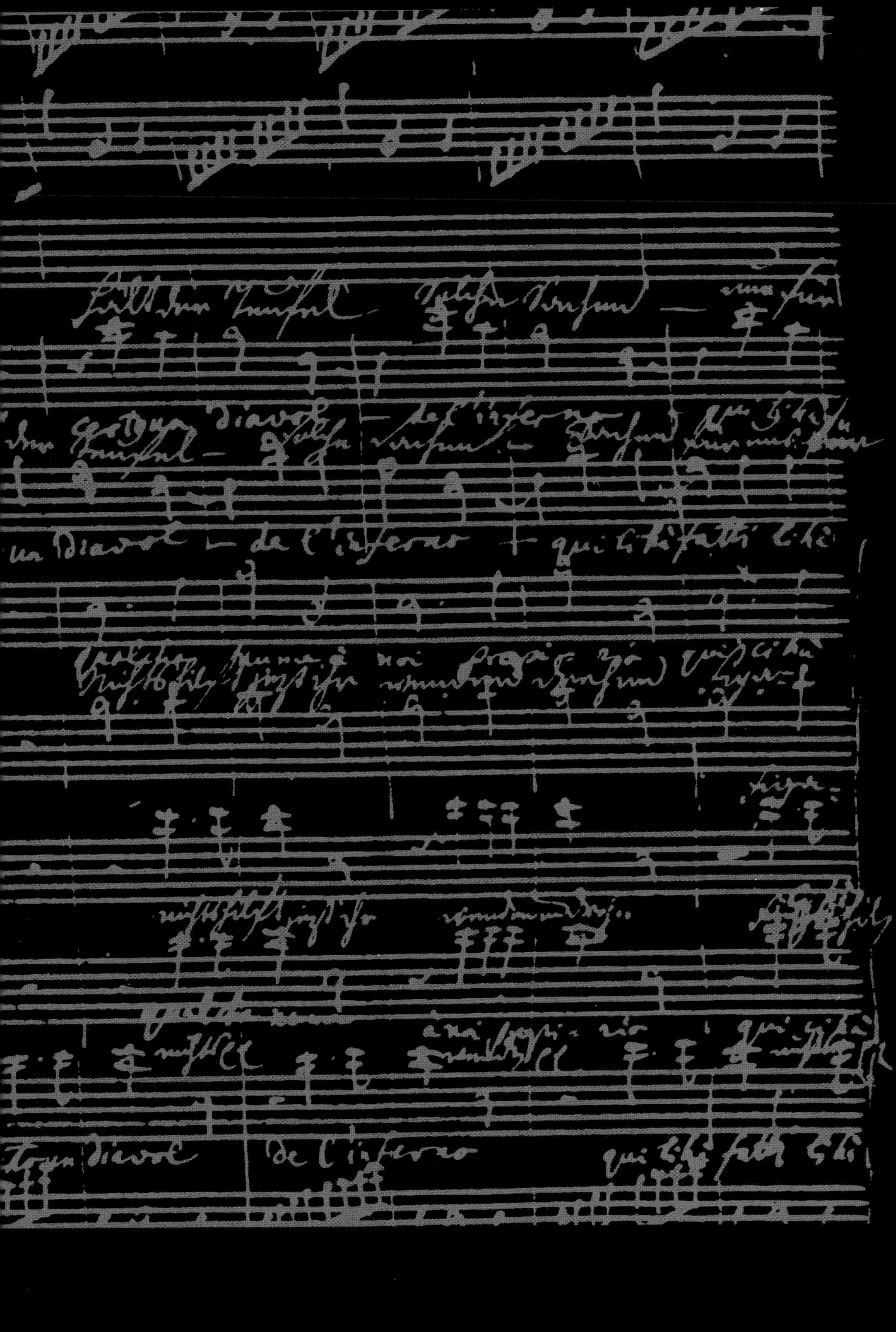

PROLOGUE

*B*ernard Levin, in a statement with which stern critics suddenly reveal themselves to be reckless romantics, once declared that when he dies, the word 'Kiri' would be found engraved upon his heart. Where the contrapuntal splendour of Bach, and the subtle half-lights of Debussy's Pelléas et Mélisande, had for years famously failed to touch him, the sound of a young New Zealand soprano singing Mozart wholly besotted him. To his ears, Kiri Te Kanawa was one of the three or four outstanding singers in the world, her voice the loveliest of them all. Of the men who were her equals, only Placido Domingo, he asserted, caressed the heart and the hearing with such intensity of joy and passion; among the women, not even Montserrat Caballé in her prime could be considered a match for her.

That was more than twenty years ago. Kiri herself was then a little over thirty. But at Covent Garden she had already sung her first Countess in Le Nozze di Figaro, and at the New York Metropolitan her first Desdemona in Otello. She has been hailed as the first Maori singer to achieve world status. Even today, in spite of her fame, people continue to mispronounce her name (the accent is on the first syllable, as in Panama).

Yet it is a name - meaning 'skin' or 'bark' - that is striking enough to have stood her in good stead. Nobody who watched her fiftieth birthday appearance on television will forget how she began with a quote from La Bohème. 'Mi chiamano Mimi', she confided, 'but you may call me Kiri.' In compliance with the suggestion, that is what I shall call her in the following pages. It was how she signed herself in correspondence before I met her, and it was what I found myself immediately calling her during the days of conversations that form the basis of this book.

But hers was not the first Maori name to have drawn attention to itself on a British operatic cast list. Inia Te Wiata, born in just as unknown a part of New

Zealand thirty years before her, had paved the way. After a limited career in his homeland, he became aware that, if he was to make headway as an international baritone, he would have to come to Europe. As Kiri herself would later do, he moved to London, continued his studies and won fame at Covent Garden. But though Don Carlos, Falstaff and Boris Godunov were to be his big roles - he died during rehearsals for a production of Mussorgsky's opera in 1971 - he often seemed happier as the endearing rascal Don Alfonso in Scottish Opera's Così fan tutte in 1967.

Kiri appeared destined from the start for the big roles, as that same visionary Scottish company, by inviting her to sing Desdemona in 1972, was uncannily quick to recognise. By then she had been in London for five years, initially to receive operatic grooming, with her mother as chaperon. The celebrated Vera Rozsa, in an act of instinctive inspiration, had accepted her as a pupil. And though going to all-night parties at that time seemed more inviting to Kiri than the drudgery, as she saw it, of the London Opera Centre, she was soon appearing in a variety of roles, among them Elena in Rossini's La Donna Del Lago at the Camden Festival, which led to her first triumph as the Countess in Figaro at Covent Garden.

The girl who had been brought up in New Zealand's emotively named Poverty Bay was by then clearly on her way. Her father and mother, Tom and Nell Te Kanawa, may not have been her natural parents - these she never knew, having been given up for adoption at birth - but they had cared for her deeply, and were of the same Maori and European mix. Though it was no secret that they had really wanted to adopt a boy, they agreed finally to accept a girl. Above all, they encouraged her to sing and were prepared to move to Auckland so that she could study music more seriously at a convent school under a dedicated teacher, Sister Mary Leo. Her options at the time - a choice between her interest in religion and her ability to make strong men weep with her singing of *Ave Maria* in Auckland's dinner dance clubs - seemed to carry a considerable whiff of Massenet's operatic penchant for the mingling of saintliness and sin.

From the prospect of a career in a place 'where every man sat with his own bottle of whisky in front of him', she was rescued by the New Zealand Arts

Council amongst others, who funded her move to Britain and her study at the London Opera Centre. Though not without an element of risk - would someone who at the time so conspicuously lacked self-discipline fulfil such a magisterial belief in her? - this was scarcely a shot in the dark. Already she had won all the main singing prizes in the Southern hemisphere, but she needed the right conditions in which her voice and personality could blossom. London gave her these, though not without initial misgivings on the part of her metropolitan teachers, who thought that she lacked a sense of application and that an element of frivolous antipodean impulsiveness might seriously damage her prospects.

She was certainly - then - impulsive. Having met an Australian mining engineer called Desmond Park on a blind date in London at the age of 23, she married him three months later. Yet the impulse was proved right. Not only are they still happily married, but her husband's keen business sense and organizational ability were just what suited her. 'With Des', she was to report later, 'I knew I was on the right road, so any conflict in me stopped. I knew if I was going to do it, I had to do it well. He would come home and ask how much I had done during the day. He knew I was a pretty wild character who just wanted a good time.'

Without her husband's support, she admits, she may not have lived up to the challenge of the London Opera Centre - 'I was a manic late arriver and I would not learn my music' - yet after three years of the Centre's four-year training period she was told by the director, James Robertson, that she knew all they had to teach her. Auditions at Covent Garden, though more protracted than someone of Kiri's dynamism had patience for, were thereafter similarly favourable. As Sir Colin Davis, in the process of casting FIGARO, was to put it: 'I just could not believe my ears the first time I heard her. I had to check that it was not a fluke performance but the truly remarkable voice it seemed.'

Kiri herself now says that, though the star role of the Countess was her ambition, she would have been perfectly happy to sing the minor role of Barbarina, the gardener's daughter, just to get into that Covent Garden production of FIGARO. The long preparation for the role was the turning point in her career. Her knowledge of the Countess' two great arias expanded into growing comprehension of the opera's ensembles and recitatives. Familiarity with the music brought an increasingly closer and closer identification with the personality of the unloved wife whose husband, under her very eyes, was pursuing her own chambermaid.

As a spirited New Zealander, Kiri could recognise that behind the Countess' veil of sadness lay at least remnants of the sparkle that had attracted Count Almaviva to his young Countess Rosina in the first place. These she was able to exploit with a characteristic vivacity; but the Countess, as she soon discovered, had opened the door for her to a type of role that would form the basis of her operatic portrait gallery. It would include Donna Elvira in DON GIOVANNI, Fiordiligi in COSÌ FAN TUTTE, the Marschallin in DER ROSENKAVALIER, the title role in ARABELLA, the Countess in CAPRICCIO, Amelia in SIMON BOCCANEGRA, Desdemona in OTELLO, Micaela in CARMEN and Tatyana in EUGENE ONEGIN.

All these operatic women, whether or not they were grief-stricken, were in varying degrees proud, dignified, trustful, and vulnerable. Hers, it has been said, is a repertoire of discretely tragic heroines, few of whom actually die (Desdemona being one exception) but most of whom suffer in one way or another, even in the midst of comedy.

Her Donna Elvira, in this respect, has become increasingly multifaceted, eccentric, pathetic, funny. Even her Pamina in DIE ZAUBERFLÖTE appeared to carry a weight of emotional experience that made her girlish freshness all the more touching. Her Arabella, the older sister awaiting and finding the right man, seemed instinctively aware that everything might go wrong. Her Countess Almaviva with which, above all, we now associate her, is another woman of experience, whose music nevertheless demands sustained beauty of tone and considerable physical stamina.

These roles, in the past, were Elisabeth Schwarzkopf's and Elisabeth Soderstrom's territory and, along with Strauss' ARABELLA, were a feature of Lisa Della Casa's flowing operatic career. They have been described as 'boudoir' roles, and Kiri Te Kanawa's gold and silver timbres - 'not a note scooped or

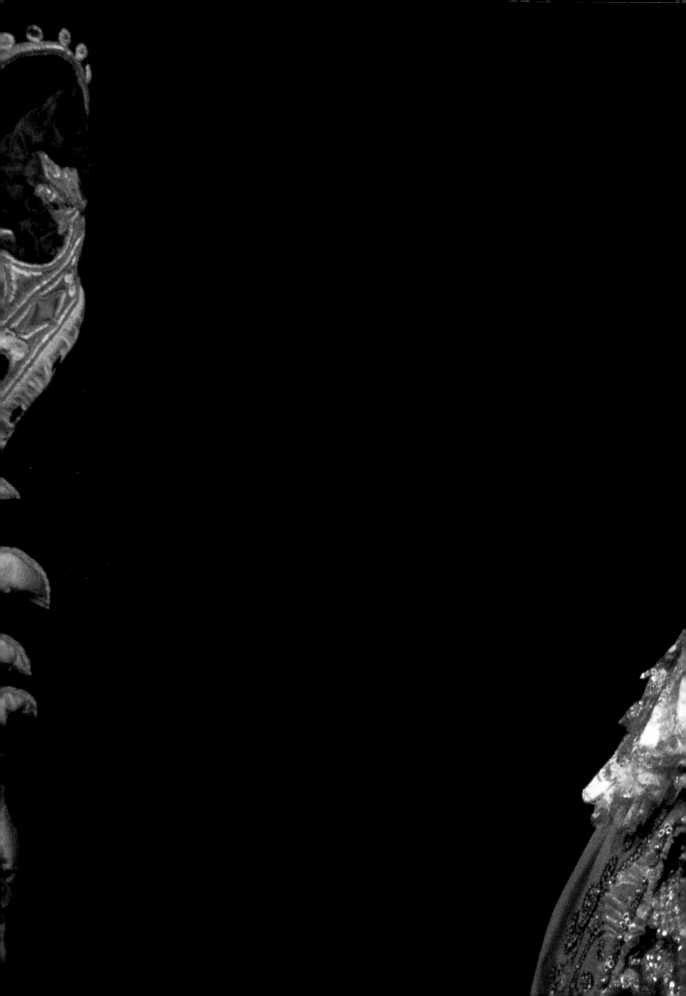

slurred, not a stress misplaced', as Bernard Levin put it in 1976 - have maintained the predominantly Viennese tradition to which these characters belong, though she has never thought of herself as another Schwarzkopf.

The sound - her own sound - is still there for all to hear. Her stamina is secured by daily exercise. Her diet includes a wide range of health food, and she exercises daily. She plays golf regularly. Golf, indeed, may one day replace singing, so clearly does she enjoy it. She normally relaxes in shorts and trainers and looks relaxed and trim. Repose, one suspects, does not suit her. Long interviews tire her quicker than physical effort. 'You come to me armed with questions', she said in exhaustion towards the end of one of our longer sessions, 'but I have to keep supplying the answers.' A few minutes later she had changed into gym gear and with the thought of an imminent vocal and physical work-out, seemed wholly regalvanised.

Yet what she says in the course of a taxing interview is almost invariably alive and responsive, revealing her own distinct, often amusing, point of view. Though she admits to being a slow learner - it took her a year to master CAPRICCIO and learning ROSENKAVALIER was 'dreadfully difficult' - she gets there in the end, and the results seem all the better for the effort that has gone into them. The snide, and much quoted, remark that she would rather talk about shopping or mowing the lawn than about music originated from Kiri herself, and it was typically self-disparaging.

Few singers, in my experience, really enjoy talking about music - as opposed to their next operatic dates and recording sessions - and Kiri is one of them. True, she is easily distracted. If you are interviewing her, mugs of tea or glasses of juice will be offered. Lunch break - smoked salmon or something similarly calorie-conscious - comes early. The afternoon is a short one. Yet while you are with her she concentrates on her answers, treats them seriously, takes time to think about them and double-checks if you have worded them ambiguously.

Her appearance at the wedding of Prince Charles and Lady Diana at St. Paul's Cathedral in 1981 brought in its wake not only the title of Dame (making her a successor to Nellie Melba, Clara Butt and Janet Baker) but even greater public prominence, wonderful in one way, dangerous in another, when you consider that more than 800 million people were watching her.

An experience she once had, when a determined fan turned up unexpectedly at her doorstep, troubled her deeply, for she is a very private person. She says that the words, 'I am your greatest fan', are the scariest words in the English language (Prince Charles, at least, called himself no more than 'one of' her greatest fans). She has two children whom - repeating personal history - she adopted after suffering two miscarriages, and she has protected them assiduously, right into their teenage years.

Yet when she sang Händel's *Let the bright Seraphim* at the royal wedding - and was compared to an 'illuminated opal fruit' - she extended her international appeal in a way which, so far, has done her nothing but good. Moreover, it reminded her that the singing of arias - with which, in her schooldays, her musical career began - could continue to be a valuable part of her career, to which, as the years pass, she is increasingly returning. Publicly addressing her at the end of her mammoth fiftieth birthday celebration at the Royal Albert Hall in London, Clive James said: 'Your voice is from heaven but your feet are on the ground.' As a mid-life tribute from a fellow antipodean, it could not have been more appropriate.

Conrad Wilson

DRESS

REHEARSAL

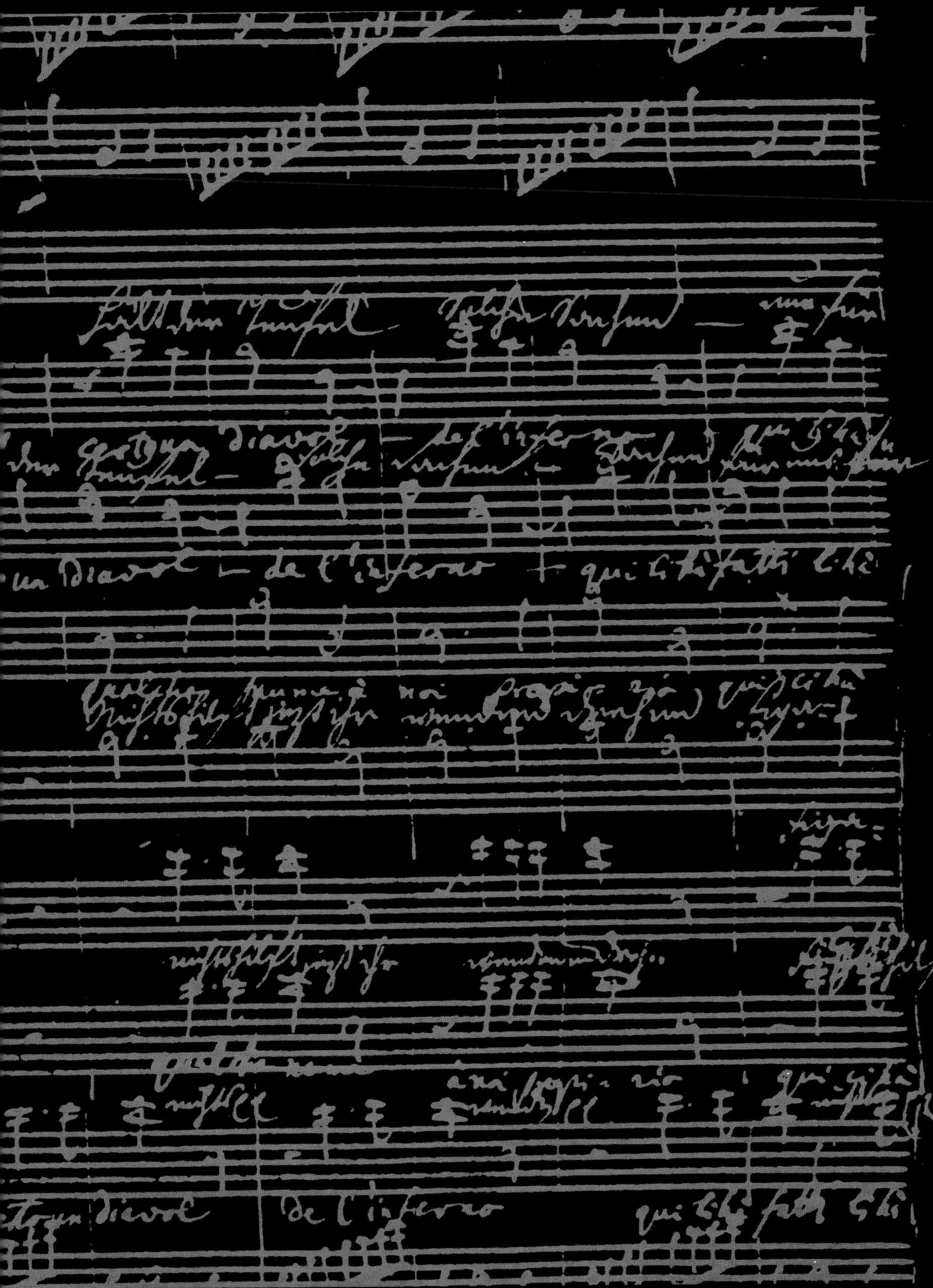

THE LOVE OF MUSIC

The gala premiere, with its swishing gowns, brilliant jewels and expensive tickets, in my experience, is rarely attended by many music-lovers. The devoted audiences, who deeply care about opera, often feel excluded on those evenings. Although the dress rehearsal might have given us performers an indication of the success of the production, I cannot gauge from the applause I get as a singer on that first night how I am doing. Most of these people are there to enjoy the glitter and glamour of the gala night. It is only thereafter, when the true opera-fans attend, that I receive feedback on my staging. Personally, I prefer to sing for audiences who care about the performance.

My love of music was instilled by my mother. Initially, she pushed me into singing, but in retrospect I feel that I was destined for a life of music anyway. I appreciate that my parents gave up so much to enable me to pursue my career, and I feel sorry for my mother who died too soon to see the results of all her hard labour.

If my mother taught me to work on my talent, my father gave me the confidence to realise this dream. He was a wonderful man. I was his pride and joy, and I could never do wrong in his eyes, no matter what I did. He simply loved me the way I was.

The very first singing teacher I had was Sister Mary. She was a nun in New Zealand and a wonderful person. She nurtured my

PAGES 16-17: *Kiri Te Kanawa taking her curtain call in John Schlesinger's production of* DER ROSENKAVALIER *at the Royal Opera House, Covent Garden in 1985. Photography by Zoë Dominic.*

voice, and taught me never to exert it. I sang in the school choir, which staged special performances twice a year, when we would get up on the platform dressed like vestal virgins. One year I was given the famous solo in the Nuns' Chorus from CASANOVA, and received many nasty, envious looks as a result - one of those things you do not forget.

Sister Mary enabled me to miss classes so that I could study music. I can now see that I might have been good at many subjects, languages, arts and crafts, which I never got a chance to study. I never received the formal education my parents sent me to school for. But I learned to express myself through song.

It was through Sister Mary's perseverance - and that of my parents - that I finally left New Zealand for London, where I was taken on as a pupil by Vera Rozsa almost thirty years ago. Like the conductor Georg Solti, she is Hungarian, and working with these two fabulous people has been essential to my musical career and a source of immeasurable joy in the bargain. Both Rosza and Solti have dedicated their lives to music. There is nothing more important than music in their lives, nothing else comes close.

Praise would come from Rosza sparingly but I have never looked to her for praise. All I have needed to know throughout my career is that I am singing as well as I can and that I am still in good shape. Vera has always made sure of that.

To start with, I went to Rosza for an hour a week, which was all I could afford. As a student, I had a scholarship of about ten pounds to spend each week, and four of them went to Vera. When I had more money, I started to have two-hour lessons. Then I went more and more often. I still need to see her.

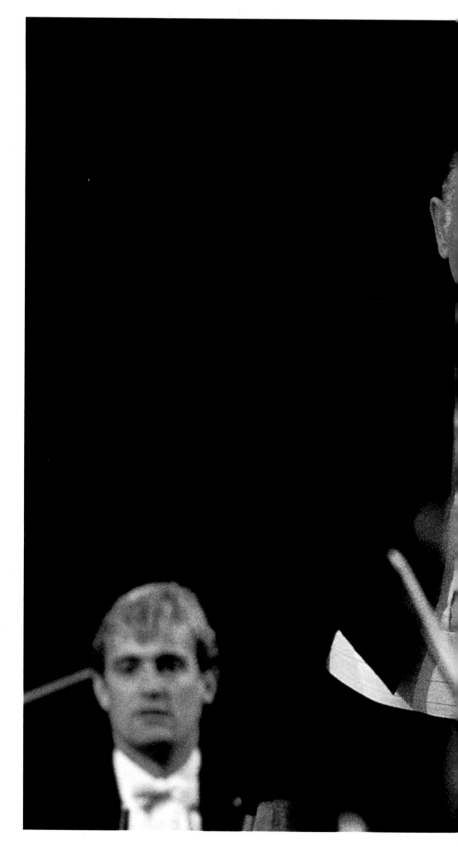

RIGHT: *Kiri Te Kanawa, with Sir Georg Solti and the BBC Philharmonic Orchestra, taking a bow at the Strauss Concert Gala in Manchester, 1990. Photography by Catherine Ashmore.*

Rosza taught me how to avoid singing flat. I also learned to breathe much lower, when I needed to take more air for the bigger phrases. I found myself able to sit on my breath as if I was sitting on a blown-up cushion. More importantly, I learned from her how to snatch a breath even in the middle of a run, so that I had enough to get through to the end of a long phrase. With this method, I did not need a great full breath in advance. I have perfected this technique to the point that people sometimes tell me I have fantastic breath control, but that is only because they actually cannot hear me breathing.

Rosza not only gave me a stable musical platform through the development of a sound vocal technique but also guided me in the selection of a suitable repertoire. Furthermore, a good instructor like Vera could teach you a lot about acting. I would say that I have gained most of my operatic intuition from her. She used to come to my rehearsals and say: 'Look, you just are not intense enough, your feet are all over the place.' That comment would be far more valuable to me than anyone complaining that I did not move here and did not walk there, or that I had been on the wrong side of the stage - which is the sort of communication that sometimes passes under the name of stage direction.

From these beginnings, my career has been inspired by a number of adorable people. Leontyne Price, Renata Tebaldi and Victoria de los Angeles have all been influential in my life but Joan Sutherland has been the greatest inspiration of all. Growing up in New Zealand, I was about as far removed from the rest of the world as this wonderful Australian soprano once was. Yet, she managed to succeed, not just in her own country but also on the international scene. Her example proved to me that our provenance from the Southern Hemisphere did not preclude a career as an opera singer.

There have been many singers who were considered overnight wonders and had embarked on terrific careers who suddenly disappeared, totally disappeared. After a while you would come across them singing in another voice category altogether. You ask yourself why. You then discover that a number of them had blown their voices out, taken the top off, taken the bottom off, or sung too many chest notes too soon.

I have been inspired by listening to great singers and learned how they protect their voices from the stresses of the job. That is a rather lonely task, because you have to lock yourself away. You cannot go to parties or to loud rock concerts without using ear plugs. You have to preserve and nurture your gift always.

It is very difficult to live a controlled life of this kind. Sometimes people will say to me, oh, we would like you to visit this particular college. It will just take an hour or so. But you know that in reality it will not just take an hour or so. You have to sit down to lunch and talk to people about nothing at all, and find that you have used up a lot of your time and a lot of your voice. So it was important for me to decide early on that I had to be very good to my voice, really look after it and stay out of smoky rooms, for instance.

I still guard my voice as much as I ever have. After a hard session, I will absolutely shut up for the next day and give myself a complete rest. It is amazing just how much a little rest can rejuvenate a voice.

My developing years were mostly shaped by Richard Bonynge, Joan Sutherland's husband and teacher who gave a master class at the London Opera Centre when I was studying there. At the time I was leaning towards mezzo-soprano roles. I remember being in total trepidation of him, but I managed to sing for him. He convinced me that I was not really a mezzo all and that it would be better for me to concentrate on soprano roles.

I had been happy enough, I must say, singing mezzo because it seemed that much easier than going for high notes all the time. However, Bonynge's advice came like the voice of God. I would probably have obeyed him if he had told me to become a contralto. In retrospect, I realise that I was right at the point of the corner and after the encounter with Bonynge, life was definitely changing direction for me.

Looking back on my years at the London Opera Centre, at the loneliness and unhappiness I experienced there, I think it was just something I had to go through. It was the first time I had ever left home. Initially, my mother came with me but then I was on my own. I had never been without my parents and had to learn to stand on my own two feet. I knew I would miss the close, nurturing care of these two people whom I loved very much. But I suppose this phase was part of growing up, as it would be for any young girl.

In my earlier days, I was a very bad learner, or perhaps I was taught badly. Sometimes, when I did not know the words by heart yet, I would find myself clutching the score until the very last moment. This was embarrassing, although I usually managed to get through the song in the end. There was one particular opera score I did not let out of my sight for a whole year, and by the time I came to the first rehearsal I still did not know it.

Rehearsals can be professional, funny or plain dreadful. I still remember a very difficult and endless rehearsal of DIE ZAUBERFLÖTE - it must have been at least sixteen years ago - when nothing was getting resolved. As it is, the opera in itself is complex enough - an opus full of magic, in which ambiguous male and female forces compete in a mysterious power play set in a fairy-tale realm, in which good and evil are never what they appear to be.

The stage director did not seem to know the direction he wanted to go. And the conductor, the dear man, obligingly catered to every changing mood and demand. At midnight, I looked down at the conductor and told him I was terribly tired and was going home. Everything had been going wrong, and the music ground to an almighty halt. We had all done enough, and everyone was on the verge of dropping dead.

All these are factors that can cast a cloud over a production long before the dress rehearsal. The ingredients that make a rehearsal work or not work do not lack variety. If half the singers fail to turn up, that certainly sets the morale on a downward spin. The fact that the conductor may be conducting elsewhere does not help either. Then, when he finally arrives from his overseas assignment, he may be tired, but the cast is not aware of this. Or else he does not know the score properly yet, so to start with, he puts his assistant in his place.

So the cast has to learn to work with the assistant for a while, even though the assistant cannot be expected to conduct in the same manner as the conductor himself. Often - most unfortunately - the assistant may not know how to keep the beat and follows the singers whose individual tempe may differ vastly from each other.

Life can be very difficult for assistants. I do not think I give them a hard time. Maybe I am wrong. I am not very good at wasting hours trying to pussyfoot around. Rehearsals often drag on, with the entire cast wasting their time and effort until the conductor arrives and takes over.

So what, in my opinion, makes a good rehearsal, or an acceptable rehearsal, is first of all that all the performers and players are present and on time. Nobody has jet lag. The conductor has arrived. He is in great shape. He is being thoroughly pampered, as is his due, and all the staff at the opera house are happy and helpful.

These days, in countless rehearsals, you get the director saying: 'We will be doing a chorus rehearsal, but we would like you to be there anyway.' In other words, you just stand on the stage, and they push the chorus around you. I suppose it is important to be there, but these are some of the most tiring sessions of all. You literally stand hour after hour standing in one position, while the stage director and his crew get the lighting right. He could use a plastic blow-up of you, and it would be good enough. It is surely no coincidence that I have had my legs operated on twice for varicose veins.

People assume that dress rehearsals have their hilarious moments, but these seldom happen. The entire cast has to be totally orderly and regimented. There is no room for much levity, though we may be allowed the odd quick giggle. When an orchestra is employed at a cost of several thousand pounds an hour, nobody is in the mood to waste time with frivolity. All the same, there can be funny premieres, like the concert performance of OTELLO I did with Solti as conductor, although the work is not exactly an opera buffa.

Luciano Pavarotti was singing the title role for the first time in his career. This opportunity of playing the role of the jealous Moor meant a lot to him, and the production on stage was deadly serious, but backstage we shared some unbelievably droll moments. Luciano had his words in front of him - no notes, no scores, just lyrics - and he had his own personal prompter to give him the cue for his entry. During the performance, Luciano knew what the rest of us were doing and he always came in perfectly as the recordings of these performances prove. To this very day, I do not know how he did it.

I remember one scene in Act Four, when the situation was getting comical. As Desdemona, I was singing the Willow Song *Mia madre aveva una povera ancella* and *Ave Maria* in sad anticipation of my murder at Otello's hand. Luciano sat on stage with a scarf right over his head as he had a cold and was trying to be discrete. Every so often, his hand would come out from under the scarf, pick up a piece of apple, and disappear again. After the apple was quietly crunched, he then, in the same manner, would reach for a drink.

All this was going on behind my back, and a member of the cast asked me afterwards if I had noticed. I chuckled: 'Please, don't tell me any more. I have to get through four performances, and I just do not want to know what he is doing.' In the end, the production was a very exciting occasion, with Solti leading and Luciano singing beautifully, in spite of his cold.

The audience can usually spot blunders during actual performances, but never when brilliant conductors like Georg Solti, or Claudio Abbado, or Colin Davis, or Jimmy Levine are guiding, because every single one of them is completely organized. There simply are not allowed to be any embarrassing situations. If the unexpected does occur, these extremely skilled conductors ensure that the involuntary mirth remains undetectable to the audience.

I do have a happy memory of the time Placido Domingo split his pants during one of the many OTELLOS we sang together. We were in Paris, I think. He suddenly took his coat off on stage and tied it round himself. During the scene change, I walked into the small backstage room where we were supposed to wait, and caught him red in the face with his pants down, shouting, 'Don't look, don't look.' I giggled: 'For God's sake, Placido, hurry up, you're due back on stage.'

There is no doubt that, in opera, your clothes do sometimes give out on you, but I have never witnessed a serious accident. There have been no broken limbs, though I remember once swishing a folding fan too close to Hakan Hagegard. He was singing Eisenstein opposite me in a performance of the operetta DIE FLEDERMAUS at the Met. I found that I had cut the inside of his eye. That was really nasty. It was a new fan, with sharp edges - and a good example of the stupid things that can occur in opera. It is very important to be working with objects you are already used to handling. I did not realise I had hurt him until I saw the state his eye was in during the break. It was terrible. Yet, Hagegard continued the performance as a true professional would, without so much as a flinch.

These incidents happen frequently. The staff gives you props, saying 'Here is your new fan', and you have two seconds to get used to it, because it is the only fan available. Or else they would say, 'We have changed your gloves tonight', and I would retort, 'Why on earth are you changing them when we are in the middle of a run of eight performances?' The designer, I expect, has decided that those new gloves would be an improvement, but usually it turns out that they are too tight or too long or too short or they fall off during the performance. Of course, the intention is good, but the results are, more often than not, disastrous.

I try to make sure, in all performances, that the costumes and props I start off with are those I stay with. Even if they are not perfectly adequate, and could be improved, at least I have the continuity of the items I have become used to, whether they be shoes or dresses.

I remember how once, at the New York Metropolitan, the designer kept on changing those small accessories. One day, I had a short pair of gloves, then I had gloves with holes in the fingers, then I had a long pair of gloves. After I felt as if I had gone through their entire assortment of accessories, I said: 'Please, stop doing this to me. Whatever I had on last, please, bring it back. I do not want any more changes.'

Performing Wolfgang Amadeus Mozart's opera of sinister sensuality, DON GIOVANNI, in France I once noticed an undue sense of amusement creeping over the audience. As Giovanni's jilted lover, Donna Elvira, I was just singing the great aria *Mi tradi*, battling with feelings of fury and compassion, when I realised that the backdrop was flying in and flying out and flying back in again.

Then there was John Schlesinger's production of Richard Strauss' DER ROSENKAVALIER at Covent Garden in 1984. As far as I was concerned, my entrance in that production never worked. The role of the Marschallin is a big one, and is spun out across a very long opera. Therefore I asked John Schlesinger if I could be given a lovely, slow entrance in Act Three, just before the great trio at the end. 'Well', he replied, 'there is this nice door you can come through.'

Unfortunately, the door was only 32 inches wide and my dress of true rococo dimensions, was 39, so I could not walk through it in the dignified manner befitting the wife of a military commander. I had to squeeze through.

Looking back, I suppose it did not matter much, but there are moments in certain productions when I feel irritated and exasperated with a stage direction, a prop or a colleague, and it is then that I think I should be getting out of opera altogether. Obviously, these moments soon pass.

I believe in opera. When I am on stage I am the character I am portraying. I cannot jump in and out of a role, suddenly becoming Kiri Te Kanawa rather than the Countess when people are applauding. Of course, the audience knows it is me, and of course, I know I am me, but the illusion on stage must be maintained at all times.

Therefore, I deeply deplore some of the traditions that opera singers and opera houses seem to cherish. One performer I played opposite - she will have to remain nameless - expected applause after a big aria, and would take a bow. I hate that. It interrupts the performance. This particular singer told me that it was a tradition at the opera house we were appearing in, and I said: 'Let's stop the tradition right now.'

But my colleague would not listen. When I found out that I was expected to do the same, I declined. Time and again I was told to go back on stage, but I refused. I always remember the advice I received from the director, John Copley, at the start of my career. He said it was just not done, and I absolutely agree with him.

Sometimes other singers make it very difficult for me to stay within the role. I recall a performance of Strauss' ARABELLA not so long ago, when the baritone who played Arabella's Mr. Right, kept coming up to me so close from the very beginning of the performance that I felt we were already married.

Yet, this was supposed to be the first meeting between Arabella and Mandryka. Therefore, he should have known to keep a respectful distance. Mandryka should have pleaded his case in a credible way. Instead, he was all over me, and I felt that, as

RIGHT AND BELOW: *An attentive Kiri Te Kanawa, with Sir Georg Solti and the BBC Philharmonic Orchestra, in a rehearsal for the Strauss Concert Gala in Manchester in 1990. Photography by Catherine Ashmore.*

ABOVE: *Sir Georg Solti giving a piano recital during the Strauss Concert Gala in Manchester in 1990. Photography by Catherine Ashmore.* LEFT: *Kiri Te Kanawa in discussion with Sir Georg Solti, during a break in the rehearsal for the Gala in honour of Sir John Tooley in the auditorium of the Royal Opera House, Covent Garden in1988. Photography by Catherine Ashmore.*

Arabella, I would not have bothered with this man. I would have walked out on him there and then.

Since I was not attracted at all by this behaviour, I tried hard to keep a distance, even putting furniture between us during the performance. At one point, I stood behind a chair so he could not get to me. Then I would move far enough down stage to be out of his reach. Improvising my steps in this manner proved difficult, because he kept pursuing me and even ended up standing right behind me, which is one of the worst annoyances a performer can cause to a fellow singer. I tried to invent new ways to escape him, and to make it appear to the audience that he was simply adoring me, but he never got the message.

We all get stage fright from time to time, and with me it usually comes from overwork. For example, just before a performance, I occasionally get this image of an absolutely empty stage, clear, with nothing in front of me, and then the audience suddenly comes swarming up and advances towards me. It is a fear of being trapped in a crowd. For this reason, I always like to have an exit in sight, preferably an open door. I have genuine feelings of claustrophobia. Once, in Paris, fans crowded into my dressing room like a swarm of buzzing bees and my back was against the wall. I could see the exit but could not reach it. This sort of situation makes me feel very afraid and out of control, and I try to avoid it.

Some singers get frightened that they might forget their words, but if that happens to me, I just make them up - I have no qualms about it. On such occasions, Solti always shouts, 'Chinese, Chinese', by which he means that if you invent Chinese words, nobody will notice, even if the audience does not understand what you are saying. So I do not get worried

about forgetfulness, though it must be terrible to have a
temporary loss of memory.

Fortunately, we usually have a prompter to help out when
such a situation arises. If there is a problem, or someone has
stopped or done something stupid, you simply look down to
the pit, and the prompter will cue you in. I am sure I have
done some stupid things in my time, but I know how to stay
calm and composed and find out what the problem is and just
get on with the performance. I have a pretty practical attitude
in this respect. If there is a problem, it is fixable. Nobody is
going to shoot you if you have made one small mistake.

True, I sometimes have arguments over whether there will be
a prompter's box or not. The people in charge will say they
cannot fit one in, that there is no budget, that there is no time
and I tell them to make room and that I cannot go on stage
without one.

The first few times I performed Strauss' Capriccio I knew I
might be in terrible trouble over the many words in my part.
So I asked for a personal prompter and the opera house
agreed to employ one. There was no way I could have sung
that role without him.

Today this happens less often, but I keep thinking of what all
those inexperienced kids have to go through on stage when
there is no prompter. I remember many years ago the three
young singers who had to play the three lovers in Arabella
once being so scared that their eyes were popping out of their
heads with fright, and they did not know where they were. I
said I was not prepared to go through with the performance
watching this fear on their faces. 'Give them a chance', I said.

OVERLEAF: *With radiant
smiles, Kiri Te Kanawa,
Sir Georg Solti and
Placido Domingo take a
curtain call during the
dress rehearsal for Elijah
Moshinsky's production of
Otello at the Royal Opera
House, Covent Garden in
1992. Photography by
Catherine Ashmore.*

'Let the singers have a prompter, let them relax, and they will perform better.'

But the music itself, at least, is always a help. Singers have a note to hold on to before they get to the next word, which gives them an advantage over actors. I would dread being an actress and having to say all those words without respite. As an opera singer, I always have a musical phrase to sustain me, or a small orchestral interlude to help me out, but actors have nothing to save them; they are very exposed.

Actors and opera singers alike have to live with the possibility that they might be affected by a colleague's stage fright, but that has never happened to me, although I have seen some unusual behaviour on stage. One particular soprano suddenly and silently vanished in the middle of an important rehearsal shortly before the premiere. I never found out why she did it, but she just went home without telling anyone, leaving all her colleagues in a lurch. Perhaps something had gone wrong, which I did not see. It might have been stage fright. I will never know. Without a word, the lady returned the next day.

Occasionally, opera also disappoints in other ways. I was looking forward to the filming of Strauss' CAPRICCIO in San Francisco. The original performances of the John Cox production were a fascinating experience, not least because the costumes were designed by Gianni Versace in the style of the nineteen-twenties and -thirties.

But when I returned to San Francisco to sing it a second time - by then it was going to be filmed - the production had all been put back into eighteenth-century costume. It seemed that the

Strauss estate had disagreed with John Cox's updated concept of the story, and would not allow it to be filmed except in the way the composer originally intended.

Yet, the John Cox production was by no means bizarre unlike some of the prevalent avant-garde interpretations today. I have never actually taken part in an extremely modern production, and I really would not want to. To avoid being taken unawares, I always ask to see the costumes and designs beforehand, so I know what I am in for. Opera has become a platform for directors to show off their vanity, and I refuse to take part in productions which are pure ego trips and which, in any case, are unfair to the audience.

I have sung in a number of productions I have disliked intensely, and others I have found merely bland. I always enjoyed working with the celebrated producer Jean-Pierre Ponnelle - everyone loved him so much, and it was sad that he died so young - but I did get a little tired of his grey Mozart productions, with costumes for FIGARO, DON GIOVANNI and COSÌ FAN TUTTE that seemed interchangeable.

I did a FIGARO of Ponnelle's at the Salzburg Festival and another one at the New York Metropolitan, and they were practically identical. I thought that for such a talented man his productions could have evolved a bit more.

Many of his productions were restricted by budgetary considerations, I assume, which necessarily must limit the purchasing or tailoring of new costumes. But one principle applied to all of Ponnelle's performances: his productions never interrupted the music, they never got in the way of the flow of the opera. That, to me, is an outstanding characteristic of Ponnelle's work.

Curiously, the country in which I have felt least at home as a singer has been Italy. I never considered my performances at La Scala in Milan a success. Indeed, I felt uncomfortable there, even though I played Amelia in SIMON BOCCANEGRA, which is one of my established parts, and I had Claudio Abbado as conductor. I was always too aware of the presence of the claque, and when you are nervous you cannot sing your best.

I had this man coming to my dressing-room door, saying he was Signor So-and-so and asking what I was going to pay him, and I thought: 'I don't think I can deal with this.' Though this incident happened sixteen years ago, I have never forgotten it. I knew that the claque was part and parcel of the Italian opera scene and most singers complied, but I had heard of some dreadful occasions when performers had refused to pay and were left standing at the curtain call without applause or - worse still - being booed.

Naturally, I paid up. After all, Milan is an acknowledged capital in the world of opera. I felt like those tennis players who come to Wimbledon, and sense that the crowd does not like them. They are on centre court being damned. So there I was with this man from the claque, wondering if I was paying him enough.

In the end, they did applaud me. I got perfectly wonderful applause, but all I could think was: 'I paid for this.' The trouble was that I felt the audience should have had the opportunity to appreciate or condemn my performance without any monetary considerations clouding their judgement. Throughout the entire series of performances, this thought troubled me and distracted me from the music.

Since then, I have seldom sung in Italy. It is a pity, because in many respects I did have a lovely time, even during my first performances there. And Claudio Abbado made me feel at ease. I love Italy, and I love singing Italian music, but somehow this incident at La Scala left me with the impression that maybe I am not someone the Italians want to hear. Perhaps, the audience does not like my voice or the way I interpret a certain role. After every performance, even though the audience seemed to enjoy it, I found myself thinking: 'Gosh, I wasn't booed tonight. This is big, not to get booed.' It was not that I sensed any real hostility. I just suspected that Italian audiences seem to prefer Italian performers. In which case I would rather sing in a country where people genuinely want to hear me. Yet, I have not wholly kept away from Italy. I have sung in Venice, recorded LA TRAVIATA in Florence and SIMON BOCCANEGRA in Milan with Georg Solti.

Opera begins and ends with the voice. Mine is a lyric soprano, nothing more than that. Various people have described it as creamy, others as silvery. Occasionally, my voice is compared to a musical instrument, an oboe, or a clarinet. I would say that it is more oboeish, with a touch of violin about it. I feel that mine is a simple voice, not complicated at all, whereas Maria Callas always seemed to have at least three different voices - coloratura, dramatic and lyric.

Opera has been - and still is - a major part of my life. The chance to sing the Countess in LE NOZZE DI FIGARO at Covent Garden initially launched my career. And portraying Desdemona in Verdi's OTELLO at a moment's notice in my first appearance at the New York Metropolitan Opera proved one of the milestones in my life. You have to sing at the Met, and be a success there, in order to have made it internationally as a singer. Today, I am pleased to have a devoted following in New York, and I am grateful to James Levine for calling me to the Met that first time.

I am an opera singer and opera must come first. Recently, I was to appear in a concert singing *O mio babbino caro* from GIANNI SCHICCHI along with *Can't help loving that man*. Then the promoter decided that all he wanted was *Can't help loving that man*. But, of course, I insisted on singing *O mio babbino caro*. If I were to give in to such demands and concentrate on show music, then the classical side of my repertoire would be lost. Opera launched my career and it remains the most important genre of music for me.

What opera means to me is going out there, and not short-changing classical music. If I had wanted to get into Broadway, that is where I would have gone in the first place. It is quite difficult keeping your resolve, because so many people do not really know what you do or how you do it. They do not know you have to look after your voice, they do not know that it goes around with you everywhere, they do not know it is a lonely life, they just think it is all parties and glitz, big posh hotels and people running after you.

Well, of course it is - for about five minutes. The rest is just like anything else. You get dumped at the airport. You carry your own suitcases. The reality hits you as soon as the curtain goes down at the end of a performance. I once went to Prague with Solti, and it was very difficult, even though there was a private plane - which may sound very nice - because of our extremely tight time schedule. We got into Prague all right, going through customs like nobody's business, and straight into town.

After the performance, matters were quite different. They left us to fend for ourselves. We got to the airport and found it completely closed. We could see our plane parked in the distance but we could not get to it. We had to call the police to let us in, and we ended up walking down long corridors carrying all our bags with us. The man at passport control was asleep, and there was nobody to help us get to the plane. I did not mind, but do not try to tell me it is all wonderful.

Of course, my fans do not often see that side of my life, although some of them try to become part of it. It makes me sad because many fans are tremendously lonely. Some of these people want to live with me, be on the same plane, be in the same hotel, have a meal with me. If my admirers just want to listen to me sing and to see me afterwards. I appreciate that. It is all part of the entertainment business.

But I am always reminded of the film ALL ABOUT EVE, in which the actress heroine, played by Bette Davis, has a fan who adores her but really wants to take over her whole identity, and in the end triumphantly succeeds in doing so, only to find that there is yet another fan waiting to follow suit. That film frightened me, because I recognised the truth in it.

OVERTURE

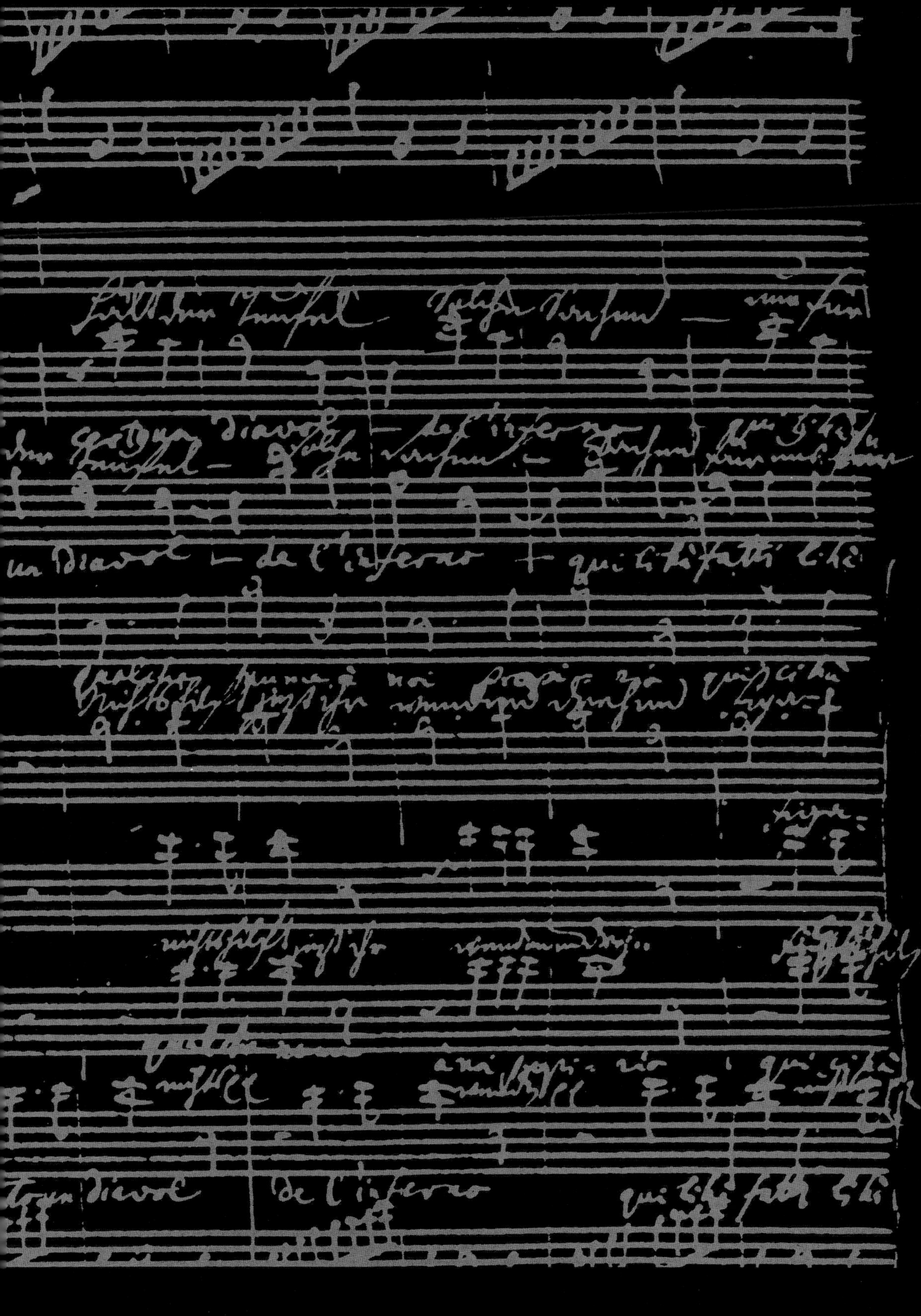

FAVOURITE COMPOSERS OF ALL TIME

The Countess in FIGARO was the first role that I yearned to have, and so Mozart became my most important composer. There were other parts I had enjoyed performing in my early days, but the chance, however faint, to sing the Countess at Covent Garden, the possibility simply of an audition, made it the most desirable role in the world to me.

I was aware at the time that the management at Covent Garden was doubtful that the Countess would be the right role for a novice singer such as myself and if I could be trusted to sustain the part. I was on tenterhooks for a long time wondering if I would get to perform at Covent Garden at all.

At one stage, I was so desperate I would have been happy to sing the role of Barbarina, the gardener's daughter. I felt that my name was on Mozart's opera somewhere, and I would have done anything to get into it.

As I was then only twenty-seven, I thought that Barbarina would have been an absolutely super role for me. Considering all the other personae in the opera, I convinced myself that the part of Figaro's cunning bride Susanna was too big, much bigger than the role of the betrayed Countess Almaviva and not within my personality or voice.

In this oblique manner, I gained confidence and began to believe that the part of the Countess in this half-comic, half-tragic play of intrigue might suit me very well. I had to audition again and again while the opera house continued to procrastinate over their decision. Weeks, then months passed which seemed like a year. In the interim, time stood still.

Meanwhile, I kept practising the Countess' arias which abound with pitfalls. They depict the person's confusion and the Countess' veiled emotion. Having previously sung them in concerts, I knew they were well in my voice, and I felt comfortable with them. Yet, when I was finally given the role of the Countess, I was suddenly seized by fear because mine was obviously a very young sound, and I wondered if I would be able to sustain that length of role and that depth of an older character in a big opera house.

Covent Garden took me by the scruff of my neck, bunged me into a room and locked me away for a year. I scarcely saw the light of day. This was the only time I ever learned a role absolutely thoroughly. From then on, I never had the time or opportunity again. I was put in a studio with Jeffrey Tate, who was a repetiteur at the time and not a conductor, and he taught me my part, day after day. I had no choice. It was like being on some sort of death row: sing or die.

I learned the Italian words - I did not speak Italian - mostly by repetition. Before I performed at Covent Garden, I was asked to sing the Countess in English in another country. Although it was easy to learn the words, singing in English can be almost as difficult as singing the part in Italian since the words often do not make the best of sense.

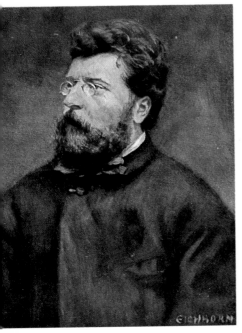

So I went to New Mexico. After several performances there, I came back feeling good about myself only to find that I had to start from the beginning to learn the role in Italian. This slow learning process proved painful, but by then, at least I knew what I was doing.

After a while I was so brainwashed that the Countess' words came out automatically. I hated the recitatives, which I found difficult to sustain and sing. So I decided that I must learn to love them. From that point on they became easier to cope with, and thankfully, the result was a great success. I had performed my first key role in a major international opera house.

In Mozart's Così fan tutte, this lengthy test of constancy of women, I have always considered the recitatives to be excessive. They are repetitive. The words and the music waft and weave as if Mozart never wanted to get to the end.

Così is fun - I would never deny that - but only if you can sustain the interest of the audience. When I am performing Così, I am forever asking myself: 'Why is it taking so long to reach the next aria?' Maybe I did not learn Così quite as well as I learned Figaro and later on Giovanni, and I remember it having been a battle. But if I find myself getting impatient and I feel the audience losing interest as well.

Some productions of Così include more of the recitatives than others, and a few include absolutely everything. My advice to other singers is therefore: 'Before you sign your contract, negotiate a few cuts.'

Despite lengthy recitatives, once I have learned a part by heart I have no problems remembering the words or the music even

Cena in casa di Margherita
Brindisi del tenore
Margherita si sente male. Tutti si dispongono
resta solo il Tenore il quale le dichiara
pensarvi!
Margherita sola.

when I have not sung the opera for some time. The text sticks, provided I have learned it slowly. 'Anything you learn fast', someone once told me, 'you lose quickly.' However, no matter how slowly or fast I learn, there always seems to be more to learn, especially about the operas of my favourite composers, Mozart and Richard Strauss, whose works are such a challenge for a singer.

I have always enjoyed challenges. Frequently, pieces of music which sound easy to the listener are fiendishly difficult to master for the singer. For instance, if someone requests a simple song, I am likely to choose a piece with piano accompaniment such as Strauss' *Morgen* because of its beautiful melody. But I also know that its first six notes are killers. I have unwittingly made many mistakes in this way. Some songs I would not sing now, for the simple reason that despite every effort they so easily go wrong, even for very experienced performers.

Giacomo Puccini's music is genuinely easier to handle for a performer. Maybe he did not trust his singers, therefore the composer made it very simple for them to remember the melody. He always has the orchestra play the tune along with the voice. As a result, you never really have to find your notes. They are all there for you. Puccini's operas save themselves at every turn. There is no way they could be sung badly, not even TOSCA. The music is stunning, but it takes over. It is out of your control. It just rolls on. If you were to miss a phrase or two when you came on stage, the opera would survive and continue. The performance would not fall to pieces.

Perhaps this reflects something in Puccini himself, an unwillingness to take risks. It is possible, I sometimes think, that originally some of his singers did not read music. If that was the case, how were they going to follow the melodic lines unless he provided an orchestral accompaniment that led the way so that they could not falter?

With Puccini, you are given what is tantamount to a whole edifice, a whole village, with the washing on the line, the fires all lit, everything in working order. Puccini always paints with realistic and compassionate brush strokes the entire scenario. The scene is set, and all you have to do is look at it.

However, you cannot touch the image, you are not allowed to touch it, because it is complete in itself. It is, I admit, enormously appealing to contemplate. The orchestration, the wonderful crescendos, are the work of someone who knew exactly what he was doing. Puccini above all knew how to create a wonderfully fluent phrasing. You do not get that with many other composers.

With Verdi for example, the orchestra at the start of an aria often gives you no indication of what follows. It is very difficult to find the tune.

Having said that, Giuseppe Verdi gave new impetus to the development of the operatic genre by fearlessly pursuing the characterisation of his roles, regardless of the beauty of the tune. His operas are filled with drama which he achieved through the

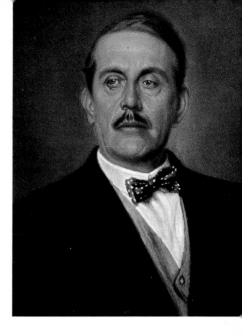

expert utilisation of bel canto and coloratura. In his operas, Verdi paints large ensemble scenes, with fine details and many shades of contrasts of human passion. There can be no doubt about it - his works added a new intensity to opera.

I have stayed away from the whole world of Händel and baroque opera. Although this period of operatic history again explores the subjects of love and duty, I have always been reluctant to perform the big da capo arias, consisting of an introduction, a middle section, followed by a full-scale repeat of the first part.

Unless the music is totally engrossing, I tend to get impatient and wish I would not have to do the da capo in order to finish the song. Going back to the beginning, I imagine the audiences saying to themselves, 'We have heard this already', and I am never quite sure that they want to hear it again.

I would, by far, prefer to sing shorter versions of these pieces, especially since the middle section of a Händel aria, which is often set in a minor key, can be dramatic and wonderful. Of course, this is not possible since present musicologists object to cuts and demand completion, completion, and completion, at any cost.

One of the bonuses of including the da capo is that you can add decorations to the melody the second time round, but again I am not convinced about the value of doing so. Basically, I always feel that to decorate too much makes you lose the tune. And if the tune is a good one and sings well as it is, what is the point of distorting it beyond recognition?

OPPOSITE: *Wolfgang Amadeus Mozart (1756-1791). Painting by L. Balestieri.* TOP: *Giacomo Puccini (1858-1924).* ABOVE: *Richard Strauss (1864-1949). Painting by Eichhorn. All three photographs by Mary Evans Picture Library.*

The over-decoration of baroque operas has deterred me from becoming more interested in this period of operatic history. Having said that, I am well aware that most people are convinced my career really took off when I sang the Händel aria at the wedding of the Prince and Princess of Wales. That was certainly one of the turning points in my life. I became famous overnight, and many people who had previously known nothing of me or my work suddenly began to recognise who I was.

Joan Sutherland gave wonderful interpretations of Händel's operas. That made me think myself foolhardy to try to follow in her footsteps. At one point in my life, I deliberately ran away from Händel. I feared being compared to this great Australian Händel interpreter when I was trying to make a name for myself, and with good reason.

There was a period in Italy, when any soprano who began to show her talent was immediately called another Maria Callas and found herself constantly compared with the legendary diva. This is unfair.

For this same reason, I have avoided doing any opera by the German composer, Christoph Willibald Gluck. The person who made Gluck famous in Britain was Kathleen Ferrier through her singing of an aria - the sad but beautifully haunting *Che faro* from ORFEO. The role of Euridice simply seemed to belong to her and to her voice.

Even if there had been an opportunity for me to sing the part during the period when my voice had mezzo-soprano leanings, I do not think I would have done it. The role was owned by someone else, first by Ferrier, then by Janet Baker. A singer needs a niche of his own. One of my niches is Strauss' CAPRICCIO. Perhaps other performers will avoid singing parts I did for a while, until they make these roles their own.

Yet, you can never make a role entirely your own. It would be dreadful if you could. People's memories, I keep telling myself, are short and selective. In due time, the audience will forget, and then you can choose your own composer and create your own portrayal of a part.

Mozart's music is full of traps for the unwary performer. When you sing a Mozart aria, you have to hit each note in the middle - you cannot skip up and you cannot slide. If you do, you miss the note. In Mozart's music, a singer's fallacies or flaws are clearly exposed.

If I were auditioning a singer, I would ask him to sing an aria by Mozart, for instance *Porgi amor* or *Per pietà*. I could then immediately hear if the voice had confidence, or if there were any breaks in it. I would also be able to pick out any inadequacies that might surface. More often than not, the singer would shy away from Mozart and reply, 'Oh, but I have got this very nice aria by Puccini.'

Mozart's music is exacting and precise - and I still find it taxing to sing even after all these years of playing his roles. To make Mozart sound truly Mozartian, a singer has to change his approach completely. He cannot sound as if he just came from singing Puccini's LA BOHÈME.

A good Mozart pianist, for example, who is perfectly at ease with his music, will produce a lovely, dry sound. There is no

crashing and bashing in Mozart, nor sentimental pretenses. His notes are very subtle and affecting and are produced merely by the slightest touch of the hands.

My singing teacher, Vera Rosza, once said to me that singing Mozart is lubrication for the voice. If you want to warm up privately, you should just sing Mozart. His music requires a performer to use the entire vocal spectrum a singer must be able to command.

Although people have come to associate me with the role of Fiordiligi in Così Fan Tutte, I find her vivacious sister Dorabella the more interesting personality. That is the role I sang in earlier days and frankly, I think my character suits Dorabella's better. She is a feisty person, not so haughty and rather naughty. She appears to be natural, someone I have always felt I would like to have as a friend.

By contrast, I find it much harder to imagine inviting Fiordiligi to dinner because she always seems to be pointing the finger constantly, in a dreadful, schoolmarmy way. Yet, I guess many people we meet who initially appear natural and lively ultimately turn out to be replicas of her personality. I do not see many people like Dorabella.

I only sing Fiordiligi. Her part is not any easier than her sister's. The big leaps in her arias fit in perfectly with the more forbidding side of her personality. The songs are some of the most difficult pieces in my repertoire and are not very often heard in concerts.

OPPOSITE: *Charles Gounod (1818-1893). Gouache by Theobald Chartran in Vanity Fair 1879. Photography by Mary Evans Picture Library.*

In most operas, arias are preceded and followed by gentle recitatives to make them sparkle against a more subdued backdrop. But Fiordiligi's arias appear chronologically in difficult positions in a sequence of several arias.

Porgi amor in FIGARO is another aria which is notorious for its problematic placing, both for the singer and the audience. At the start of Act Two, most of the other characters have already appeared, with the exception of the Countess herself. She then walks onto the stage, cold from the break and - without the slightest possibility of warming her voice up - goes straight into a slow and serious aria.

The first of Fiordiligi's arias, *Come scoglio*, is positioned reasonably well, but by the time *Per pietà* is reached the work is in danger of becoming a succession of arias. At this point in Act Two I find myself longing for a duet, tercet, any ensemble piece, whatever. I always wonder if the audience is not too tired to listen to the aria by the time I reach it.

You can see why cuts are made to Act Two of Così. To be brutally honest, I do not think the libretto contains much of a story-line. The opera, also called 'The School for Lovers' is a caricature in essence, a pathetic manipulation of people's lives and emotions. Despite the opera's comic qualities, the work ends in a bitter experience, unmasking ardently sworn feelings as hollow words.

For all the beauty of its music, Così is not as interesting a masterpiece as FIGARO or DON GIOVANNI. The ending of Così, with both, Dorabella's and Fiordiligi's fiancés, apparently pursuing Fiordiligi, remind me of Strauss' CAPRICCIO, in which Countess Madeleine is courted by two admirers. And that, perhaps, is what it really is, a caprice, a lovely but extremely long caprice.

Fortunately I have never found it difficult feeling my way into Fiordiligi's personality, or out of it again. But the inhibitive trait of her character and her moral superiority bring a constraint to my performance. By comparison, I can do anything I like when singing the passionate Donna Elvira in Don Giovanni. It does not matter what is happening around her on stage, Elvira is a law unto herself.

Playing the innocent Pamina in Mozart's Die Zauberflöte was a role that I loved in my younger days. The role is perfection for singers as long as they look nineteen. Much as I adore the part, I have not sung it in the past ten years.

Among other Mozart roles, I have always steered clear of Constanze in Die Entführung Aus Dem Serail despite her beautiful arias. The character as a whole does not appear to suit my voice and personality. But the lovely role of Ilia in Idomeneo might have interested me.

Whatever part I am playing, even in an extended run of performances, I am usually able to switch off quickly after the show. That, in my experience, is the main difference between singers and actors. Singers must devote much of their attention to the vocal element. The music does intervene with the depth of the dramatic characterisation and thus functions as a support system for the singer.

Actors cannot help being the characters they portray. An actor might find himself delving so deeply inside a character that it is hard for him to emerge from the role after the performance. Often when I have met an actor offstage after he has been portraying a difficult character, I cannot recognise him as the

ABOVE: *Giacomo Puccini's signature* La Bohème, *1897, London. From The Lebrecht Collection.* RIGHT AND OPPOSITE: *Excerpts from the original draft score of* La Bohème *by Giacomo Puccini, 1896. From The Lebrecht Collection.*

person I know. He is a stranger. For this reason alone, I would not want to be an actress. I do not like to lose myself. Once the final curtain falls, I step back into reality.

The Countess Madeleine in Strauss' Capriccio, who has to choose between a poet and a composer, and the resigned Marschallin in Der Rosenkavalier by the same composer, are operatic parts which, if they have not actually taken me over, have deeply preoccupied me because of the problems that these characters have to deal with. However, neither the sad, middle-aged Marschallin with her staid life nor the cold, court-holding Countess Madeleine are anywhere near my personality. This makes it easy for me to re-emerge to reality once the final curtain is down.

Sometimes I become mesmerized by the sheer task of learning. I wish I could insert a floppy disc in my brain, which would immediately install the music and the words in my mind. Unfortunately, the moulding process in opera is slower than that. I used to think that the libretti of the Strauss operas were very long, yet I suspect if one did a word count, Mozart's operas would be found to contain both more words and more notes, than Strauss'.

Of Mozart's operas, I found Figaro the most tiring to learn, no doubt because it was my first Mozart role. After I had learned the first of my Strauss' roles, Arabella, ten years later, the rest of the Strauss operas became easier. I suppose a performer has first to become thoroughly acquainted with the style of a composer. Later, a musical leitmotif begins to emerge in all his works.

People do not always realise that their brains do not stop working when they go to bed. Mine goes into overdrive like a mental tape recorder. You put it on 'pause' for a while, and then it suddenly starts playing again, like an echo in the middle of the night. When I am learning a role I lose plenty of sleep. There are times when I wake up automatically at 3.30 every morning, no matter where I am. The only means to get back to sleep then is to read a book.

On some occasions I have become a chronic insomniac. I do not sleep well, even at the best of times, if I have something musical on my mind. Mozart's operas contain what I call these unbelievable mind-haunting twists. Just before you reach the end of a Mozart aria there is often a descending phrase, and then it ascends again, to complete the aria. In my semi-sleep, I try to work out such problems. The result is often an even bigger mess.

A girlfriend of mine once got caught in the *Allelujah* from Mozart's Exultate Jubilate and went round its circuit three and a half times before she finally escaped from it. This is the sort of nightmare performers dread. Every time I sing Mozart's *Allelujah* now and reach that passage, I cannot help thinking of my friend and fear: 'Is it going to happen to me?' I have become increasingly aware of the dangerous obstacles that lie in my musical path, especially in any piece written by this extremely challenging composer.

The process involved in memorising the words and the music can resemble learning the alphabet or mathematics. I need to remember how to enter and shape notes and words, and I need to be prepared for tricky passages in the melody.

To retain the lyrics - the alphabet of opera - in my mind, I first concentrate on recurring words, which reflect the thematic

OVERLEAF, LEFT: *An excerpt of the score from the finale in Act Two of* Le Nozze di Figaro, *written in Wolfgang Amadeus Mozart's own hand, 1784. From The Lebrecht Collection.* TOP RIGHT: *An extract from Act Two of Mozart's* Don Giovanni, *1787. From The Lebrecht Collection.* BELOW: *A page from the handwritten score of* Der Rosenkavalier *by Richard Strauss, 1911. From The Lebrecht Collection.*

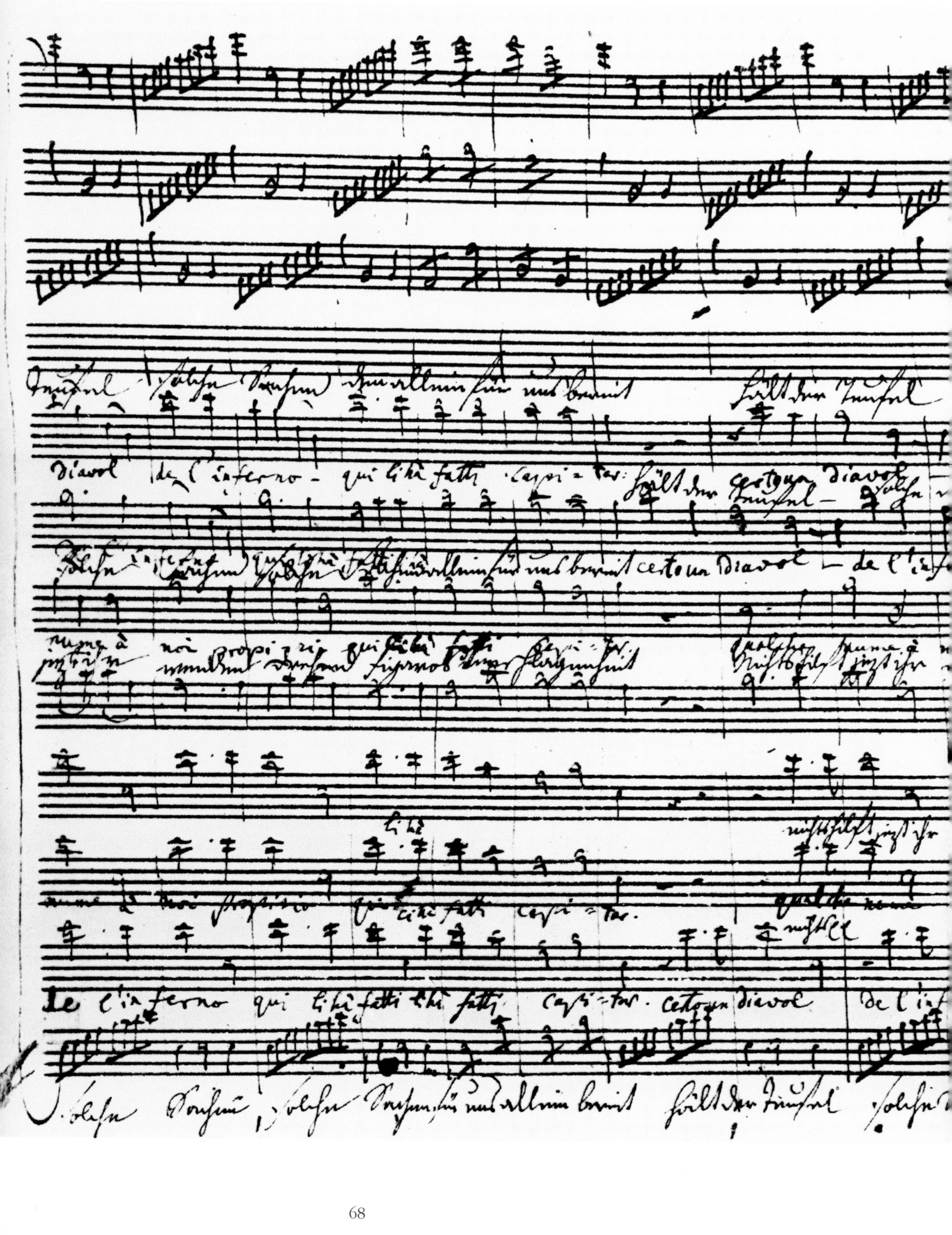

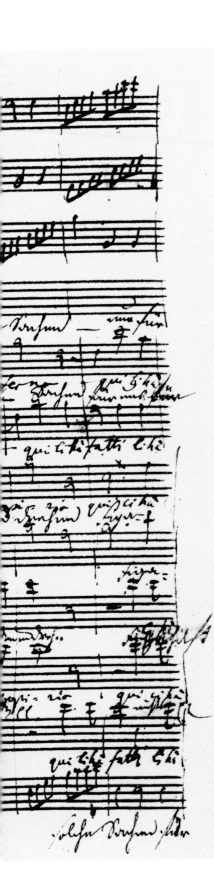

leitmotif of the story. The mathematical aspect lies in the music. I might say to myself: 'There is a four-bar rest at this point and then I descend, then there is an eight-bar rest and I ascend to the end.' Learning music is, or should be, as simple as that.

If you know a piece of music too well, however, you might become complacent about it. When you go into cruise-control and find yourself not concentrating, it is easy to take a wrong turning. You think momentarily that you have passed a certain point and suddenly realise you have not even reached it. At this point you can get into a mess. You have to keep your focus especially on works you have known for a very long time.

This phenomenon can be compared to the recital of a piece of poetry you have been familiar with all your life. You have recited it with ease for years and years, then out of the blue, someone asks you to recite it and, strangely enough, you discover that you have forgotten it. You have to consciously drag it out from the depths of your brain. Little mishaps like this occur in any singer's life.

In a few concerts, I have unwittingly skipped a whole section of music. It has not happened often, and, thank God, never with an orchestra. When a singer is accompanied by a pianist. He can retrieve the situation easily and put the performer back on track. Nonetheless, if I have made a horrible blunder, there is no point in trying to conceal it from the audience. I then say simply: 'My sincere apologies. I have made a mistake.'

My toughest assignment was learning the role of the Countess Madeleine in Strauss' CAPRICCIO, which is an opera of an elegant charade that resembles a game of chess. The German text was complicated enough, but, worse still, the role had no apparent structure. I could not find a starting point, or anything to get my teeth into.

As I had done with many parts, I learned the part of Countess Madeleine from the middle of the piece outwards. I start from the centre of the score, move gradually from there to the end, then go back to the beginning and shuffle the pieces together, never concentrating on the beginning of the score any more than I do on the end, or vice versa. I give them equal attention. As a result, I can pick up the music from any point.

I began to develop this method of studying because I found that many singers perform an aria wonderfully but the recitative surrounding it is less well presented. The effect tends to be that the aria, no matter how well it is performed, loses its lustre. It is not good enough just to concentrate on the aria and then let yourself drift back to sleep for the rest of the opera.

This made me wonder why some colleagues could not sing the sections before and after the aria just as well as the aria itself. It appears that they took the aria as the most important element of the opera, whereas I have always considered the overall concept of the music and the role to be infinitely more important. It takes a long time to recognise the importance of the recitative, as I discovered. But once I did, it made a world of difference to my performances.

Neither of Strauss' female roles has a close similarity to my character, although these three roles have formed part of my repertoire for many years. Arabella, for instance, the young woman looking for the right husband, may well have Mandryka under her thumb, once they are married. I always feel that her sister, Zdenka, is the more likeable person, the one with the heart. Despite her age, Arabella has a rigid martiality about her, which is only softened by the sheer beauty of the music, when she appears on top of the staircase with a glass of water to acknowledge Mandryka as her future husband as she slowly descends towards him.

Der Rosenkavalier is a perfect operatic comedy of manners with a large orchestra of a hundred players, which Strauss showed great ability by using effectively. Its protagonist, the Marschallin, is a beautiful, sensitive woman. Despite the romantic music in the style of the nineteenth century, the character of this powerful woman in her majestic ambience is rather tender and resigned. I can picture this sad and lonely, middle-aged lady today in Vienna or Munich, having a nice little lunch here, a nice little tea there, a nice little young lover on the side, and essentially just plodding along towards old age and death. I definitely cannot identify with her character.

Countess Madeleine of Capriccio is the coolest of my roles. She is strangely aloof and shallow, apparently only interested in the contest between music and lyrics, personified by her two admirers. Although Strauss loaded the dice in favour of music in Flamand, the tenor and composer, I found Olivier, the poet, the deeper and darker personality, quite apart from the fact that his role is sung by a baritone. At the end of the day, however, both rivals lack masculinity, looking for a surrogate mother in the Countess who - as John Cox pointed out to me - may well be in love with her Majordomus. I rather liked that idea.

OPPOSITE: *Excerpt of the score of* Habanera *from the opera* Carmen, *in Georges Bizet's own handwriting, written in 1873-74. From The Lebrecht Collection.*

In the final analysis, it is the music that sparks my enthusiasm for the roles. The long, last aria of Countess Madeleine, for example, when she is alone on the stage, with the solo French horn imitating the life-beat of the character is heart-rending. Der

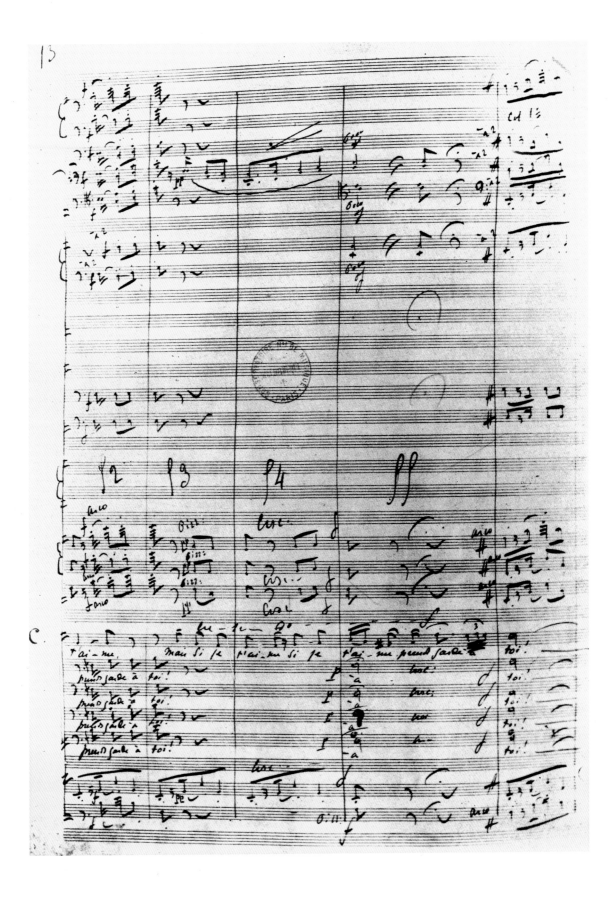

ROSENKAVALIER, on the other hand, flows like an anachronistic Viennese waltz through the witty libretto of Hugo von Hofmannsthal, blending allusions of folkloristic ballads with the cold pomposity of the Marschallin's lever.

After the prolonged frustration of learning my Strauss roles, and the feeling of not getting anywhere, there has always been for me the moment of victory when it has all come together. Then I feel like exclaiming: 'Why did I ever think there was a problem?'

I consider I was well taught in pronunciation, though the way I was trained to explode on certain consonants seemed exaggerated. Hearing certain German singers today or Luciano Pavarotti can be quite an education. I realise that I do not pronounce the consonants as precisely as they do. Rather than following their example, I tend to sing the consonants with a softer impact as I fear that harsh Germanic or Italian pronunciations would not sound as appropriate or authentic coming from a non-native singer.

I have been criticised for understressing my consonants. But flow, melodic line, and beauty of sound go hand in hand, and I have never felt I was doing music an injustice by paying attention to the whole. The voice is a musical instrument, after all. Maybe in my case the language tends to suffer, but I always go for the musical phrase rather than the necessary or unnecessary word because I have found that the music provides its own explanation.

Music has such beauty of flow that I refuse to break up the lines with words. It would seem like an act of vandalism to do so. And that, of course, is the subject of Strauss' CAPRICCIO, is it not?

Which is the more important, the word or the music? Which, in the end, do you choose? When performing CAPRICCIO, I have to choose between the personification of these two art forms. The two young men, a poet and a composer, are the rivals for my love. However, I really have no need to choose between these two competitors. If I had to, I would invariably opt for the music, which, of course, is what Richard Strauss suggests.

Having sung Strauss' operas over a long period of time, I have discovered passages of music, which, I have to admit, are less interesting to me than others. Strauss appears to be lingering on a melody while barely maintaining the tension and without any apparent direction. These passages do prompt me to question, 'What is he doing here? Why is he holding matters up? Why does he not get on with it?'

Then suddenly I hear what I can only call a golden flood of tone and I think, 'Ah, perhaps he was delaying to make you feel impatient with him, so that when the great moment arrives, it sounds all the better.' A prime example of his postponing the culmination of a work is the grand Act Three tercet *Hab mir's gelobt* at the end of DER ROSENKAVALIER.

After Baron Ochs, the unsuccessful suitor of Sophie, storms off the stage followed by waiters and musicians, the three protagonists are left alone. After some passages which sound, to me, suspiciously like padding, the Marschallin sets her young lover Octavian free and encourages him to marry his paramour Sophie. At that moment, all I feel is, 'I forgive, I forgive.'

You have to have words to sing, I am well aware of that. Whenever I perform Sergey Rachmaninov's *Vocalise*, which contains no words at all, I find myself regretting their absence, gorgeous though the music is.

There are wonderful musical uses of words, such as Franz Liszt's *Oh quand je dors*, which I also sing. During the course of a performance, I find it hard to imagine anything lovelier. The poetic melody to which Liszt sets Victor Hugo's words is out of this world. If you just heard the words spoken, you might say: 'Nice words.' The music makes them dreamy and haunting, yet you have to have the words to express the music, and vice versa. The combination of the two is the whole point of a beautiful song.

For me, phrasing makes a song or an aria. If you were going for a walk, and needed to cover five miles as quickly as possible, you would do your best to go in a straight line. But if you are interested in the walk itself, you look for the flowers on the way and listen to the song of birds.

In music, the phrase provides you with that opportunity. It is the licence in the hands of the interpreting artists to show the music to its best advantage. I am not talking about holding on to a long, high note for the sake of effect. I am in fact talking about being able to go through that high note because there is another and more important moment coming. You can make the music more interesting by phrasing in such a way that the audience consciously awaits the climax.

When I sing Liszt's *Oh quand je dors*, I imagine I am performing to a person who cannot see and with whom I am communicating through the words and music only. Since the time I sang years ago in Washington to an audience with a number of visually handicapped people, I have realised that music-lovers like to come to a performance in spite of, or perhaps because of, their disabilities. To share the beauty of the music, which is so much a part of my life, I like to help them understand what I am doing. In fact, I think that that is a performer's responsibility.

I have listened to much music and many performances that do not achieve this aim. I can hear a conductor going through phrase after phrase after phrase, and think, 'Well, if he would only just relax, or take his time here, he would make people consciously want to hear that next note.' It should be like a flower coming into bloom.

Often the music sounds rather like a blossoming flower as seen in time-lapse photography, whereby the bud may be observed minutely for several days until suddenly, in a split second, it blossoms. If that were the way you always saw flowers opening it would become very boring. You need to see them gradually opening, changing colour and shape, with the sun shining on them one day and not the next, until the day comes when the flower is fully open and the full beauty is revealed.

To me, that is what phrasing is all about. You need to take the time to explore the intention of the composer and try to do them justice.

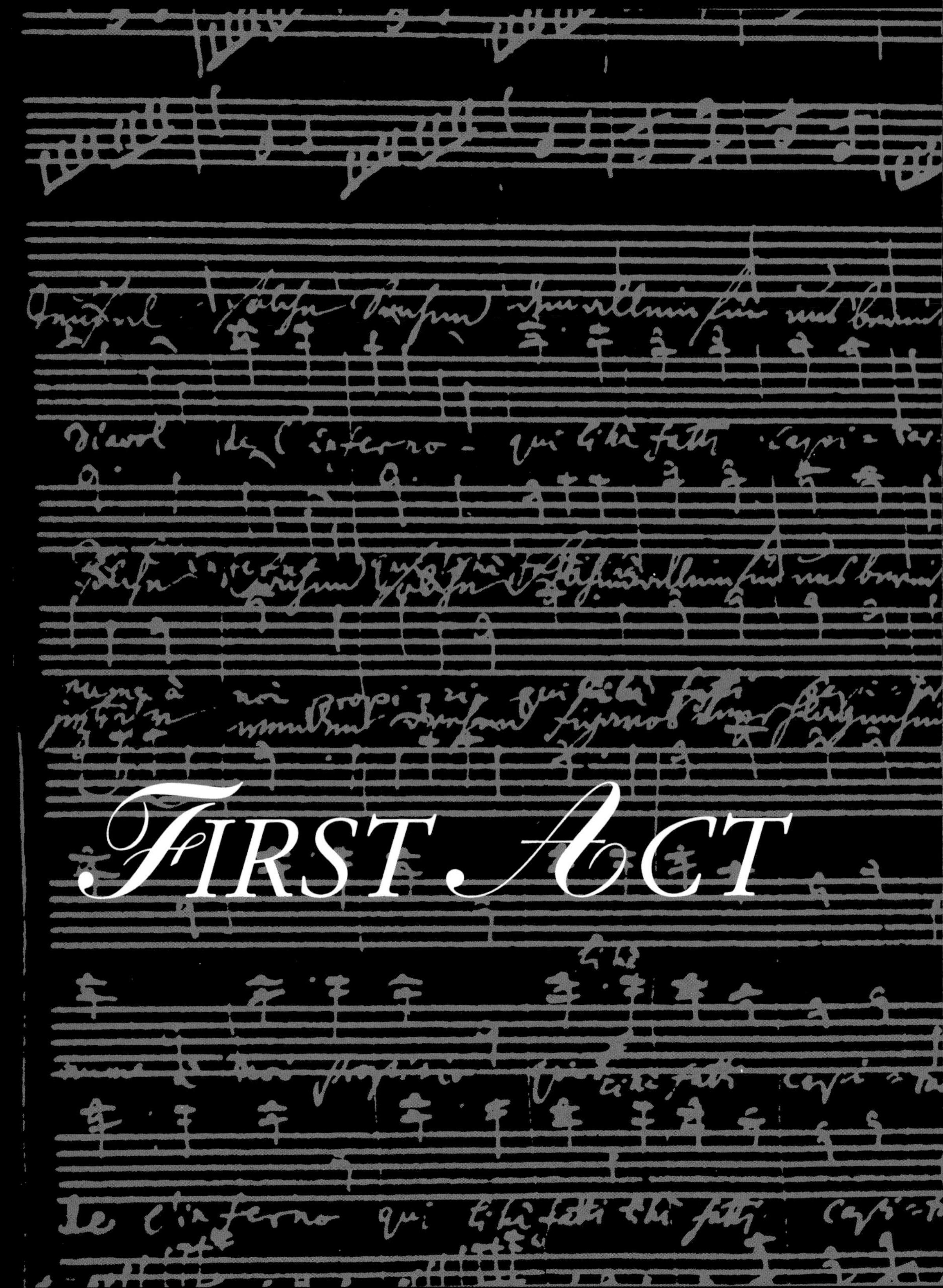

FIRST ACT

THE DRAMATIS PERSONAE
FALL IN LOVE

y first experience with Così fan tutte was singing the role of the lively Dorabella at the London Opera Centre, I was still a mezzo-soprano. Since those days, I have only performed the part of her more staid sister, Fiordiligi.

However, falling in and out of love throughout three or four acts of different roles and operas caused me to listen very closely to the scores of music for the minute variations in feeling the composers convey. I have noticed, for example, similarities between Fiordiligi's music and the Countess' motifs in Figaro.

For instance, one duet in Così has its direct equivalent in Act Three of Figaro, sung by the courting Count and flirtatious Susanna who keeps him at bay. The characters are quite different, of course. The banal and bored Fiordiligi is a bigger, more domineering character, requiring a wide range of musical techniques in *Come scoglio*, whereas the Countess has the pathos, warmth and tenderness Fiordiligi lacks.

OPPOSITE: *Kiri Te Kanawa in a contemplative mood during the New York Metropolitan production of Richard Strauss' romantic opera,* Arabella. *Photography by Winnie Klotz, New York Metropolitan Opera.*

Yet their arias do have almost the same structure, and I have occasionally wondered what would happen if I put the Countess' slow and sad *Dove sono i bei momenti* - where are the beautiful moments - into Così fan tutte and sang it with the same determination required by Fiordiligi's *Come scoglio* - like a rock - or else put *Come scoglio* into Figaro. I am just fantasising, of course, as the works are distinct variations of the same subject -

80

love and betrayal. However, these two Mozart operas contain so many similarities that they keep me pondering every time I perform them.

There is no doubt that the characters devised by most composers are identified by their musical motifs which are quite easy to pick out. The echo of a certain phrase tells you the thoughts in a character's mind at a particular moment, but it also alludes to the workings of Mozart's mind, or Strauss' or Verdi's, for that matter.

Singing a number of operatic roles of each of these three composers, I recognise recurrences and cross-references between their pieces. When performing Strauss, for instance, I enjoy hearing him repeat wonderful scores he has used in previous operas such as SALOME.

Did the composer insert these quotations of other works into his operas consciously or unconsciously? Is Strauss saying 'Remember this?'; or do certain emotions call for the use of similar motifs? Since I'm not a musicologist, I can't provide an explanation for this phenomenon, but every time I come across familiar scores of music as a performer, I feel I am part of an intimate conversation with the composer, sharing allusions and memories with him.

I sometimes wonder what will ultimately happen to the character I have been portraying. I find myself in the same quandary when I watch a classic film and ask with a sense of loss afterwards, 'Is that the end?' wishing that the film had gone on a bit longer. But the skill of a good composer and librettist is to end a play so that the audiences are left in the mood to think about what they have just seen.

Mozart's operas especially keep me wanting to go on singing for another act to learn what the future has in store for their characters. The events following the performance of DON GIOVANNI are told in the epilogue, though no doubt a big question mark will hang over the future of Donna Anna and the cowardly Don Ottavio whom she asks to wait for another year so that she may reconsider their long-standing engagement all over again.

Equally unclear is the destiny of Zerlina and Masetto, the young couple whom Giovanni almost separated. I wonder if their relationships have all been destroyed by Don Giovanni, and, if so, whether it was for better or for worse.

Neither can I imagine Pamina and Tamino living happily together in the cold, regimented world dominated by the tyrannical Sarastro after the curtain has closed on DIE ZAUBERFLÖTE. A possible sequel and a likely beginning to the story-line of LE NOZZE DI FIGARO are explained in the other plays by Pierre-Augustin Caron de Beaumarchais, on whose comedy the libretto for the opera was based.

How the characters of COSÌ FAN TUTTE get along after the opera, or even during it, is shrouded in ambiguity. When I sing Fiordiligi, I find myself switching allegiances between Fiordiligi's own fiancé Guglielmo and Ferrando, the beloved of her sister Dorabella. This switch of lovers is, of course, part of the trick that both men are playing on the damsels.

But I get this feeling not only because the opera dictates my behaviour, but because it is an aspect of life that we always look elsewhere with envious eyes and keeps pondering chances we did not take and wondering about the consequences if we had.

Kiri Te Kanawa in her role as the Marschallin in two different productions of Strauss' DER ROSENKAVALIER. ABOVE: The Marschallin expresses her reluctance to release her lover, Octavian, played here by Frederica von Stade, in a production conducted by Andrew Davis at the Paris Opera House in 1981. Photography by Agence De Presse Bernand. RIGHT: Octavian, this time played by Brigitte Fassbaender, embraces the Marschallin in the same Act, under Hans Neugebauer's direction staged for the San Francisco Opera in 1985. Photography by Ron Scherl, San Francisco Opera.

Was Mozart in Così FAN TUTTE simply celebrating a game which people played and still continue to play? We all know that, in his operas, women are susceptible to being conned by any good, handsome, well-mannered man. But does Mozart imply that the women are simpletons to be so easily influenced or that, in his days, women were economically so dependant on men that they had to take their every whim and fancy seriously?

In Così, this caricature of a drama, it is not clear how serious the men in fact are, first about their original sweethearts and - after they have exchanged one sister for the other - about their new partners. Of course, Ferrando and Guglielmo are too pathetic and colourless to dream up the intrigue by themselves. I never see much difference between the two officers though Ferrando may be a softer character than Guglielmo, but in the final analysis they could be twins.

The sisters, on the other hand, are taking the men's stratagems at face value. Mozart in the final ensemble puts the relationships neatly back to where they were at the beginning, but many directors today refuse to see this ending as the true conclusion. They want to imply a more doubtful future for these two shattered couples.

I tend to agree with them. Someone once cynically remarked to me that a marriage can only be successful if a man decides of his own volition to marry a woman. Once a man has made up his mind, his decisions are - as a rule - final. But if a woman tricks him, manipulates him, and persuades him through guile to marry her, he may just turn around and say: 'Well, I did not want to marry you but you forced me to.' Men are extremely good at putting the blame for failed relationships on women.

In many ways, I am a frustrated director. I believe the roles of Don Alfonso and Despina as puppet masters in Così FAN TUTTE could be explored in greater depth than is usually the case in the better known productions. Alfonso controls the whole opera. As a matter of fact, he turns the innocent women into victims and leads the men on to place bets on the constancy of their fiancées, putting their own fate on the line along with the future of the women they claim to love.

Despina, who is being paid to run some pretty unsavoury errands, and the cynic Alfonso have malicious fun at the expense of the others. The latter in particular is a cunning professional in this game of intrigue. Alfonso is skilled and tremendously experienced, as is obvious from the way he manipulates anybody and everybody.

Although husbands, in Mozart's lifetime, ruled as heads of the family, they were outwitted by their servants in many of his operas, notably Count Almaviva in FIGARO, who must always fear the exposure of his infidelities. The same happens to Don Ottavio, Donna Anna's fiancé, in DON GIOVANNI and to Masetto, Zerlina's fiancé. Mozart's servants seem to know better than their masters how to flatter, manipulate, affect and dissemble in order to fan the flames of love.

The most exciting and passionate of Mozart's women is, in my estimation, Donna Elvira. I have played that role with so much temperament that some of the Don Giovannis I have played opposite became annoyed with me, because they say my portrayal is far too extreme. But to me, Elvira is that absolutely wild card, a completely unconventional character. She appears to be entirely independent of any male dominance by either

OVERLEAF, LEFT AND TOP RIGHT: *Kiri Te Kanawa and Ingvar Wixell take on the leading roles of Arabella and Mandryka. In this scene, Mandryka declares his love for Arabella for the first time in this 1980 production for the San Francisco Opera. Photography by Ron Scherl, San Francisco Opera.* BELOW RIGHT: *Kiri Te Kanawa is seen here again as Arabella who has just returned from the ball, much to the chagrin of her father and her jilted lover in Silvio Varviso's production at the Paris Opera House, 1981. Photography by Agence de Presse Bernand.*

father, fiancé or brother. I did not develop this interpretation of Elvira's role gradually from production to production. I saw her as a free, spirited personality from the beginning. Since nobody has ever stopped me playing her in the uninhibited, vivacious way I see her, I have just kept on going. I enjoy behaving wickedly. This is one role I will never give up, and it is such fun to perform.

Of Mozart's men, Don Giovanni is the strongest and most complex character, an erotic demon, similar to the way Mozart was portrayed in Peter Schaffer's play and film, AMADEUS, as an intriguing comedian and a scoundrel, who liked to play around with the characters in his life, and with their emotions. In a letter to his wife Constanze, Mozart wrote on September 30, 1790, 'If people could see into my heart, I should almost be ashamed.'

Apart from Elvira, many of Mozart's operatic women are pale by comparison. The female characters were more stereotyped. Maybe it is because men did not understand women any better in Mozart's or Strauss' time than they do today.

For instance, Mozart's disillusioned and unhappy Countess Almaviva in FIGARO resembles the melancholic Marschallin in Strauss' DER ROSENKAVALIER. Their stories differ entirely, but both women must accept their husbands' negligent behaviour because they do depend on them. In the end, both women have to resign themselves to a loveless life. Strauss and Mozart, separated by over a century, invented the very same destiny for these characters.

As for DIE ZAUBERFLÖTE, I must confess that the rites of passage of a strictly patriarchal culture fail to fascinate me. The opera has strong anti-female rites and restrictions, characterising Sarastro's realm. DIE ZAUBERFLÖTE reminds me of some secluded sects and societies still existing today which elevate men to the exclusion of women.

It appears to me that the more the members of these communities get involved with the church or temple, the more they are ruled by the priests. If a young couple was to be married in such a culture as happened once to a Christian lady friend of mine, the man and the woman had to vow celibacy until they were married. More than that, if they thought non-celibate thoughts, or if they held hands, or kissed each other, or stood too closely together, they had to confess it to the priests. My friend was driven almost to desperation because of these sexual inhibitions.

These young people were not allowed even to think about sex in the marital context and became very troubled. I sometimes think that marriages under these circumstances do not survive because of the intense pressures that are put upon them by the society they live in.

For me, DIE ZAUBERFLÖTE represents the same repression of female power and sexuality under the brute despotism of Sarastro, and it makes me wonder what hope the naive Pamina and her beloved Tamino actually have.

In performing the work, I always tried to close my mind to its implications and to concentrate in the purest and simplest sense upon the performance, without becoming involved in the underlying aspects of the plot. Otherwise I might have refused to sing the opera at all. And that would have been a pity, as the

OVERLEAF, LEFT: *The anguish which Amelia Boccanegra, portrayed by Kiri Te Kanawa, feels is seen on her face as she turns away from her suitor, Paolo Albiani, in Elijah Moshinsky's production of* SIMON BOCCANEGRA *at the Royal Opera House, Covent Garden in 1991. Photography by Clive Barda, Performing Arts Library.* RIGHT: *In Verdi's adaptation of William Shakespeare's play, Desdemona, brought to life by Kiri Te Kanawa, looks lovingly upon her husband, portrayed powerfully by Placido Domingo in Elijah Moshinsky's 1992 production of* OTELLO *for the Royal Opera House, Covent Garden. Photography by Clive Barda, Performing Arts Library.*

opera is musically very beautiful. Pamina is one of Mozart's loveliest roles.

In FIGARO, the anti-female element is less strong, though the Count is definitely a philanderer. Like Alfonso and Despina in Così, Figaro and Susanna are the puppeteers, outwitting the Count. In spite of his abject apology to the Countess at the end, when he gets down on his knees to her to say he is sorry for having been caught red-handed, we know it will not be long before he moves on to the next lover who might very well be Barbarina, the gardener's daughter.

Verdi's men and women show more independence of character. Amelia in SIMON BOCCANEGRA is a survivor. Desdemona, if she did not have that evil Iago in her life, would also have survived. But in this case there are additional factors. Are we supposed to look on Otello as a black man or simply as a man? It is very difficult to know.

When I am staging Desdemona, I see him as a deeply jealous man. But is he is going to murder me because of his jealousy of me, his beautiful blonde wife, or because of his paranoia about being black in a white society? Furthermore, his nemesis, Iago, is white as well. No matter how often I sing Desdemona, I am never quite sure how to read Otello's behaviour.

You still see Otello's insecurity in people every day. The truth of Verdi's opera, the truth of Shakespeare's play, was and is and will remain valid.

I always feel the role of Iago is rather subtle, almost underwritten. The paranoia of Otello is there for all to see, but the viciousness of Iago seems deliberately understated - yet he is the very devil himself. You meet people like that, they hide what is going on within themselves, and mislead you to think they are at peace with the world, when, in reality their life is in turmoil.

There are also hidden meanings to Verdi's TRAVIATA, even though the events appear plausible enough. It is such a simple and touching story, after all - the young man from a good family who falls deeply in love with a high-class courtesan, so his father intervenes.

Every time I sang Violetta, I wondered about the father. His actions seemed so unlikely that I began to feel that he also was attracted to Violetta and that he wanted her even more than did his son.

So, here is another example of extreme masculine jealousy, leading a man to destroy a woman. On the surface, the reasoning all seems so straightforward but I feel that Verdi's music hints at other meanings. Among the female roles of this composer, the personality of Violetta has always struck me as the most humane.

Aida attracted me, but the part would have been difficult for me to sustain against the background of a grand orchestra filled with trumpets and drums and fortissimo scores. More than once have I said to a conductor: 'The music is absolutely wonderful, and if you were to keep the orchestra down, I could get through the work.'

That is the theory. But in fact, you know that the moment you get up on stage, the orchestra will explode. More often than not,

OVERLEAF, LEFT: *Kiri Te Kanawa and Michael Devlin, as the Count and Countess Almaviva, in John Copley's production of* LE NOZZE DI FIGARO *at the San Francisco Opera House in 1986. Photography by Ron Scherl, San Francisco Opera.* PAGE 97: *Kiri Te Kanawa as Arabella and Violetta in different productions.* TOP LEFT: *Portraying the doubt and anxiety Arabella feels over the choice of a husband in the opera of the same name. Photography by Axel Zeininger, courtesy of Österriechischer Bundestheaterverband.* TOP RIGHT: *Violetta sings a powerful aria in John Copley's production of* LA TRAVIATA *at the Sydney Opera House, 1978. Photography by The Australian Opera.* BELOW LEFT: *As Arabella at the New York Metropolitan Opera. Photography by Winnie Klotz, New York Metropolitan Opera.* BELOW RIGHT: *As Arabella under the direction of Silvio Varviso at the Paris Opera in 1981. Photography by Agence de Presse Bernand.*

the conductor's hand does not come up to quieten the orchestra. Many conductors are apparently too timid to ask the players to keep it low.

Mine has never been a monstrous repertoire, and some operas I shall never sing again. I have no desire to perform Puccini's LA RONDINE in public, even though I recorded it not so long ago. The funding suddenly became available and I agreed to sing the role. I panicked as I had only three short weeks to learn the complex role of Magda de Civry. However, when you hear me sing her aria on the soundtrack of the film A ROOM WITH A VIEW, you might think I had been singing that radiant music almost all my life.

LA RONDINE is seldom staged, as is Gustave Charpentier's LOUISE, which I once considered seriously. However, I never had a chance to see the opera performed, and for good reason too. The story-line is thin - a banker's mistress falling in love with another man and renouncing him because of her past. A few beautiful arias such as Louise's, *Depuis le jour*, which I love and sing in concert halls, do not and cannot sustain an opera enough to justify a staging.

As a rule, I only record operas I have already performed. So I declined to record MADAMA BUTTERFLY as it would have taken me two years to get that part properly into my voice. My motto has always been simple: 'Why try to do everything when not everything works?'

Though my voice is still in good shape, I have become very selective in my planning for the forthcoming years. However, I intend to keep on singing the three Strauss operas ARABELLA, DER

Rosenkavalier and Capriccio of my existing repertoire, along with Otello, Simon Boccanegra, Le Nozze di Figaro and Don Giovanni for as long as I can.

I have recorded Strauss' *Four Last Songs*, which have so much in common with his operas, with Solti and Andrew Davis and always hoped to record the work for a third time to show the development of my voice from the beginning of my career through the midpoint to the final stage. My instinct was to choose a young conductor for my last recording, though on reflection I probably would not. Novices in the profession have to have years in the harness to become the relaxed conductors they should be. Then again, I must say that all those years of hard work never relaxed darling Solti. He is as strict as ever.

I regret that the Tosca I recorded with Solti was much too frantic to be exactly what I would have liked it to be. I could also have done a better Traviata, but I was thrilled how Die Zauberflöte turned out with Neville Marriner. He had a manner of making me feel that I was the only singer he had ever worked with or would want to work with. I get this treatment from Solti, too, but not always from many other conductors. I feel they are thinking of themselves most of the time.

Though I sing Amelia in Simon Boccanegra, I have never looked at Verdi's other Amelia, the one in Un Ballo in Maschera. I would love to have been able to add Salome to my list of Strauss roles, but - for the same reasons as Aida - I do not think it lies within my voice.

I might turn down a part if it is too big for me, or does not lie well within my vocal range, or I do not empathise with a

OVERLEAF, TOP LEFT: *Dimitri Hvorostovsky plays Valentin to Renée Fleming's Marguérite, in Frank Corsaro's production of* Faust *for the Lyric Opera of Chicago in 1996. Photography by Robert Kusel, Lyric Opera of Chicago.* BELOW: *An enraptured Anna Tomowa-Sintow as the Marschallin and Annie Sophie von Otter as Octavian in Act One of Willy Decker's production of Richard Strauss'* Der Rosenkavalier *for the Chicago Lyric Opera in 1989. Photography by T. Romano, Lyric Opera of Chicago.* TOP RIGHT: *Giuseppe Sabbatini's Alfredo Germont holds the fatally ill Violetta, played here by June Anderson in the 1993 production of* La Traviata *directed by Frank Galati at the Lyric Opera of Chicago. Photography by Dan Rest, Lyric Opera of Chicago.* BELOW RIGHT: *James Morris takes the title role opposite Carol Vanessa's Donna Elvira in Matthew Lata's 1995 production of* Don Giovanni *for the Lyric Opera of Chicago. Photography by Dan Rest, Lyric Opera of Chicago.*

character. I might look at it from a different angle altogether and simply ask, 'Can I get through four weeks of rehearsals and dress rehearsals before the first night?' Often I can, often I cannot. It is like athletics. You have to pace yourself, and a lot of singers get as far as the first night and then find that they cannot do it. That is terrible, just terrible - all that hard work and not being able to give one's best on the first night.

I enjoyed playing Manon Lescaut in Giacomo Puccini's opera of the same name, but I have always had mixed feelings about Mimi in La Bohème. I have difficulty empathising with her, although I love the music. Her personality is not the easiest to portray. Most of the time she never does anything, and her passivity irritates me. I think it is only in Act Three, the dawn scene at the gates of Paris, that she reveals what little strength she has.

Much depends, it is true, on who is singing Rodolfo. A very ardent Rodolfo can make it simple for the soprano to play Mimi as someone who is adored by him. But if he is merely worried about his next aria, Mimi will have a problem since Rodolfo will be distracted from her. I had the wonderful Pavarotti, playing opposite me at Covent Garden, who was as sweet and adorable a Rodolfo as I could possibly have imagined. He is a very gentle person, unaffected in the happiest sense of the word, the kindest of men.

Micaela, Don José's cast-off sweetheart in Georges Bizet's Carmen, can seem as weak as Mimi in La Bohème, but it depends again on who is playing the part. In reality, she is strong and decisive, as her appearance in Act Three proves. This is a role I have enjoyed, ever since I first sang it with Placido Domingo as

Don José, Shirley Verrett as Carmen, and Solti as conductor. It offers far more scope than you would think. I would like to have performed the role of Micaela more often, but lately people do not want to see me in what is known as a secondary role. Personally, I would love to sing Micaela again. Unfortunately, it never seems to happen, though I do sing her aria in concerts.

Francis Poulenc's LES DIALOGUES DE CARMILITES, a fabulous and very modern French opera, is a work I would like to go back to, but I have never been asked. On the other hand, a dear friend of mine, a conductor, recently suggested that we do Jules Massenet's MANON. I reminded him that it was five acts long, and I could not bear the thought of learning it, and boring an audience with it, at this stage in my career.

Puccini's heroines - including his Italianised Manon Lescaut - are delightful and probably never lost their appeal for the audience. But for the singer, performing them regularly could become boring. I have enjoyed doing Tosca, although the part does not completely suit my voice. I suspect if I had sung it at the start of my career, I might have done myself serious vocal damage.

In addition, the opera as a whole does not excite me musically. In the works of Mozart and Strauss there is always some little technical hurdle to be conquered, which keeps you on your toes and prevents your concentration level dropping. Their works always contain a twist, you always worry that you might falter at the next difficult passage.

One Strauss role I would love to have done, but could never do, was Octavian in ROSENKAVALIER. It is a very appealing role for a

OVERLEAF, TOP LEFT: Emily Golden and Neil Shicoff play the ill-fated lovers, Carmen and Don José in Vera Calabria's 1990 production of CARMEN at the Lyric Opera of Chicago. Photography by T. Romano, Lyric Opera of Chicago. CENTRE: William Shimell and Felicity Lott as Count and Countess Almaviva, reunited in the final act of Sir Peter Hall's production of LE NOZZE DI FIGARO for the Lyric Opera of Chicago in 1991. Photography by T. Romano, Lyric Opera of Chicago. TOP RIGHT: Playing the devoted couple, Figaro and Susanna, are Samuel Ramey and Marie McLaughlin in Sir Peter Hall's production of LE NOZZE DI FIGARO for the Lyric Opera of Chicago in 1991. Photography by T. Romano, Lyric Opera of Chicago. BELOW LEFT: Maria Chiara and Giorgio Merighi portray Manon Lescaut and Chevalier des Grieux, for director Giorgio De Lullo in the 1977 production of MANON LESCAUT at the Lyric Opera of Chicago. Photography by T. Romano, Lyric Opera of Chicago.

LEFT: *Dimitri Kavrakos, in his role as Prince Gremin, holds the hand of Anna Tomowa-Sintow, who plays his princess, Tatyana, in Pier Luigi Samaritani's production of* Eugene Onegin *for the Lyric Opera of Chicago in 1990. Photography by T. Romano, Lyric Opera of Chicago.*

woman - perhaps the only breeches role I have ever truly coveted. It would have been a lot of hard work. As the Marschallin, you have your rest periods. You sing for most of the admittedly very long first act and for part of the last act, but between these appearances you have an hour and twenty minutes in which you have nothing to do.

Octavian would also have been far too low for me. The role requires a mezzo-soprano with a good, high top. You have to have that extra bit of mezzo weight to sing it, especially to get through the sound of the orchestra.

As a student, I played a small role in Le Roi L'a Dit by Léo Delibes. It was fun, but probably more so for the singers than for the audience. In a student production, which the audience pays almost nothing to see, you can get away more easily with such an opera - especially if it is as witty as Le Roi L'a Dit. The work has the added advantage of being so rarely staged as to have a certain novelty value.

But in a big opera house, you cannot help but think of the audiences who have paid for an expensive seat to see an interesting piece. They may not be able to appreciate how much a work as slight as Le Roi L'a Dit would cost a good company in a notable opera house to produce.

When someone tried to tempt me into singing Richard Wagner, I simply refused the offer. Solti once did his best to persuade me to sing Sieglinde in Die Walküre, and in general, if Solti suggests I do something, I tend to do it. I went home over the weekend, with everyone gone and, in peace and quiet, looked at the score, tried my voice out on it, and played recordings non-stop.

Singing it with Solti of all people would have been wonderful. But it was not for me. I have to feel as though I could do justice to a role, and I just believed I could never sing Sieglinde.

I love Wagner, but as a performer I find him an almost untouchable composer. Apart from my youthful moments as a Flower Maiden in PARSIFAL and apart from the tiny role of the Woodbird in SIEGFRIED, I have always avoided him since.

It was the same with Strauss' DIE FRAU OHNE SCHATTEN, which Solti also wanted me to try. The music seemed simply too heavy, and the same could be said for the title role in ARIADNE AUF NAXOS, which people are forever suggesting, but which would put me straight into the arms of Bacchus - not necessarily my idea of fun. His voice would not be the ideal match for mine.

I have always insisted on protecting my voice, not least from heldentenors, and I am sure I have been right to do so. For the past ten years, my voice has remained unchanged. The higher part of my voice is in place. The lower part has never been very strong, and I now have to work at it a little harder than I did. I have consciously avoided parts which are very heavy on chest notes as they cause serious wear and tear to a voice.

A long time ago someone tried to push me into doing THE MIDSUMMER MARRIAGE. For a budding soprano, it is quite difficult to refuse an enticing opportunity suggested by a renowned conductor. However, I refused the part. Later, Georges Bizet's LES PECHEURS DE PERLES was proposed to me by a recording company. However, I could not see anything worth doing in the work with the exception of the famous duet between the tenor and the baritone.

OVERLEAF: *Kiri Te Kanawa in her role as Micaela, sings a duet with Placido Domingo who plays the dashing Don Josè in Michael Geliot's 1973 production of* CARMEN *at the Royal Opera House, Covent Garden. Photography by Zoë Dominic.*

I have never been attracted to any of Gluck's operas, not even to ORFEO during the time I was tackling mezzo roles, but I do love singing Händel, even if it is just the occasional aria, as at Prince Charles' wedding.

I once did a Händel collage for television with Christopher Hogwood and the Academy of Ancient Music. They called it THE SORCERESS. It was assembled from several of Händel's operas and issued on video. I was the only singer required for the recording which consisted of a series of seven arias, with a plot loosely based on that of ALCINA, Händel's great witchcraft opera, which Joan Sutherland used to perform so well.

Only one of the arias actually came from ALCINA itself. The rest were extracted from JULIUS CAESAR and other operas. The collage was rather strange and difficult to sing, but I think it worked. One piece, which I called the aria from hell because it tormented me so much, lasted about seven minutes.

This particular piece had three passages of recitative in it, and so much coloratura that I recorded and filmed it in a series of separate sections. The producer had cameras sweeping round relentlessly, and there were so many twists and turns in the music that I thought I was going to die. It reminded me of Joan Sutherland who said that in a difficult piece she could go from one cadenza to the next and never know where she was.

Sutherland has always been one of my great heroines. But I have special memories, too, of Frederica von Stade as Cherubino in FIGARO - she was one of the best Cherubinos. Tatyana Troyanos' Octavian in ROSENKAVALIER was in the same league, as was Agnes Baltsa in this role. It would also be hard to choose between Mirella Freni and Ileana Cotrubas as Susanna in FIGARO.

Thomas Allen's Marcello in LA BOHÈME filled me with admiration, as did Hakan Hagegard as Papageno in the Ingmar Bergman film of DIE ZAUBERFLÖTE. No less memorable for me was the experience of hearing Leontyne Price sing Aida at the age of fifty-eight, complete with a tremendous *O patria mia* in the Nile scene. Singing of that quality was an example to us all.

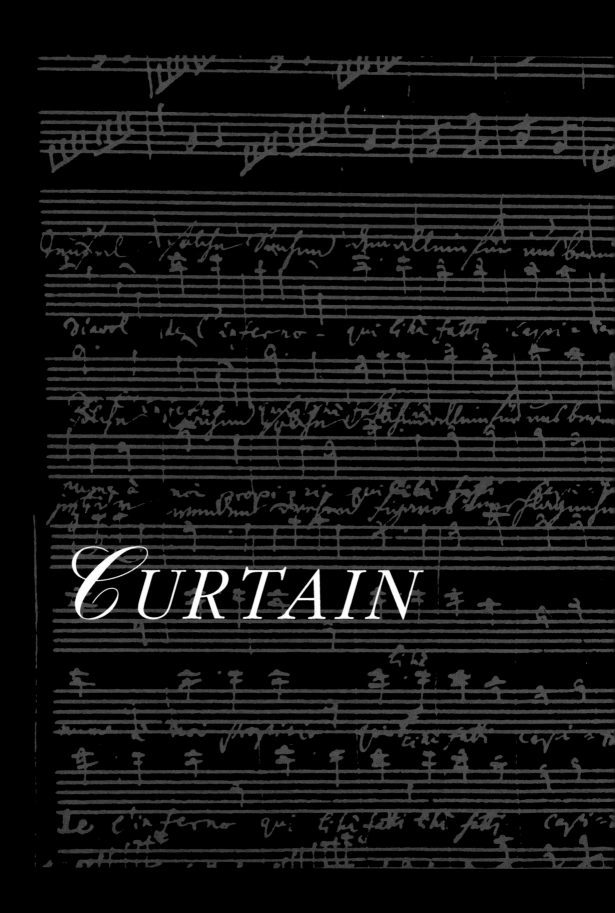

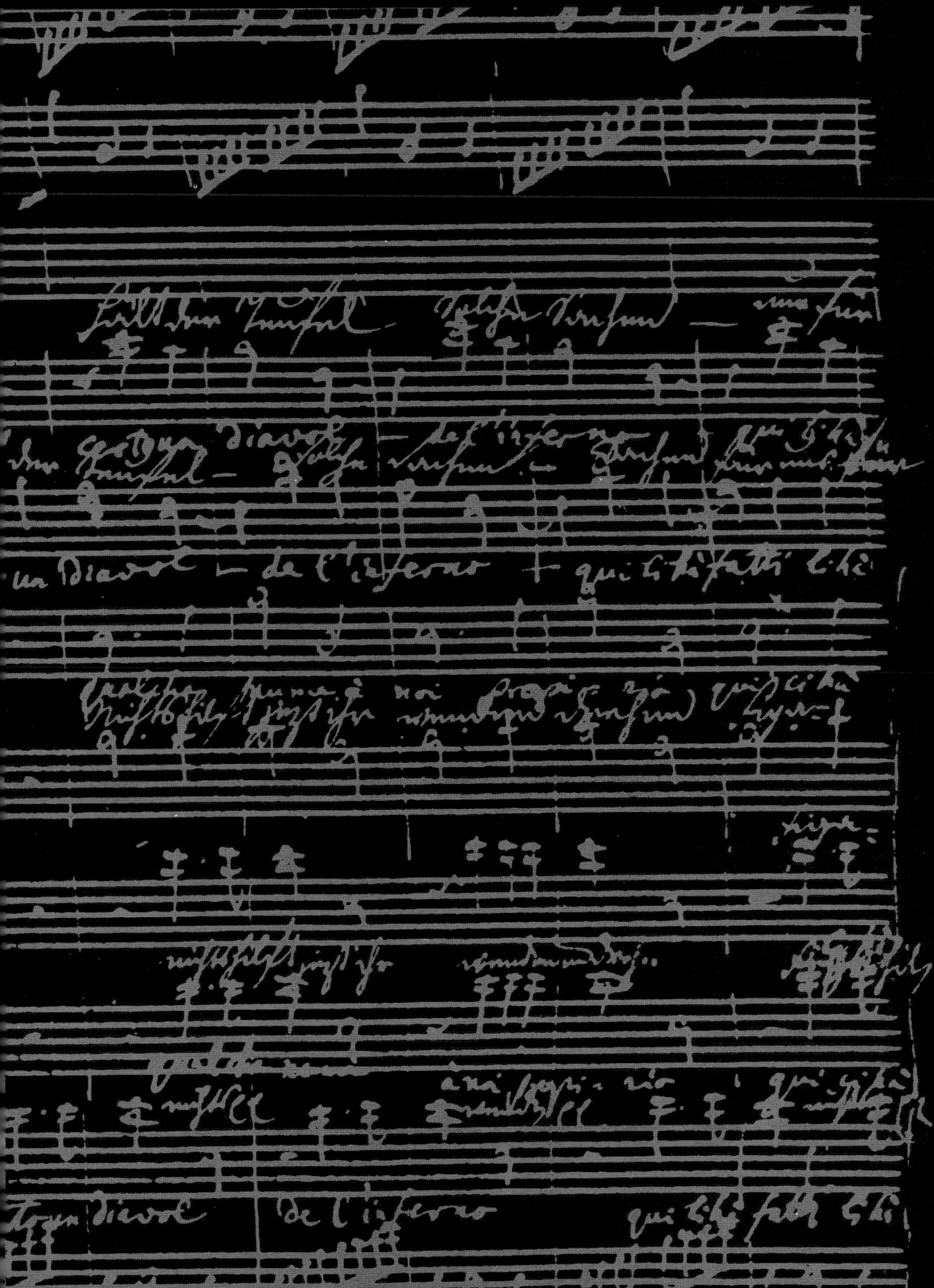

MUCH ADMIRED CONDUCTORS

To be a great or even a good opera conductor, it is said, requires the qualities of a mythical god. Most singers have a list of their favourite conductors - the ones they have learned to trust, the ones who have nurtured them, are patient with them, understand them, make them feel loved, tolerate their foibles, give them clear signals, keep them calm, know instinctively when their voices need nursing, subdue the orchestra on their behalf and simply show they care.

These do not have to be great conductors in the conventional sense. Some of them have sacrificed starry careers for the sake of the singers whose voices and personalities they have recognised, like Tullio Serafin who encouraged Maria Callas in her early days.

Serafin was an expert conductor, wondrously knowledgeable about opera and how it should be sung. He was reputedly modest and retiring, and much happier in the orchestra pit than on the concert platform.

Joan Sutherland received similar devotion and advice from her conductor husband, Richard Bonynge. Both Serafin and Bonynge have achieved international acclaim as conductors dedicated to the performers they worked with. They could be hailed as 'singer's conductors' in the best sense.

These conductors knew about the human voice and all its problems. Both of them seemed more content to play the attentive and inspirational leader to a great singer than to seek their own fame. As Dame Janet Baker has said of the late Sir Alexander Gibson: 'He was a master of the art of accompaniment, and it is becoming a lost art.'

Being one of today's star sopranos, I have reached the position where I have the option to work only with conductors I admire and feel in tune with. But it was not always like that. In common with other singers, I have had the experience of conductors who let the orchestra play too loudly, who fail to breathe the music in the same way as I do, who shape a phrase with the rigidity of band masters.

My favourite conductor is, unquestionably, Sir Georg Solti, with whom I have performed or recorded most of my favourite roles. Here is a conductor whose career has been sensational. He has successfully straddled both opera houses and concert halls, who exudes power, lives on his nerves.

At the age of eighty-four, Georg Solti seems an unlikely opera singer's chaperon, at least in the Serafin sense. He can be impatient, and strikes fear into the hearts of many singers. A perfectionist is not easy on his co-workers, but the effort is rewarded by a brilliant performance.

Solti is the one of the few conductors I would happily fly the Atlantic to work with, and he, for his part, is the one who, on the spur of a moment, calls me for a performance. What makes Solti different from other conductors and so wonderful to work with, is that I always know exactly what he wants. We are on

ABOVE: *Andrew Davis in
a studio portrait, 1993.*
ABOVE RIGHT: *Sir
Neville Marriner, 1992.*
RIGHT: *Sir Colin Davis in
a rehearsal at The
Barbican, 1991.* FAR
RIGHT: *Riccardo Chailly
conducting during the
performance of* LE NOZZE
DI FIGARO *at the Royal
Opera House, Covent
Garden, 1994.
Photography on this page
by Clive Barda,
Performing Arts Library.*

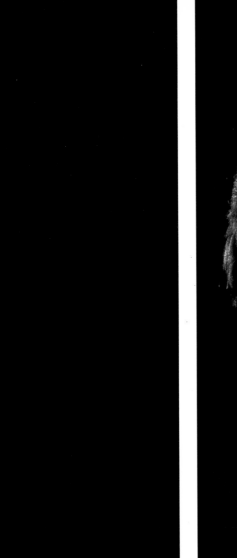

the same wavelength. Despite all his demands, he is a person who actually seems to like what I do. Working with him can be difficult - of course it can - because he is a very exacting man and a great perfectionist.

Solti has been said to treat opera like a military operation, which is perfectly true. His organisational ability is one of the characteristics I admire most in him. As a singer, I like the thought of being completely disciplined, so that no problem can arise during a performance. Solti is always there and at the ready to do all that needs to be done to establish a clear communication between the stage and the orchestra pit which is the prerequisite for a good performance.

The ability to create harmony between the cast and the orchestra players is one of the best attributes an opera conductor can have. Many of the newer conductors let me know that their time is very limited. They say at the start: 'You sing well, you phrase well, you will make the performance work, so let's do the job together.'

The trouble is that though these conductors know what they want, they do not always take the time to explain and demonstrate to the cast what they expect. The performers are often at a loss and have to guess how to make it all happen. And the conductors do not find out if their intentions suit the performers. By contrast, Solti always takes the individual qualities of the performers and the players into consideration.

Solti's ability to see your point of view, at least if you are someone he respects, is one of his endearing characteristics. If I want to mould a certain phrase and need a lot of time to do so,

Solti can grant that even though his beat is as tight as it ever was. During rehearsals with Solti, I just take my time, take my breath, and, if necessary, start the phrase again. This possibility makes all the difference between a phrase that lives and breathes and one that is lifeless.

On the other hand, inexperienced conductors often cannot accommodate these requests. They are like clockwork. To put it simply, these conductors may be able to slow music down slightly, or quicken it up, but a singer needs more than that. Novice conductors I have known are seldom able to allow a performer this freedom, because they lack experience.

Solti's pacing is to my taste, especially in Wolfgang Amadeus Mozart and Giuseppe Verdi, but above all, in Richard Strauss, in whose music he is completely at home. My work on DER ROSENKAVALIER with Solti at Covent Garden was followed by a video of the opera.

Regrettably, apart from DER ROSENKAVALIER and our recording of the *Four Last Songs*, I have not sung nearly as much Strauss with Solti as I would have liked. We have not even managed to do an ARABELLA together, though it is an opera he knows and loves. I once tried to get him to do CAPRICCIO with me - I longed to perform that work with him - but he simply did not want to do it. Maybe he prefers the challenge of a more demanding work like DIE FRAU OHNE SCHATTEN with its vast contrasts between Strauss' opulent instrumentation for the emperor's domain and his suggestive portrayal of the misty fairy world.

Solti is undoubtedly my Number One. Today there is nobody like him, nobody so strongly linked with the past, or through

ABOVE LEFT: *Zubin Mehta, conducting the resident orchestra at the Maggio Musicale in Florence, 1993. Photography by Clive Barda, Performing Arts Library.* ABOVE CENTRE: *Jeffrey Tate, 1992. Photography by Michael Ward, Performing Arts Library.* FAR LEFT: *James Levine in Vienna. Photography courtesy of Österreichischer Bundestheaterverband.* LEFT: *Lorin Maazel, at the Royal Festival Hall, with the Philharmonia Orchestra, 1993. Photography by Clive Barda, Performing Arts Library.*

whom musical history flows. Who now can say that he studied with Bela Bartók and Zoltán Kodály and Arturo Toscanini?

I loved working with Karl Böhm, the great Austrian opera conductor who also formed part of the same great tradition that Solti belongs to. Böhm was renowned as interpreter of the works of Wolfgang Amadeus Mozart and Richard Strauss. Karl Böhm was a close friend of Richard Strauss who dedicated the opera DAPHNE to him. The maestro's death brought a particular era of Mozart and Strauss conducting completely to an end.

Wilhelm Furtwängler was a conductor I would have enjoyed working with. No one else could phrase quite as flexibly as he. Unfortunately, this eminent expert on the works of Richard Wagner and Mozart died more than ten years before my time. Furtwängler who also composed several symphonies and concertos was likewise part of the tradition.

Among the conductors who are now at the height of their careers James Levine stands out. I always look forward to singing at the New York Metropolitan, of which he has been the Managing Director since 1976. He is a fine Mozartian, a particularly good pianist and excellent accompanist as well.

I have not worked with Claudio Abbado for many years, and certainly not since he became Herbert von Karajan's successor with the Berlin Philharmonic, but I admire him, too. Abbado has become reputed especially for his interpretations of the operas of Gioachino Rossini, Vincenzo Bellini and Giuseppe Verdi.

I did some lovely Mozart with Sir Colin Davis in his Covent Garden days, but I have not worked with him for quite some time either. Solti is the one I have most consistently sung with, but Davis also has the right operatic qualities and is always on the singer's side. I know that my phrasing is totally in tune with his, and that is very important. As far as I am concerned, almost everything in opera goes back to Davis. If anyone has formed my Mozart style, it is him. When I originally learned FIGARO with Davis, I accepted Colin as God and did what I was told. I suppose it is amazing that years later I still want to perform Mozart with Colin's strict attitude and a lack of decoration. Everything that I learned from Davis, ever since that time I first worked with him at Covent Garden, I have carried with me to this day.

Other Mozart conductors occasionally suggest that I jump the gun all the time. Davis always made me anticipate every phrase. A singer could never be too early, or, for that matter, early enough for Colin. Yet, there was never once any sense of rushing through a rehearsal or a performance with him. His tempi always seemed to remain consistent, meticulous and precise. Despite the lack of ornamentation in his productions, they had colour.

Ornamentation has become a fashionable element of the so-called 'authentic' Mozart performances. The question of adding a mordent, a double mordent, a trill, a turn, an inverted turn, a Nachschlag, an acciaccatura or an appoggiatura and a grace-note to Mozart's scores is hotly debated among conductors, producers and singers today. What happens to the original tune through the addition of the note next to it, either below or above, and the duplication or triplication of the original note in a wide variety of different rhythms and tempi, can be imagined. The entire character of the work changes.

OVERLEAF, LEFT: *Seiji Ozawa with the London Symphony Orchestra, 1994.* TOP RIGHT: *Kent Nagano with the London Symphony Orchestra at The Barbican, 1990.* BELOW: *Leonard Bernstein at the Royal Festival Hall, 1979. All photography on these pages by Clive Barda, Performing Arts Library.*

Though these ornamentations are not written into the score, some are indicated on the margins. However, since these marks were not standardized until well into the nineteenth century, conductors and performers today are left to their own devices to guess the meaning of these symbols. Furthermore, embellishments like the trill and the Nachschlag were played in the seventeenth century in one manner and in the nineteenth century in another.

Some conductors claim that decorations were implied even if they were not noted on the score. They beautify the shaping of a cadenza and enhance the melodic line, or so they claim. And quite a few conductors embellish every line of music they get their hands on.

I accept that there are times when ornamentation can add flavour to the music, making the tones sound more positive by including an appoggiatura from above the note, or more mournful by adding one from the note beneath. Yet more often than not, there is no need for them. I would not contemplate adding decorations to most arias. I like the melodies exactly as they are written.

Davis did not like ornamentation, and neither do I. To this day he uses very few decorations, and prefers the melodic line to stand as the composer wrote it. My philosophy is similarly simple: 'Why decorate and spoil a beautiful tune?' Embellishments are usually put in by somebody who wants to leave his mark on the notes.

Sometimes decorations are just added mechanically. How many appoggiaturas do you have, Susanna? Should you have more or fewer than the Countess? I think you have to consider what the music is trying to say to determine whether appoggiaturas are suited or not. Since decorations tend to be pre-planned, I find them too calculated. Opera needs spontaneity and fluidity.

There are conductors who never look at you while you are singing, who keep their faces in the score which I find totally uninspiring. When that happens, it is not a performance, not a proper collaboration, not a joint statement of love for the music.

I like it when I see a conductor looking up at me expectantly from the pit, and I know he senses that I am going to do something different. At such times, I can see the look in someone like Solti's eyes. He knows that I have signalled him in some subtle way, said something to him silently, and as the phrase comes up, the conductor will be ready for me and will give me a little extra time if that is what I want. Then he will signal that it is his turn, and off we will go again.

That is the wonderful contact I love during a performance, a feeling of give and take. That is what staging opera is all about. I get this sense of communication with Colin Davis, and had it also with John Pritchard. By the end he was so much on my wavelength that his responses were almost instinctive and his hands would go slowly down or up to convey his messages to the players. It was all I needed to excite me as a singer, a small acknowledgement that the conductor was with me, and that he loved the music the way I did. After all, conductors have such a big job to do, it is nice to know that they have time for me.

What can be truly disappointing, however, is when you have conductors in the pit who do not care. They are too busy, they are distracted by personal matters, they prefer one of the other sopranos to you, or the tenor or the baritone. Working with the producer may be hell, but you are finally in the conductor's hands. He calls the tune. If you have someone in the pit who just yawns when he looks at you and shows no concern, you would rather go home.

A conductor is not always a singer's potential enemy, albeit some singers invariably thinking of him in that way. Although a conductor may make demands, much is likewise demanded of him. Normally, he is expected to attend all rehearsals. He, of course, also has to lead all the performances. He needs to keep the cast and the orchestra together and motivate the players and performers with praise and critique.

Rightly or wrongly, we all do need and expect praise and a support system to keep us going, whether or not we ask for it or deserve it. Colin Davis is one conductor who has the knack of making every member of the team feel good.

Yet, nobody seems willing to compliment a conductor on his efforts. It must be a lonely life for them, and occasionally it begins to show. There are moments when you can see that conductors would like to have their self-esteem boosted as well and then I feel that they deserve more sympathy than they get. Having said that, the egos of some conductors are more than big enough already.

I have never worked with the great but reclusive Carlos Kleiber, not even on Verdi's OTELLO, which is one of his specialities. I have not worked with Riccardo Muti either, or with Carlo Maria Giulini which I regret.

ABOVE: *Claudio Abbado in action at the Queen Elizabeth Hall, 1988. Photography by Clive Barda, Performing Arts Library.* LEFT: *Karl Böhm taking a break during a recording at Henry Wood Hall with the London Symphony Orchestra, 1980. Photography by Clive Barda, Performing Arts Library.*

I did once a FIGARO with Herbert von Karajan at Salzburg, but found it difficult to relate to him and never had another chance to improve our communication. Usually, I have to do two, three, or four performances with a conductor to know what is actually happening, how a production is created and how the music is made.

Karajan's was a fabulous performance. I know that he always provoked divided opinions among critics, some of them admiring his polish and his perfectionism, others thinking him too much of a superb, high-powered machine. But the greater a conductor is, the more likely he is to attract criticism.

Andrew Davis is of a younger generation of conductors. He stands out in my mind as an outstandingly fine Straussian. I like working with him. I also admire Julius Rudel, a good conductor, better known in America than in Europe, with whom I have done Così FAN TUTTE and numerous concerts. Perhaps I am wrong, but I have the impression that there not many conductors in the top ranks these days, and they are getting fewer all the time.

Neville Marriner, with whom I recorded DIE ZAUBERFLÖTE, is a quiet Englishman with a pleasant nature. Marriner has never been a fiery conductor like Solti and, yet, he is inspired. Every time I have worked with Marriner I found it very meaningful music-making. He has a way of making me feel that he totally believes in me, and I do not get that from many people. There is a sensitivity about Marriner that I really love. He is a terrific conductor, now in his seventies; a great man.

Working with Giuseppe Sinopoli, was uncomfortable for me. I found I could not access his music. We were doing Puccini's

MANON LESCAUT at Covent Garden. He is excitingly controversial, but working with him proved difficult. I was unwell at the time, and probably should have cancelled.

However, the management would not entertain this suggestion , and I struggled through the performances with a bad case of flu. Later we both recorded MANON LESCAUT, I performed the opera with Riccardo Chailly and Sinopoli conducted Mirella Freni. Chailly was a pure pleasure to work with.

Karl Böhm could be slow, but his slowness was always intense - that was the beauty of it. He was often criticised for his slowness - and still is when his recordings are reissued - but there was always a structure to it. With some conductors, there are speeds that literally seem to wind down to go nowhere. But Böhm always managed to hold the musical tension throughout the entire performance.

In essence, as a singer, you do need a singer's conductor. Claudio Abbado is one who always conducts from memory, a practice which some performers worry about, because they fear Claudio might not be able to retrieve the situation if something goes suddenly wrong. Yet, I thought that he was absolutely fabulous. His performance demonstrated flexibility, he communicated with the singers and most definitely was not stuck with his head in the score.

Some conductors go to the other extreme and never take their eyes off the music so that they lose the necessary flow of communication with the members of the cast.

Since these conductors never look at you unless something has gone wrong, they do not know where you are, especially if you are moving around the stage which I suppose must be equally frustrating to them. Sometimes a conductor suddenly looks up and when the singers are not where he expects them to be, he wonders in exasperation why the singers are not with him?

A conductor must be able to constantly phrase with me, and breathe the same sort of breath, know how long my notes can stretch, and be able to anticipate me. He must also have the strength to keep the orchestra down, because orchestras in general are too loud.

Moreover, though this may seem strange, a good conductor must not be too tall, because a tall conductor's arms are too long which is something I discovered long ago. As a result, his beat is too long, consequently, the sound of the orchestra inevitably starts to grow.

I prefer a conductor with a short beat, a small, economical beat, which is something that tends to go with smallish men. And, of course, my ideal conductor must be mature. Young conductors have not settled in their style and have much to learn. Years of experience are needed to get the relaxed nature and knowledge that are the keys to good conducting.

Solti, above all, is the one man who fulfils these qualifications, even though nobody could call him relaxed. He has an economical beat, he is very well organised, he is extremely efficient in everything he does, he never picks on the orchestra yet knows how to keep it down. And I love his never-diminishing enthusiasm for life, which recently prompted him to phone me and ask if I would be free to perform in Verdi's SIMON BOCCANEGRA in two years' time. 'But Georg', I exclaimed into the

receiver, 'we might both be dead by then!' and he replied
impatiently, 'Not going to die, no dyings, you come and sing.'

I have happy memories of singing TOSCA in Paris with Seiji
Ozawa as conductor. He was extremely kind, patient and
supportive but at the same time very dynamic and dramatic in
his interpretation. I wish I could have worked with him on more
occasions. Unfortunately, our schedules never seem to coincide.

The only time I worked with Leonard Bernstein was the
recording of his own WEST SIDE STORY a few years before his
death. A lot of the background details of these sessions and the
stress we all went through have been preserved on video, which
many people have seen. The video shows the now notorious
altercation between Bernstein and a tired José Carréras which
has been retained in the memory of the public to the exclusion
of many more harmonious moments. Yet, working with
Bernstein was a delight and a privilege, because he cultivated an
atmosphere of dedication and enthusiasm which inspired the
performance as a whole.

For our recording of WEST SIDE STORY, Bernstein hand-picked
every single member of the orchestra. He selected the
percussionists with particular care, because they had to put on
track shoes to dash from one instrument to another in order to
cope with all the percussion parts. And the orchestral players,
these hardened musicians, would not leave the session when it
was finished. They sat there totally absorbed in the presence of
this magnificent man, just wanting to be with him. I still cherish
the memory. Singing WEST SIDE STORY was something outside my
previous range of experience, and it was certainly not a light
sing, as some listeners may assume it to be. Nobody should

underestimate the depth and complexity of WEST SIDE STORY. It may take the form of a Broadway musical, but it is a serious composition, with massive orchestration and an undertaking for the most competent of voices.

Bernstein certainly had a personality. Indeed I would say he had a multiple personality. He enjoyed being able to play with people. I would wonder, 'Is he all right today?' and was never quite sure.

I shall never forget an occasion when my phone rang at home and it turned out to be Bernstein. Sometimes I think I may have dreamt the whole incident, but I know I did not. We talked for half an hour. He said he had been listening all day to my recording of the LES CHANTS D'AUVERGNE, trying to get inspiration to write music. He kept on talking to me, saying: 'I cannot write any music. I have been sitting here for hours and I have not put one note down on paper.' It was a wonderfully candid moment with this difficult man whom I adored.

Bernstein was one of the great musicians of this century, yet, he felt that people underrated his WEST SIDE STORY, which he considered an extremely important piece. And I agree. Some of the rhythms in it are amazing.

Though the conductors with whom I have worked most productively are Georg Solti, James Levine, and in earlier years Colin Davis and Karl Böhm, there are surprisingly few operas I have sung with all of them. With Solti I have sung DON GIOVANNI but not FIGARO. With Levine I have performed FIGARO and COSÌ FAN TUTTE but not DON GIOVANNI. With Karl Böhm I did DIE ZAUBERFLÖTE but none of Mozart's Italian operas. I wish I were able to compare in detail the manner in which one conductor and then another worked with me on one particular opera, but, sadly, it is not possible.

As there is normally a considerable time gap between the performances of any particular opera with different conductors, I cannot always remember the small variations of interpretation between one conductor and another. This is especially so when my portrayal of a character is fully worked out, and completely established in my voice, mind and body.

An opera singer's life by its nature tends to have its own priorities. It is a hectic and strenuous life, and often certain aspects of a performance remain more vividly in the memory than who was conducting and how he was conducting, on any particular night.

I may remember that one conductor - Otto Klemperer for sure - was very slow in a magisterial manner, and that another conductor could be very fast. None of these approaches to tempo is necessarily good or bad, or suitable or unsuitable for the rhythm of a piece of music, always provided that speed is consistent. It is easy, in both instances, to lose the tension of a work and let the passages fall apart.

However, to produce a performance sparkling with life, the most important task of a conductor is to ensure that the colour and the light of the notes are shining through the phrasing of both, the orchestra and the singers.

I am often reminded of the old story of the orchestral player who said, after a conductor had explained in exceedingly long, boring, and tedious detail how he wanted a certain passage performed, 'Yes, maestro, but do you want it loud or soft?' It may seem unappreciative of me to say so, but many of the conductors with whom I have worked have seemed alike in the way they have tackled a work.

Frankly, I cannot even remember the names of some of them - even those who have done things very differently from the rest. There are people you encounter only once in the course of your life. I recall others, who struck me as rather good at the time, but whom I have not seen or heard of since.

SECOND ACT

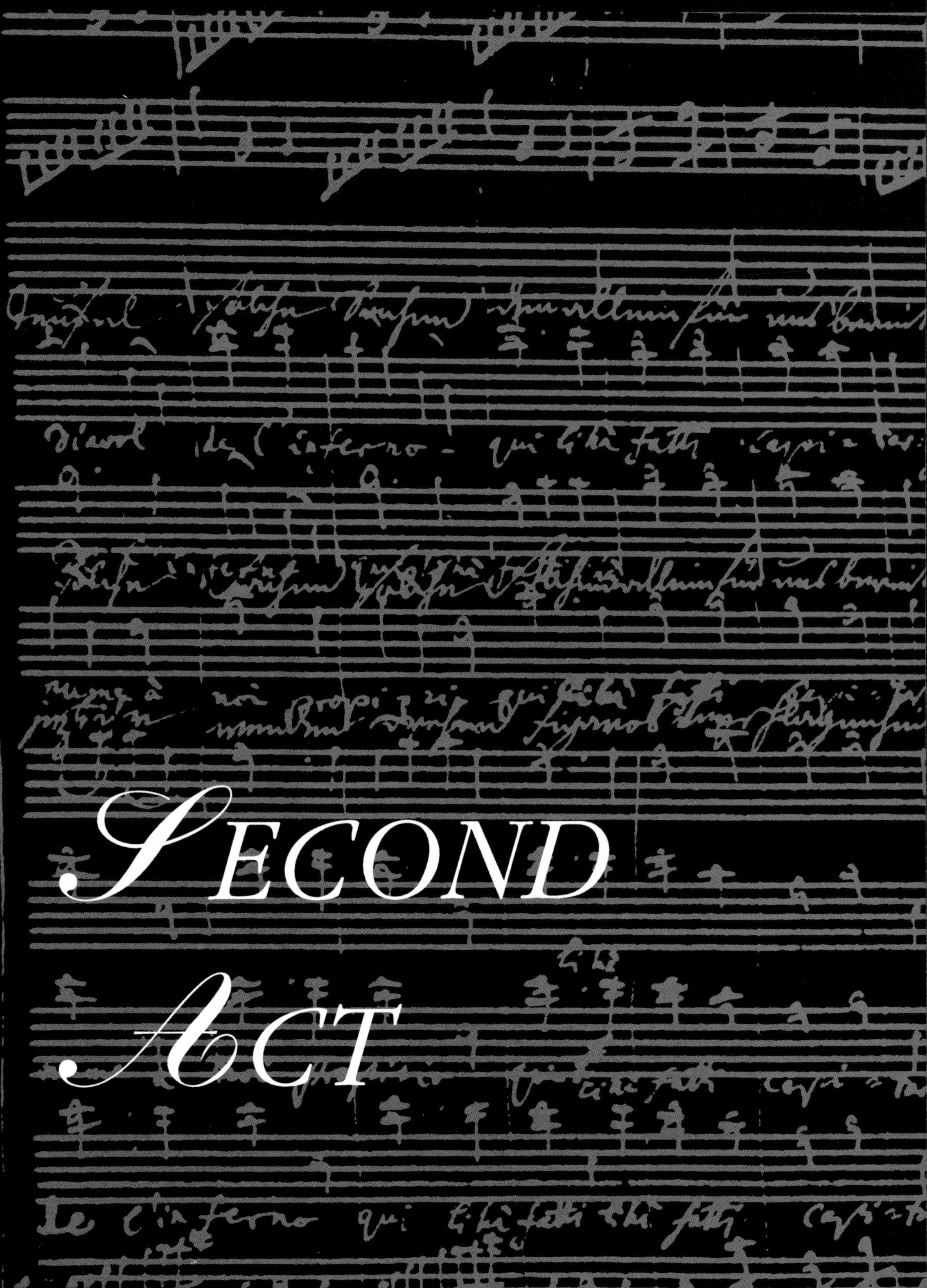

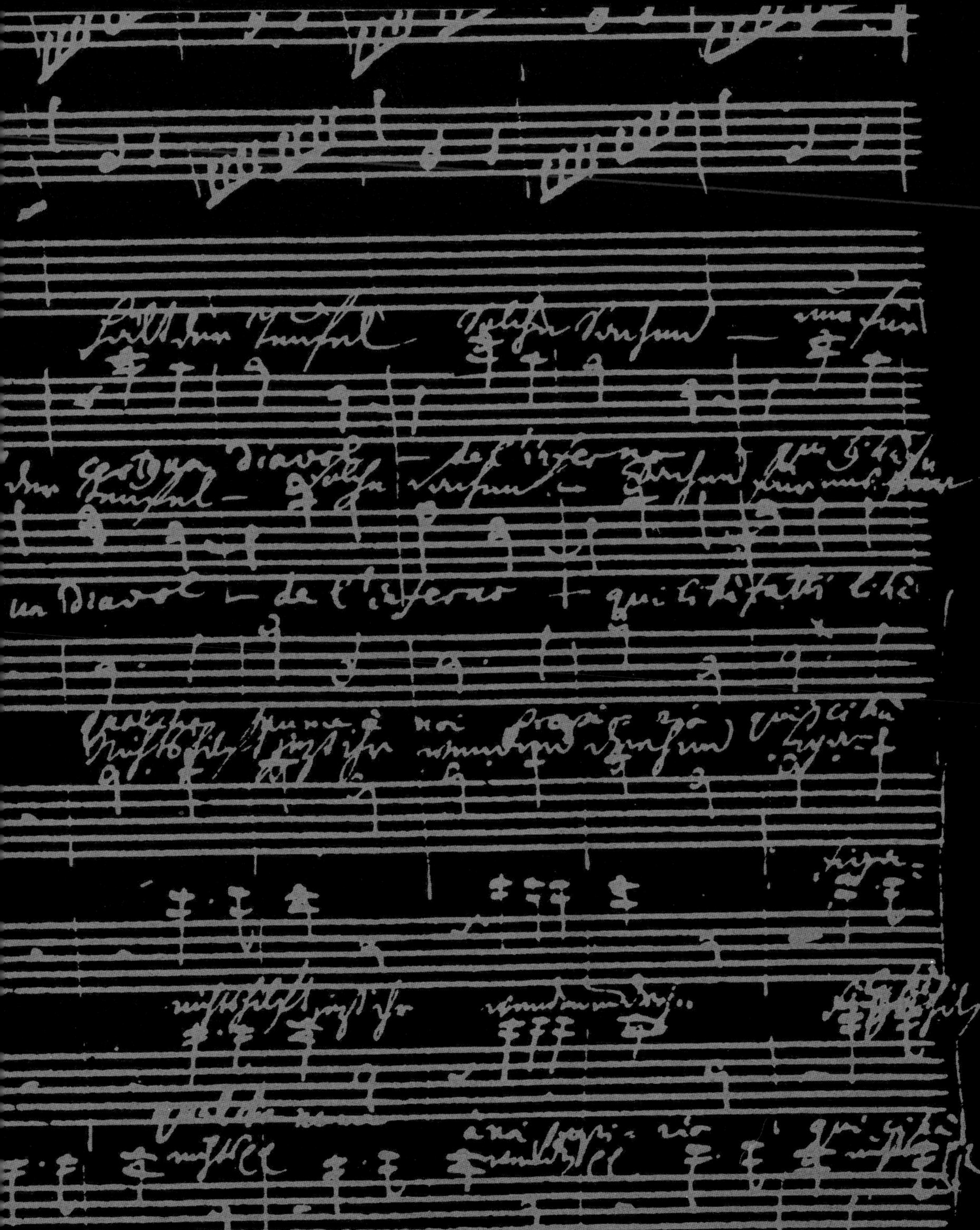

THE LYRICS OF LOVE

T throughout history, operas have been treating the theme of love in its many tragic and comic variations. The libretti may tell of the fortunes and misfortunes of kings and queens, as in Händel, or of mythology, as in Christoph Gluck, or of countesses and servants, as in Mozart or Strauss, or of heroes and villains, as in Verdi, but in the end, they are lyrics of love - love versus duty, sacrifice versus love.

The personae involved are not necessarily similar characters, but there is undoubtedly a language of opera, with operatic archetypes which can create this impression. Consequently, I sometimes wish that the characters I am portraying would behave differently, react differently and act in less convoluted manners once in a while.

OPPOSITE, ABOVE: *Kiri Te Kanawa, Stuart Burrowes, Edda Moser and Geraint Evans in Charles Mackerras' production of* DON GIOVANNI, *staged at the Paris Opera House, 1975.* BELOW: *Kiri Te Kanawa and Ruggero Raimondi in the same production by Charles Mackerras. Photography by Agence de Presse Bernand.*

I can get impatient and annoyed when I see two or more operatic characters heading into a state of prolonged confusion over a misunderstanding, which could be sorted out between them with a few simple words of explanation. When I think of Otello's unjustified jealousy of Desdemona, or Figaro's of Susanna, or Susanna's of Figaro, I sometimes feel like saying to them: 'Speak your mind. Get your act together.'

Opera explores its themes in an indirect manner to conclude with a direct impact. Love, duty, temptation, morality and

strength of character in a closely confined society are illustrated, varied and commented on in words and notes. A quagmire of charades, masquerades and intrigues in multiple sub-plots add new twists to the story-line before the grand finale. The wonderful music often provides its own interpretation of the subject, sometimes in harmony with and occasionally in contrast to the lyrics.

A good performance adds its own special magic to this great operatic experience. But when the performance is lacking in quality, I am less patient with all the verbal operatic rigmarole and wish that the characters would just get on with the plot. A good example is when Figaro's parents are finally identified as Doctor Bartolo and Marcellina and we get endless repetitions of *Sua madre* and *Suo padre* going round all the different characters. I can become rather irritated, even though the music is beautiful at that point.

Everything clearly depends on how the composer deals with the structure and controls the plot. If he is not able to add music to words without slowing down the action disastrously, the audience begins to lose interest. This ability to handle a situation and to pace the music accordingly is what made Mozart and Strauss the geniuses they were. It is amazing how great composers hold your attention time after time despite the very limited range of subjects and situations you find in opera.

Some libretti, especially eighteenth-century ones, have been used again and again by different composers. The good versions have survived in the repertoire, and the others are occasionally revived at obscure opera festivals. A good libretto is rarer than a bad libretto - the whole history of opera tells us that. But no libretto, however good, will survive bad music, whereas good music may help to hide the flaws of a bad libretto. The libretto of Verdi's MACBETH is a poor substitute for Shakespeare's poetry, but the music makes it worth performing. We listen to Verdi's MACBETH because of Verdi's music, not because it is based on Shakespeare's masterpiece.

A great composer is able to change and enhance a familiar operatic situation by writing better music than others and by throwing his own personal light on the characterisation. He may use musical ambiguity - the so-called hidden language of opera - whereby the music provides different undercurrents which your ears pick up while the words tell you something else.

This conflict between music and libretto gives opera its special tension. You find it often in ensembles in which each character may be saying something different or expressing contrasting moods. Spoken drama can never replicate this phenomenon, when people speak simultaneously you can never pick out what is being said, whereas when the words are sung, it is perfectly possible to do so.

Mozart, especially, has the ability to convey two or more meanings or moods at any one time. Every note of music denotes a feeling or a thought and psychological aspects are expressed by musical implication. The singers, the director and the conductor must be equally aware of the double meanings, otherwise the interpretation is lost.

Consider Così FAN TUTTE. The traditional productions treat the opera purely as a joke, taking the libretto literally as it appears on the surface. Farcical disguises and comic interplay between

OVERLEAF, PAGE 144, TOP LEFT: *Poster for Bizet's* CARMEN, *1901. Photography by Explorer, Mary Evans Picture Library.* TOP RIGHT: *A sketch of Carmen and Don José in their final scene, 1903. Source: Adolf Munzer in Jugend. Photography Mary Evans Picture Library.* BELOW: *An artist's impression of Bizet's* CARMEN *at the Blackpool Opera House, 1938. Fortunino Mataniva in a souvenir booklet. Photography by Mary Evans Picture Library.*

Carmen

OPPOSITE, TOP LEFT: *A painting of Madame Bressler Giandi in her role as Carmen, 1900. Source: Le Theatre. Photography by Mary Evans Picture Library.*
TOP RIGHT: *In Act One, Carmen and Don Josè, played by Emily Golden and Neil Shicoff, meet for the first time in front of the cigarette factory in Vera Calabria's 1990 production for the Lyric Opera of Chicago. Photography by Dan Rest, Lyric Opera of Chicago.*
BELOW: *Denyce Graves takes on the title role of Carmen in Nuria Espert's authentically Spanish production at the Royal Opera House, Covent Garden, 1994. Photography by Henrietta Butler, Redferns Music Picture Library.*

the characters carefully conceal the fact that these people might have feelings. Numerous productions work perfectly well with this rendering of the work.

More recently, however, there has been a trend towards more serious productions of Così, with few laughs and an implied air of doom hanging over the story. It could be argued that both these approaches to Così are wrong, since they bring out only one aspect of the opera and disregard many other possible paraphrases which a good production should recognise and respect. A deeply serious production of Così, I feel, is simply a reaction to the many comic performances that have been staged so far.

One of the many recurring elements in opera is dissimulation, the use of masks, and masquerades, notably in Così FAN TUTTE, DON GIOVANNI, and FIGARO. These ploys are also used in Strauss' ROSENKAVALIER, in Verdi and Johann Strauss' DIE FLEDERMAUS. Quite often the whole plot of an opera depends upon concealment, mistaken identity or deliberate disguise. I generally enjoy this aspect of opera, though in purely practical terms it can be a bit of a nuisance.

The audience may be unaware of the fact, but it is all too easy for a singer to lose his orientation when he is wearing a mask on the stage. He has to tilt or turn his head in peculiar angles in order to identify his position in the scene and among the props he needs to manoeuvre around. His peripheral vision is also impaired limiting the breadth of his view .

It can be uncomfortable to have a mask on your face for a long portion of a performance. If you are wearing a hand-held mask, you can move it about and you can look round the sides. This helps as in many productions you can miss your footing on a staircase or a ramp, if you do not have clear sight-lines.

Love has been the most frequently recurring theme of opera covering just about all periods of operatic history from Henry Purcell onwards. I sang his DIDO AND AENEAS when I was a student but have not sung it since, although I adore the music. The opera tells of their intense love which is dashed by a cunning word of an evil sorceress tearing the two apart and leaving Dido to die of a broken heart.

Obsessed with love and hatred is the vehement Donna Elvira in DON GIOVANNI, which is my favourite role of all. However, opera leaves much room for interpretation by both the producers and the performers.

I remember once seeing a Donna Elvira so placid and passive that the effect was unbelievably boring. Absolutely nothing of the psychological complexity of the character came across to the audience. This tedious and misleading production did the opera a disservice. It was not the singer's fault. She had obviously been told to behave in a certain manner. Her performance was utterly different from the way I love to sing Elvira. But then, my interpretation is not necessarily the only method of portraying the character.

To survive an operatic career, you need to do things your own way. You need to be entirely unpredictable. By this I do not mean being unpredictable simply for the sake of it. I mean making a conscious effort to avoid being categorised. You should always keep your audience in suspense, never be

The interpretations of the Marschallin in different productions of DER ROSENKAVALIER differ historically as well as from production to production. FAR LEFT: Julie Schutzendorf-Koerner plays the role in Düsseldorf, 1927. Photography by Mary Evans Picture Library. CENTRE LEFT: Kiri Te Kanawa as the Marschallin in John Schlesinger's 1984 production at the Royal Opera House. Photography by Clive Barda, Performing Arts Library. LEFT: Kiri Te Kanawa, with Brigitte Fassbaender as Octavian, reprises the role for director, Hans Neugebauer at the San Francisco Opera House in 1985. Photography by Ron Scherl, San Francisco Opera. BELOW: A sketch of the Presentation of the Rose in Act Two, as it was staged during the performance of the 1925 production at Covent Garden. From: Das Theater. Photography by Mary Evans Picture Library.

predictable, never let them know what you are thinking. Only then will a performer be able to keep the attention of the audience throughout an entire evening.

When serious modern composers attempt to transform plays into operas, the end result usually makes you yearn for a theatre performance. However, on Broadway we see the same old operatic plots enduring and taking on fresh life. Bernstein, with West Side Story, proved that the subject of Romeo and Juliet, which has been the theme of many operas, still has plenty of life in it.

One of the reasons for the perennial success of modern adaptations of well-known stories is the fact that their subjects are problems of enduring validity, such as the nurturing of love under adverse circumstances. Miss Saigon is a modern Madama Butterfly in disguise. The lyrics of love occasionally undergo several transformations, but works such as the musical My Fair Lady, based on George Bernard Shaw's version of Pygmalion, has stood the test of time and still forms part of the repertoire of many opera companies. In the case of Andrew Lloyd Webber, he did an amazing job of successfully adapting Sunset Boulevard from the film.

Once I realised that my audience responded favourably to my renditions of pieces from other musical genres like operetta, musicals, jazz, blues, folk ballads and popular songs, I became courageous. I disregarded the critics' opinions about the duties of opera singers. I told myself that nobody could stop me from singing whatever I chose to sing or dictate what I can or cannot do. Music is music. As Luciano Pavarotti has said, 'We do not have barriers any more.'

When I first sang at Covent Garden, those barriers were still up. As an opera singer, you sang in the opera house and you only sang opera. You never went elsewhere. If you were a concert singer, you generally stayed in the concert hall and maybe from time to time broke into opera in a small way. And if you were an oratorio singer, that was certainly what you sang. Every performer was thus conveniently categorised into these neat little boxes.

I finally had the courage to break free from these conventions. I think it takes a lot of fortitude to do that. Singers who lack courage to venture out and leave one category of performance never find out what they can or cannot do.

Singing in the concert hall has become part of my life. Mozart's concert arias, which form an important part of my repertoire, are really operatic arias - often poignant little operatic scenes. Some of them were written as inserts into the operas of other composers, as was the custom in Mozart's time. These arias are special, because they were written for particular singers, whom Mozart knew well.

The lyrics for *Chi sa, chi sa, qual sia*, for instance, were written by Da Ponte for the singer who first performed Dorabella in Così FAN TUTTE.

The aria tells of a woman whose husband has fallen badly into debt, but he has not confessed this fact to his wife. She cannot understand why he constantly seems to be so angry with her and she wonders if she is to blame for his behaviour.
Vado ma dove reflects the plight of the same unfortunate and distressed woman.

Kiri Te Kanawa convinces as an actress as well. ABOVE, ABOVE RIGHT AND RIGHT: *Here she is seen, in the role as the Countess, at the beginning of Act Two singing the hauntingly sorrowful aria,* Porgi amor, *resigning herself to the philandering nature of her husband.* BELOW RIGHT: *Subsequently, the Countess conspires with Susanna, played by Gianna Rolandi, to dress up the page-boy Cherubino, played by Susan Quittmeyer, as a girl to teach Count Almaviva a lesson. These scenes are taken from John Copley's production of* Le Nozze di Figaro, *performed for the San Francisco Opera, 1986. Photography by Ron Scherl, San Francisco Opera.*

Non temer, amato bene was written for a private performance of IDOMENEO in Vienna, with a beautiful violin obbligato. I have never sung IDOMENEO in the opera house, but this aria has brought me close to the work. *Resta, o cara* was written just after the first night of DON GIOVANNI in Prague for the singer with whom Mozart was staying as a guest and who is said to have locked him into his room until he completed the aria for her.

Though these lovely Mozart arias are not easy to sing, I feel that my voice is comfortable with them. These pieces are little music dramas, in which I am the one and only character. I do not need to interact with anyone, other than the conductor. The arias come from inside me, which I enjoy, compared to the constant give-and-take and tensions of an opera production.

Singing these arias makes me feel that I am the instigator of my own destiny, as it were. I can express the music one way, or sing it in another way and phrase notes in different modes with a spontaneity impossible in an opera house, where my portrayal of a role must fit in with the phrasing of my colleagues. The timing of the action takes complete control.

There is another benefit of concert work. It keeps my voice in good shape in a way that opera does not. I find that I have to keep returning to concerts for my voice to remain healthy.

Opera does not help at all, as you are not necessarily singing in a controlled manner. You often have to make sounds that are not normally compatible with beautiful singing. You have to act out a role, be a character for hours at a time. And your voice can tire, not least because in an opera house you have to push your voice to get over the orchestra.

PRECEDING PAGE: *Kiri Te Kanawa as the melancholic Marschallin, dressed resplendently, in Act One of John Schlesinger's production of* DER ROSENKAVALIER *at the Royal Opera House, Covent Garden, 1984. Photography by Clive Barda, Performing Arts Library.*

Straining the voice can easily damage the vocal cords, especially if an aria or a role which, no matter how strongly you identify with it, does not suit your voice completely. Particularly if it is too low, as sometimes happens in my case. The Marschallin in Der Rosenkavalier, for instance, is quite a low role for me. I suppose it was intentionally composed by Strauss for an older singer, whose voice may have dropped.

A constant diet of opera, therefore, can be a positive danger for a singer's voice. Concerts are the antidote. The chance to perform a work like Canteloube's Les Chants d'Auvergne which I sing often can bring a wonderful sense of relief. These love songs are not operatic in any sense. They are just lovely pieces of music, rustic in origin - the sound of France - and full of atmosphere. These are songs I can respond to completely, especially when the accompaniments are played by a chamber orchestra rather than a full orchestra. If I had to name my favourite among all the recordings I have made, I would probably choose these songs.

INTERMISSION

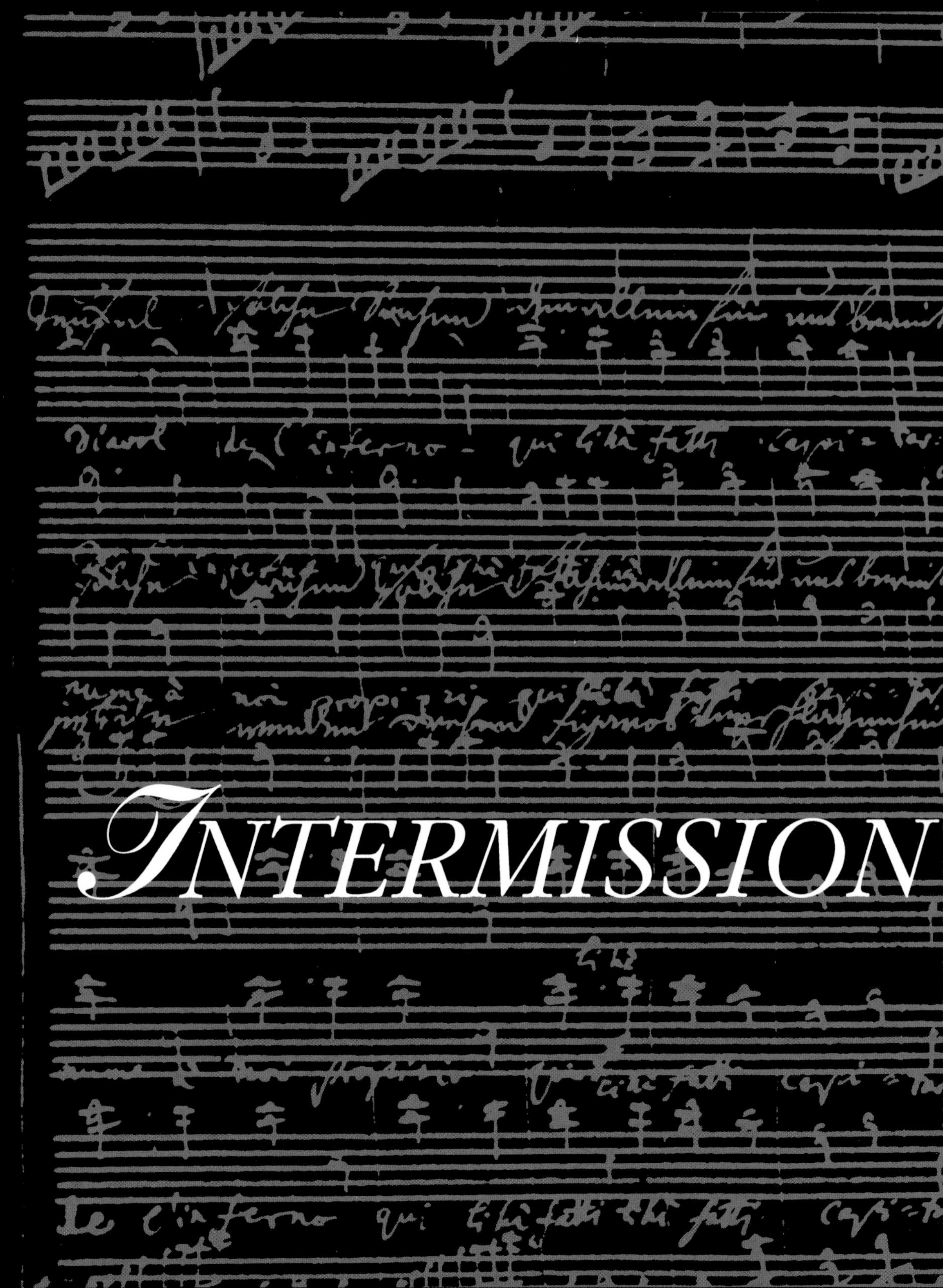

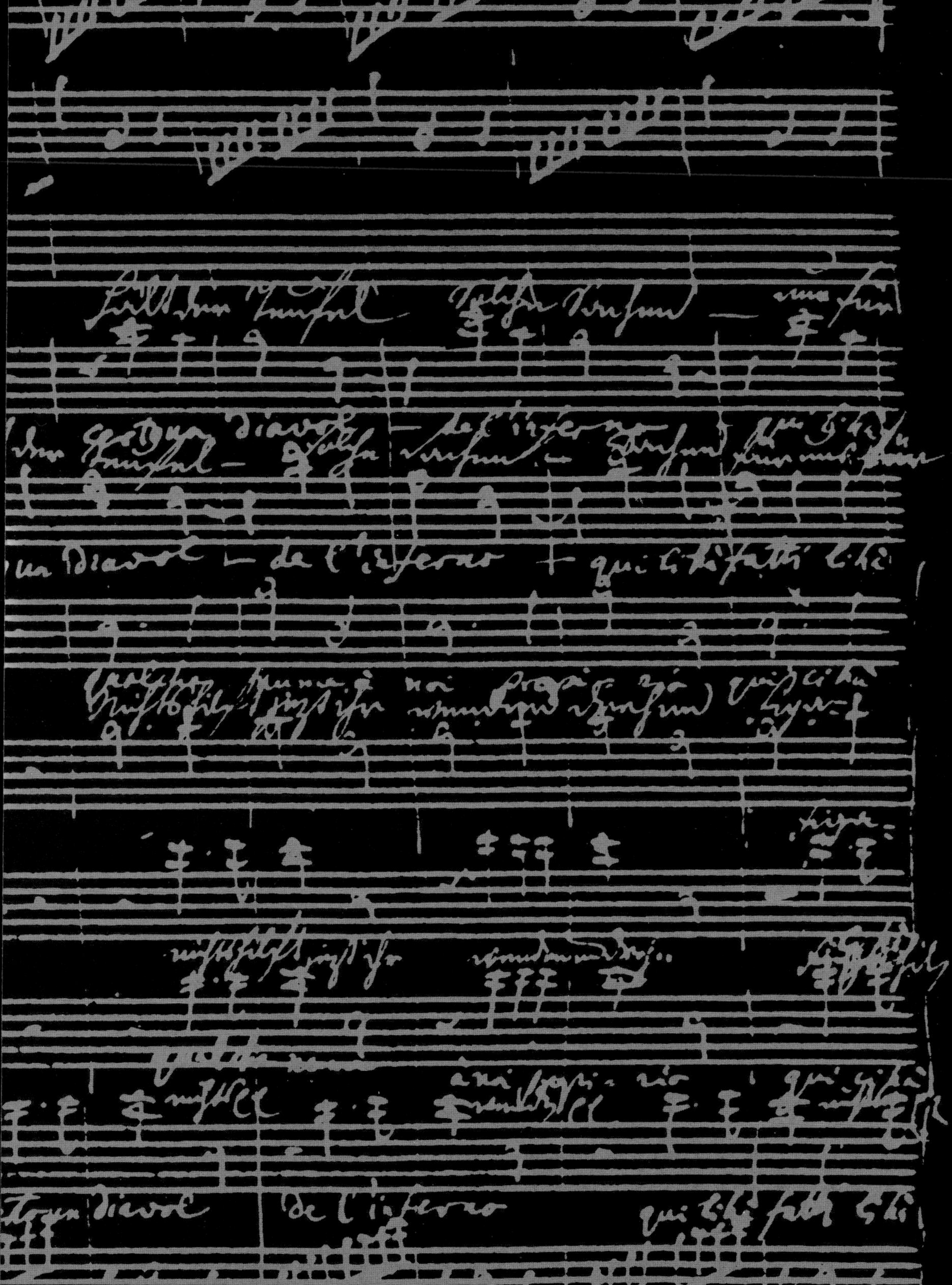

CRINOLINES AND CASTRATI

*P*eople claim there have been three clearly defined ages of opera. The era of the singer was followed by that of the conductor, and finally the period of the producer or director. Opera began as a singer's art. It was for the voice that composers wrote their operas. It was singers who made opera what it is - a drama with music. They dominated the stage through the beauty and intensity of their tone and the power of their presence.

In the early days the great castrati, the male sopranos and contraltos strutted around like peacocks, and were always given the star roles. They did not need producers to tell them how to act, and they would not let anyone boss them about. Händel's operas belonged to the age of the castrati, although female performers were rising steadily in importance. The operas of Mozart, Gioacchino Rossini, Vincenzo Bellini, and Gaetano Donizetti were inspired by the great voices, both male and female, as were the works of Giuseppe Verdi, Richard Wagner, and Richard Strauss.

By this time the age of the conductor was dawning. The orchestra had grown in importance, and people like Gustav Mahler and Arturo Toscanini reigned over the performances, with singers and players obeying their command. Today, in comparison, it is increasingly the producer who rules, and who decides how an opera is going to be staged. If any altercation arises, it is likely that the producer will prevail. There are exceptions, of course. I cannot imagine anyone dominating Georg Solti. But then, Solti comes from the Mahler tradition, when the conductor was in charge. Performers, players and producers treat him with respect.

The rise of the producer and the increasing importance of his ego has led to many changes during the quarter century of my career. The look of a performance rather than its sound has come to matter more. The decor, the action and the visual credibility of a singer count much more today than they did in former times.

More importantly, every production of an opera today has to look different from the previous one. Preferably, a performance should shock the audience and excite the press. The sound of music is no longer sufficient for the success of a staging.

The key word is 'concept', which every production needs to have if critics are to take it seriously. Often the concept is so bizarre that the producer and designer are booed off the stage, when they take their bow at the end of the performance.

Why are such productions allowed to happen? Since few new operas are staged at present, which even fewer people want to see, all operas - no matter how old - are made to look new, even if they cannot sound new. A modernised version of a well-known opera can provide a new experience and in the process gain new significance.

One way of literally giving an opera a new look is to update its contents and to perform it in modern dress. This fashion is not

Various producers and directors interpret the essence of an opera such as DON GIOVANNI *differently, as do the performers involved.* FAR LEFT: *Gilles Cachemaille plays the title role in Deborah Warner's extremely controversial and modernised production staged at Glyndebourne, 1994. Photography by Clive Barda, Performing Arts Library.* CENTRE LEFT: *Kiri Te Kanawa as the fiery and radically different Donna Elvira, intruding upon Don Giovanni's supper in the finale of at the Royal Opera House, Covent Garden, 1983. Photography by Clive Barda, Performing Arts Library.* LEFT: *Kiri Te Kanawa, again as the vibrant Donna Elvira during one of her quiet moments, in Peter Wood's 1988 production at the Royal Opera House, Covent Garden. Photography by Zoë Dominic.* BELOW FAR LEFT: *The final scene after the death of the Don in a 1995 production at the Lyric Opera of Chicago. Photography by Robert Kusel, Lyric Opera of Chicago.*

necessarily to be despised. However, producers often choose to transfer the opera to the nineteen-forties and nineteen-fifties. I hate the period and its style, though I admit that this is a purely personal reaction.

If a more appropriate or stimulating period is chosen for the setting of an opera, the result can be wonderful. When I sang Strauss' CAPRICCIO with John Cox as producer, I loved the way he updated the work by using Gianni Versace costumes which brought the performance into the twentieth century, even though Strauss himself had decided to set the story in the eighteenth. But I am also perfectly happy to appear in CAPRICCIO in the way the composer intended it to be staged.

As a singer, I love the eighteenth century. What soprano wouldn't? I admire the elegance and the grand style of the era. It is next to impossible to look ungracious or unfeminine in the hourglass shaped robes of the rococo period, with its pastels of silks and satins, its decolletages, corsets, crinolines, laces and ruffles. A singer cannot possibly slouch across the parquet clumsily when her costume of majestic brocade induces her to sweep onto the stage. I like to see the wonderful long train and admire the way the curls of the wig are draped to flatter the neckline and shoulders of the performer. I enjoy the fantasy and the illusion of a graceful past.

I tend to wear very safe costumes, so that nothing I do on stage can interfere with my singing. At times I have worn costumes that have been too heavy, too long or terribly unbalanced - but I object to wearing any outfit that hinders my performance. If a producer asks me to run in crinoline and lace, I tell him I am sorry but he has made my costume far too heavy and cumbersome for that. If he wants me to run - and I am not unathletic - he will have to give me a different costume.

All opera singers are bothered with their bodies. They are too short, too thin, too fat, too wide. The performer's figure can become a problem when the costumes for a production are selected from existing inventory. A producer must look at the individual singer and then determine which is the best part of the body to show off and which are the weak points to be concealed. The costume must make the singer look good and not provoke an adverse audience reaction. Yet, that is precisely what producers, with their concepts, more often than not, unwittingly do, especially if the play is transferred to a historic period with particularly unflattering fashion.

Some female singers are - let's admit it - extremely large. But quite often these very large ladies have really beautiful faces. So a producer - through his choice of costumes - should emphasise her good features and hide the unattractive ones. But I know this can work both ways. Occasionally, a very big lady thinks she has a petite eighteen-inch waist. Then it is hard to tell her she has not, especially if she has her mind set on a particular robe of a diminutive size. The designer has to get round the problem very tactfully by convincing her that she will have immense difficulty getting into a dress which does not suit her and would not do her justice .

It is generally helpful to be slim because it makes everybody's life easier in the costume department. I once sang Mimi in Bohème in Germany and inherited someone else's enormous costume, whose corset could not be tightened to my size and dug into me in all the wrong places. The hips went too far

OVERLEAF: *An opera can be updated in many ways, one of which is reflected through the costumes designed for each production. The three different productions of* LA BOHÈME *show performers in costumes ranging from the late eighteen-hundreds to the early nineteen-hundreds to the nineteen- nineties.* LEFT: *This thoroughly modern production featuring David Hobson as Rodolfo, Cheryl Barker as Mimi, Roger Lemke as Marcello and David Lemke as Schaunard was produced by Baz Luhrmann, 1990. Photography by Branco Gaica, The Australian Opera.* TOP RIGHT: *The starving Bohémians, dressed in clothes from the nineteen-hundreds, cheer as Schaunard brings victuals in a 1996 performance at the Royal Albert Hall, London. Photography by Henrietta Butler, Redferns Music Picture Library.*

ABOVE: *The cast is, this time, dressed in costumes faithful to Puccini's original concept. This scene, with Kiri Te Kanawa as Mimi, Luciano Pavarotti as Rodolfo, Thomas Allen as Marcello and Maria Pellegrini as Musetta, takes place in the Cafe Momus. The performance was under the direction of John Copley and staged at the Royal Opera House, 1976. Photography by Clive Barda, Performing Arts Library.*

down, and the layers of skirts and underskirts refused to stay up. Despite all efforts by the theatre staff the problem could not be solved satisfactorily. So in the end, I went on stage looking like an extremely ugly and bulky old lady rather than a young seamstress dying of consumption.

I much prefer seeing the graceful costumes of eras long passed than a soprano in modern dress plodding in on her visibly flat feet. If a performance is being staged in modern dress, you see the feet of the female singers moving around at eye level from the stalls. I must confess that I do not find that a particularly fascinating sight. Worse still, I hate to hear the painfully distracting 'click, click, click' of the modern, high-heeled shoes while the music is playing to another beat.

I do not like productions that bring operas up to date unless the producer has a justifiable reason for doing so. Too often, I suspect, operas are modernised for the sake of effect or to challenge the public. For small opera companies without much money to spend, the question of costume drama versus modern staging also becomes an important financial issue. It is , of course, cheaper and easier to dress people in current fashion. If the production in itself is so compelling that the costumes do not matter much, then obviously this decision can be a worthwhile economy.

I disagree with the theory that modernised productions assist in bringing opera within immediate grasp of the audience. Opera singers - their voices, their actions - are more important than the clothes they wear. In my opinion, the best way to make opera more directly accessible is to make the performances easily available to the general public at a reasonable ticket price.

FOLLOWING PAGES, PAGE 168 AND 169: *Costumes play an important role in the historical placement of an opera. In these pictures, taken from Richard Strauss' last opera,* CAPRICCIO, *the performers are seen in clothes designed to reflect the nineteen-twenties.* TOP LEFT: *Kiri Te Kanawa, playing the Countess Madeleine, is dressed in an evening gown designed by Gianni Versace for the closing scene. This production was directed by John Cox for a performance at the Royal Opera House, Covent Garden, 1991. Photography by Catherine Ashmore.* BELOW LEFT: *In the same production, the Countess with Thomas Allen as the Count. Photography by Clive Barda, Performing Arts Library.* BELOW RIGHT: *Another scene from the*

Surtitles greatly assist an audience in understanding the plot. Not everyone has seen the opera many times before or spent hours studying the libretto. We must cater for the general public possibly attending an opera for the first time.

Gala premieres, on the other hand, turn opera into exclusive events. Special nights for invited guests exclude the general audience. An everyday person would feel out of place - like a gatecrasher at a birthday party where he did not know anybody - in an exclusive opera house on a gala night.

The words 'avant garde' and 'modern' have come to be synonymous with 'radical' or 'explosive' for knowledgeable opera patrons. I do not think that there is anything wrong with being radical, but 'explosive' tends to go beyond entertainment. Do we really need to state the obvious through opera? Do we need to be bombarded with a producer's personal ideas, through this art form, on the ways the world is heading for destruction? The audience is being taken for a ride when they pay to attend an opera and end up seeing a performance which is just a producer's ego trip.

Producers often seem to be exorcising their personal problems through their productions. Consequently, they wilfully obscure the subject matter, not merely by setting it in the wrong century, which may be excusable. But often the opera is transferred into the wrong country, the wrong region or circumstances. The scenery does not reflect the instructions of the librettist or the composer. Worse still, in some productions, the characters themselves are completely distorted. This sort of producer is delivering his own personal philosophy, rather than that of the composer, compromising the entire opera.

1991 production at the Royal Opera House, Covent Garden, featuring clothes by Versace. Here we have Kiri Te Kanawa as the Countess, Thomas Allen as the Count, Anne Howells as Clairon, David Rendall as Flamand and William Shimell as Olivier. Photography by Catherine Ashmore. TOP CENTRE: In a production also directed by John Cox, but with costumes designed by Martin Battersby. Felicity Lott and Emily Golden play Countess Madeleine and Clairon respectively. RIGHT: Here the Countess is seen in conversation with the composer, played by Kurt Streit, and the poet, played by Rodney Gilfry. Both these pictures are taken from the 1994 production at the Lyric Opera of Chicago. Photography by Dan Rest, Lyric Opera of Chicago.

Sometimes I think I would like to go back to the old days, when singers created or helped to design their own portrayals. The art of the producer, as we now know it, was not considered necessary during that period. The result might lack the dedicated sense of direction which a single mind today can impose on the dramatic side of an opera. Without a producer, a singer would have no real guide, apart from the other members of the cast, and of course, the conductor. Then the performance might get out of control.

I wonder what it would have been like to produce an opera with Maria Callas. I wish now that I had seen more of her great talent. To listen to her live recordings - especially her Traviata with Carlo Maria Giulini as conductor - is most inspiring. Hers was the greatest portrayals of Violetta, with her voice alone conveying all the happiness and despair of the woman, the whole range of mood and colour.

I do not think any other singer has come close to expressing the pathos as she did in the role. I cannot imagine another performer - except perhaps Ljuba Welitsch before her - surpass Callas in exuding this intensity of feeling, which came from inside her and could not have been taught to her or imposed on her by any producer.

I have sung lovely music. I have used my voice to sing enchanting phrases that suited me. Never have I been able to put that particular Callas quality into my voice, a sound she could always produce when the music needed it, and which belonged entirely to her.

That Callas-sound was one of the wonders of opera, and remains so even to today. Her intonation had breadth and depth, but it was the air in her voice that gave her the unbelievable ability to sigh and to cry that lingers in the memory. Callas displayed - very convincingly - aggression, too, in roles like Bellini's Norma, the druid priestess, who sacrificed her life for her unfaithful lover, and the mad queen Medea in the opera of the same name by Luigi Cherubini.

In her live TRAVIATA recording, Callas stood perhaps a little distanced from the microphone, because the sound possesses a veiled quality that renders it even more moving. I never thought she sounded quite so heartbreaking in any of her other recordings, not even in her *Casta diva* from the opera NORMA.

Maria Callas was always Violetta to me. She had the total character within her grasp. Her pianist once told me that toward the end of her life - and she was only in her early fifties when she died - she became more and more like Violetta, almost to the extent that she was Violetta, waiting in a darkened room in Paris for Alfredo to arrive.

Then, when the man in her life came through the door, the curtains would go back and the room would be filled with light and she was a young girl again, and happy. But the moment he left the room, she would sink into depression, and it all went into terrible blackness again for several days at a time.

Callas was said to be difficult, but managements are notorious for causing the problems. I remember once being contracted to sing - I had better not mention where or with whom - and the management granted me all of one hour and a half with the conductor followed by two and a quarter hours with the orchestra. What was left of the afternoon I had to myself, just about enough time to change for the performance that evening.

OVERLEAF: *Kiri Te Kanawa playing Manon's death scene in the desert during the Opening Gala of* MANON LESCAUT *at the Royal Opera House, Covent Garden, 1983. Photography by Zoë Dominic.*

171

To do even remote justice to the programme would have required at least three rehearsals of three hours each.

Increasingly, I like to be in charge of my own destiny. I was once quoted as saying that, irrespective of what a producer is demanding, I tend to develop a character from day to day during the preparation of an opera and that at the dress rehearsal, I may change my whole approach to a part. In other words, however much I may have worked on a role with my singing teacher, with a coach and with a producer, I often come up with an entirely different interpretation in a performance. My attitude certainly changes sometimes.

I frequently seem to wander through rehearsals like a sleepwalker, as if I were not quite sure of what is going on. Basically, I am observing the other members of the cast and the interaction among us all the time. A performer has to develop the character in his own heart first because the music limits the scope of possibilities for interpreting a part.

Movements also confine the projection of a role. It is a challenge trying to slot a performance into these two different restrictive elements. The moves and the music guide a performer in the portrayal of the character, but singing the notes leaves little time for all the small gestures and steps and transactions that a singer has to act out on stage. In the end, you have to fit your own vision of the character into the various restrictive parameters which are inherently opera.

For me - and I am not the only singer to have said it - productions frequently do not begin to take off until the producer is completely out of the picture. This is especially true if a producer or designer keeps changing stage directions, scenes and props. You may find that your costume has suddenly had layers of fabric or other paraphernalia added to it or your wig has grown heavier, while the producer is asking you to change your attitude to the role and the first night is approaching fast.

As we near the end of the rehearsals, tensions mount and everyone gets short with everybody else. In the midst of all the chaos, you succumb to temptation and indulge yourself with a display of bad manners. With the opening night just around the corner, nobody much cares about flaring tempers and expressions of frustration and disapproval. This period is the best and the worst time for us all but with luck, it generally works out well in the end.

There are times when you see and feel the nervous stress running through the rehearsals right up to the first night when all the puzzle pieces of the performance begin to come together, and yet people are screaming, or being screamed at, because they are still thought to be not good enough. I find this truly astounding. I think to myself: 'They look absolutely gorgeous. They are singing well, so why are they all complaining? All will be well for the premier performance.

Flashpoint is reached for all manner of simple reasons. For example, I was doing a scene during which a drink was passed to me. I was about to burst into song and raised the glass and instead I almost burst into a shriek. I noticed a great green lump at the bottom growing fuzzy-looking mushrooms. It turned out that nobody had cleaned or replaced the bottles or the glasses for several days in a row.

OVERLEAF: *Masks are used to deceive and confound other personae in the play and form an essential part of any operatic plot.* TOP LEFT AND RIGHT: *A scene taken from Puccini's* TOSCA *performed at the Wembley Arena, 1991. Photography by Mick Hutson, Redferns Music Picture Library.* BELOW LEFT: *Behind the masks are Donna Anna, Don Ottavio and Donna Elvira, as portrayed by Luba Orgonasova, Frank Lopardo and Carol Vaness respectively. This scene is taken from Matthew Lata's 1995 production of* DON GIOVANNI *for the Lyric Opera of Chicago. Photography by Dan Rest, Lyric Opera of Chicago.*

The great leap from the battlements in Tosca is a perennial source of hazard which I approach with apprehension. In my case, I was supposed to land on a pair of offstage beds with mattresses pushed together. As likely as not, they would not stay together and I would fall straight through and crash onto the floor.

Despite my pleas, the management never accommodated my suggestion of shifting the mattresses to cover the bed-frames so that I might have a fighting chance of escaping uninjured. Opera singers get used to sprains and bruises, and consider themselves fortunate that they seldom suffer anything worse.

For many reasons, the rehearsal period can be extremely painful. Some producers are totally organised while others seem inept and incapable of utilising their and our limited time efficiently. They need months to do a production and would easily absorb a whole year if they were given the chance. They forget that time is a luxury. For me, the moment of relief comes when at last, the producer has gone off to his next opera and I think to myself: 'Thank goodness, now I can get on with being my own boss.'

Even if I realise after the first rehearsal that the production is not going to suit me - that I have made a terrible mistake - I still have to give it a chance, I cannot walk out. Critics often ask why a particular production has ever been staged, why it was allowed to happen, why it was not stopped sooner. The answer is we do not have the foresight at the beginning to realise that we are on a road to nowhere. Performers need to give the rehearsals time to develop.

Some productions I have been involved in do make me wonder if opera houses have accepted them without an inkling of what the performances were intended to look like. The management may admire the chosen producer and designer. So once they have been appointed, both of them are left to their own devices. Terrible productions are staged in which members of the cast are required quite inappropriately to perform some appalling, unpalatable, almost obscene acts. During the staging of such a production, a singer becomes increasingly aware of the audience's deep hostility.

I have always carefully kept away from productions which may be viewed as controversial or which have unsuitable or unnecessary content inconsistent with the theme. I do remember being in a DON GIOVANNI with two horses way up stage. The poor beasts were made to stand there all night.

I saw no point in displaying the backsides and the flicking tails of two white horses throughout the evening - and there was the most dreadful smell into the bargain. If I do by chance find myself working with what turns out to be a difficult producer, I do my best to avoid him thereafter.

Indeed I find producers pretty unsympathetic as a species. The good ones really stand out. The bad ones are best forgotten. I do not find many producers genuinely creative.

There was one producer in particular with whom I once worked. He always had everything written down. 'Now at this point you will sing this phrase,' he would say. 'Then you will go over there at the point and you will sing that phrase.' His stage

OVERLEAF, TOP LEFT: *Simon Keenlyside plays the lead role in David Massarella's updated version of* DON GIOVANNI *at Glyndebourne, 1993. Photography by Clive Barda, Performing Arts Library.* TOP RIGHT AND BELOW LEFT: *A highly controversial version, with stark*

modernistic backdrops, of Mozart's Don Giovanni *with Gilles Cachemaille in the title role. This production was directed by Deborah Warner and staged at Glyndebourne, 1994. Photography by Clive Barda, Performing Arts Library.* LEFT: *A more traditional approach to the same opera, with Carol Vaness as Donna Elvira and Bryn Terfel as Leporello, is Matthew Lata's 1995 production for the Lyric Opera of Chicago. Photography by Dan Rest, Lyric Opera of Chicago.*

directions were mechanical, with absolutely no logic to it, just a timetable of moves and positions.

I last performed a Mozart opera with him, an unbelievable experience. It was just so difficult to remember where you were supposed to be when you were moving all the time quite unspontaneously, step after miserable step. If you sang the next phrase and suddenly found yourself in the wrong position, then you had to scamper to get to the right one. The whole performance was a positive minefield of maddening little jigsaw bits. Happily, I have not seen him around for a while.

However, working with Peter Brook on DON GIOVANNI was pure joy. Not only is he a sweet man, but you can always discuss things with him. He will try your suggestions out. He is highly intelligent and there is never any feeling of rigidity in one of Brook's productions.

Another GIOVANNI with a famous maverick producer took me outside the opera house altogether, when I worked with Joseph Losey on his film of the opera. The portents in some respects were bad. Recording sessions of the orchestral sections but not of the recitatives were done in a church in Paris with abominable acoustics. No one had any time. Lorin Maazel, who conducted, was trying to fulfil several commitments around the globe, while doing the recording. The whole film came together very quickly. It was a real circus act.

Finance was a problem. Joe suddenly came to us and said: 'Look, I'm afraid we are going to have to drop it, we've run out of cash.' Just as suddenly they found some more money and they continued with the film, though the financial situation still appeared to be shaky. There is no way to know whether the production was going to be good or not despite its tremendous flamboyant style.

Joe was an introverted person. He was one of the people who had been ousted from America during the anti-communist period, which had affected him deeply. He was extremely secretive, sometimes having half-conversations with me, then saying: 'Oh well, no, we won't talk about that.' He spoke in - how can I describe it? - a sort of hyphenated way. You could never be quite sure where he was going.

Joe always welcomed advice and we became very close. We used to sit for hours on end and chew the fat on the subject of DON GIOVANNI and its various characters and possible interpretations, and the difference between the opera and the spoken drama. Perhaps as a result of our rapport, my scenes all came out much better than I expected.

The beautiful, haunting pictures only Joe knows how to produce impressed me deeply. Every shot in the film was remarkable. He had a wonderful way of secretly getting the camera into the right position for what he wanted to do. He had hit on the idea of using the glorious Palladian villas as the background, the Rotonda outside Vicenza being Giovanni's villa, and mine was the Valmarana, with its grotesque little statues on the wall, a short way up the hill. The images were very strong and memorable, its costumes and make-up brilliantly over the top. I felt proud to work with Losey.

To begin with, nobody had any idea what Losey's concept was, or how the film was going to be pieced together. So there we were, flying through the night in private planes, being escorted by somebody who, we hoped, knew where they were going and what they were doing, travelling mile after mile. The experience was altogether disconcerting.

Sometimes we were made to get up at two in the morning to get to our destination by three. Then we would sit in our elaborate make-up while the rain poured down, and would stay there all day in cold autumnal weather - September, October, November - wearing the same make-up. I had not known beforehand how people like Losey made films. It was very interesting, but at times it drove me crazy.

As this was a film and not an opera performance, everything was done in the wrong order, adding to the sense of disorientation. At four in the morning we would all be on the set, having been up since I cannot remember when, and suddenly I would find myself having to sing some complicated recitative because it happened to be the right time of day for the shooting of the scene.

I do not know why they had to do things at four in the morning, but there it was. You never knew where you were half the time. I just prayed that Losey would finish a scene quickly, so I could get home to bed. I remember we stayed in a hotel outside Vicenza. In fact, apart from the villas on the outskirts of Vicenza, I do not remember being near any town at all.

Much of the time I felt as if I was in a trance, being driven around, plonked down somewhere, to the point that I ceased to look where I was. It appeared I was only preoccupied by the idea of trying to snatch a bit of sleep. Days and nights otherwise consisted of getting ready, endlessly getting ready. I am sure that is the way everyone does it in shooting films, but I certainly was not used to going to bed at six o'clock in the evening, waking up at midnight, doing my job and coming home. It all felt entirely surrealistic.

In comparison, my small contribution to the film of Edward Morgan Forster's A ROOM WITH A VIEW was child's play. Two previously recorded arias by Puccini's arias were used. One was from his opera buffa GIANNI SCHICCHI, *O mio babbino caro*, and the other was *Il bel sogno di Doretta* from LA RONDINE.

The producers inserted these pieces at points in the soundtrack. They knew exactly where the music was to go, and incorporated the pieces very artistically. I was very pleased with the results. I loved the film, and many people presently associate the aria from the LA RONDINE more with A ROOM WITH A VIEW than with the original opera.

Although *Il bel sogno di Doretta* is only about a minute and a half long, the aria was an incredible struggle to learn. Prior to the composing OF LA RONDINE, Puccini's music style was deeply influenced by the first French impressionist composer, Claude Achille Debussy. The aria exudes a lyrical sensitivity. To emulate precisely the lightness with which the music floats in the air, like a hint of perfume, is unbelievably difficult.

I became anxious when learning the piece, thinking I could not get through it. However, I managed to stabilise the area of my register where the music lies. I do not find it a struggle any more. Perhaps it was all a matter of brain and nerve rather than voice. Now, at the end of a concert programme, I often sing the aria as an encore. And the piece is becoming second nature to me. I have now been performing it for more than twenty years.

Another special recording, which I found inspiring, was ROSENKAVALIER with Bernard Haitink. His enthusiasm was totally infectious on the entire cast. Unlike in an opera production, there was no manager, director or producer to interfere with or distract him.

Producers, in my experience, tend to get dreadfully in a conductor's way. That rarely happens with the two extraordinary producers whom I have most liked working with, John Copley and John Cox. I have learned a lot from working with both of them, more than I ever learned from any of my acting teachers.

Copley was ideal for TRAVIATA. His great virtue is that he gives his cast an overall view of what every member should be doing as a singer and as an actor, with precise stage directions. When he is rehearsing you in a role, he becomes the character himself. In essence, you just have to copy him and gradually pare down the exaggerated portrait he has given you.

Cox was wonderful for operas like DER ROSENKAVALIER, ARABELLA, and CAPRICCIO. He tends to give you an in-depth view of the entire production, offering the singers options of various stage directives but leaving it up to the cast to create their own imagery. Ultimately, the characterisation has to be yours. You start out with an idea or two of the persona you want to create and from this basis begin to develop the role within yourself.

During quite a few productions, I was left with a feeling that if I was not directing myself in a performance, nobody else was going to. I thus was thrown back on my own resources to embody the role I was to play, and I had to use the technical skills and the confidence such producers as Copley and Cox had given me.

Cox focuses on a detail, holds it and makes the entire cast watch as you are groping towards the interpretation of your part. He is a direct opposite of the extrovert and physical Copley. Cox's approach is introvert and demands your intuitive involvement. As such, the rehearsals with him can be hard work. So much so that I once said to Cox: 'If you pay me for the rehearsals, I will give you the performances.'

I also greatly admire Peter Hall. Together we performed a FIGARO at Glyndebourne. Hall, in my experience, is a thoughtful producer, very detailed in the right manner, and his was a wonderful production. I went into the rehearsals full of ideas.

But then I was not allowed to have any ideas for three weeks. Afterwards, suddenly I had to have ideas again. Hall seems to work with a breaking-down-to-build-up method.

I hold Hall in the highest esteem. He is deeply musical and a great producer. I always considered it sad that he withdrew from his opportunity to run Covent Garden with Colin Davis. That would have been, artistically, an amazing partnership.

OVERLEAF: *Kiri Te Kanawa as the Marschallin in the famous production of Richard Strauss' opera* DER ROSENKAVALIER, *by the film director, John Schlesinger at the Royal Opera House, Covent Garden, 1985. Photography by Zoë Dominic.*

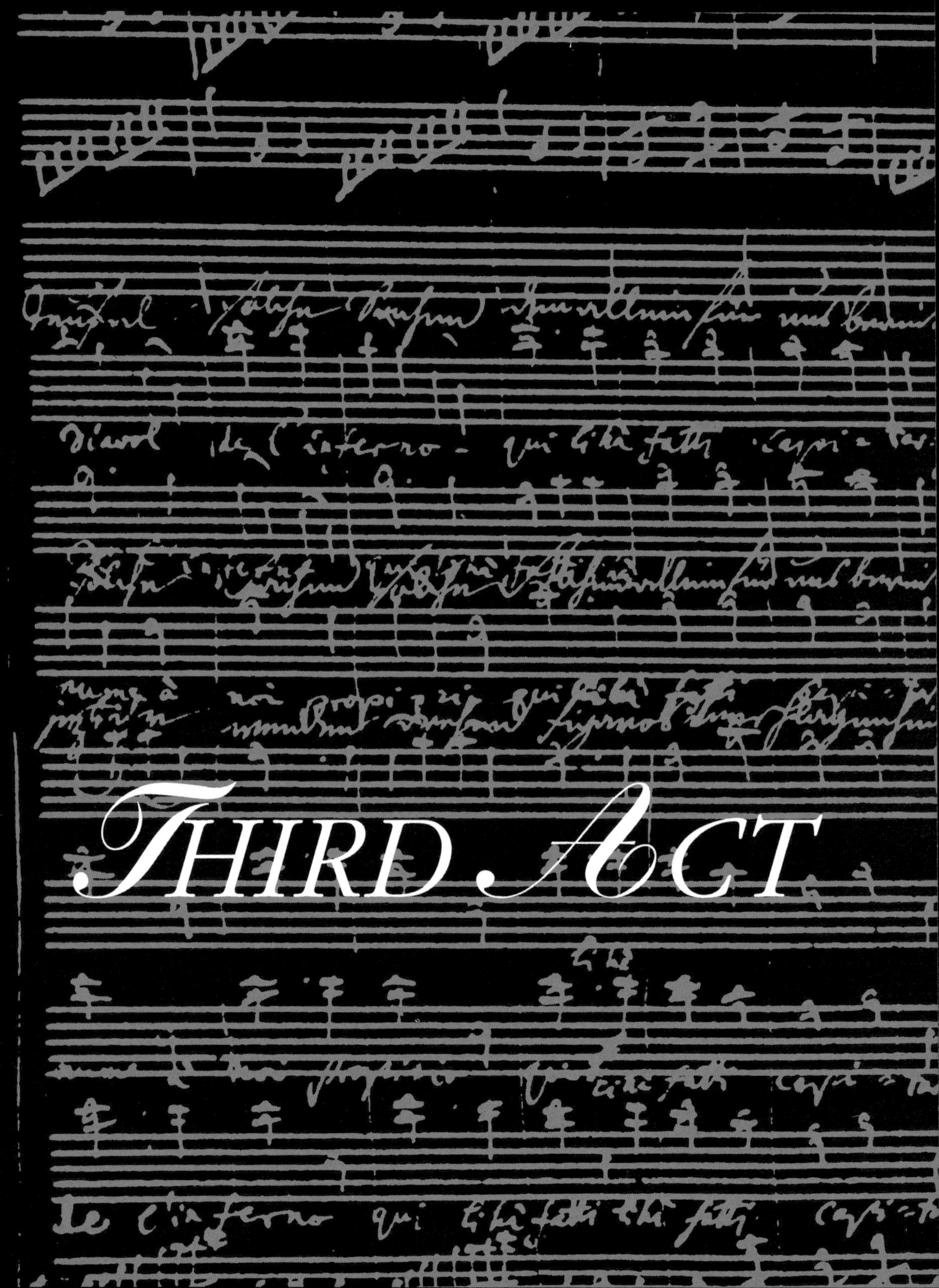

THIRD ACT

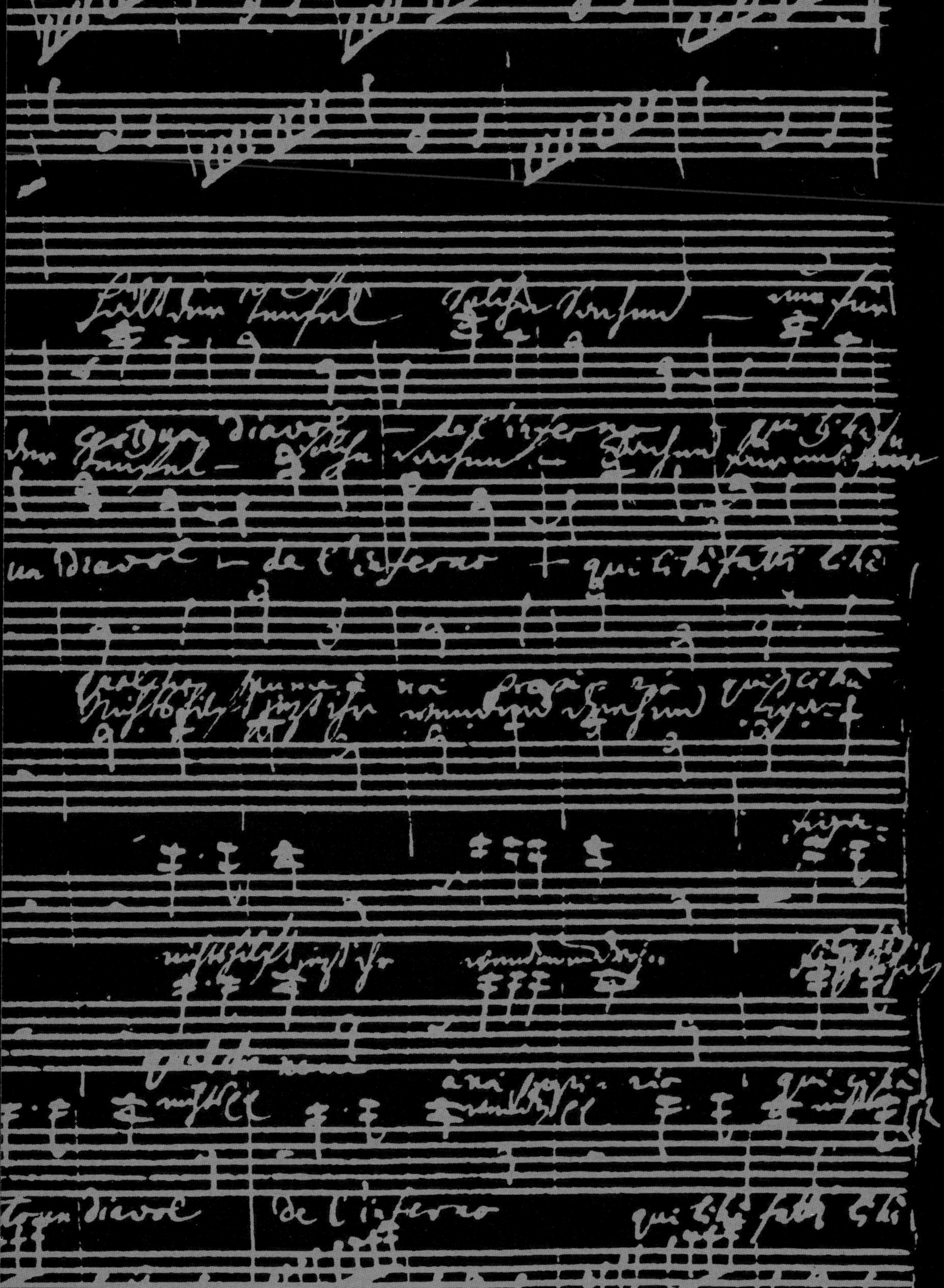
un Diavol — de l'inferno
de l'inferno

THE BIG ARIA

The aria is opera's most powerful form of emotional expression. Many different shapes and sizes are employed to convey as many varying moods. In Händel's era, the aria tended to have a strictly symmetrical layout, into which the composer poured a wealth of melody. The structure grew less formal and more spontaneous during Mozart's time. Most arias are in essence a monologue, which is the aspect Verdi and his contemporaries concentrated on. In the operas of Strauss and Richard Wagner, the aria expanded into whole scenes, such as the Countess Madeleine's closing scene in CAPRICCIO, which, right at the end of the opera, is a very difficult sing for any performer with the stamina to tackle it.

As someone who has always felt most at home in lyrical opera, I have spent much of my career singing arias. They form the heart of my repertoire, both in the opera house and concert halls. Since the female soprano has long replaced the male castrato as the principal high voice in opera, I am lucky to have within my range many of the finest arias ever written.

There is no doubt that DER ROSENKAVALIER, with its three great women's roles, glorifies the female voice. We think of TRAVIATA as Violetta's opera, certainly not Alfredo's; and LUCIA DI LAMMERMOOR and NORMA are just two of the many bel canto operas in which women take the lead. Verdi's DON CARLOS stands out as notable exception for featuring mostly male roles.

OPPOSITE: *In Verdi's* LA TRAVIATA, *Violetta Valery is a woman with a multi-faceted personality. Violetta's aria allows us to explore the psychological depth of her character which is part of the overall painting of Paris as a city. Shown here is an excerpt of Violetta's aria,* Sempre libera, *from Act One, expressing her exuberant joy of life in the composer's handwritten score from 1852. From The Lebrecht Collection.*

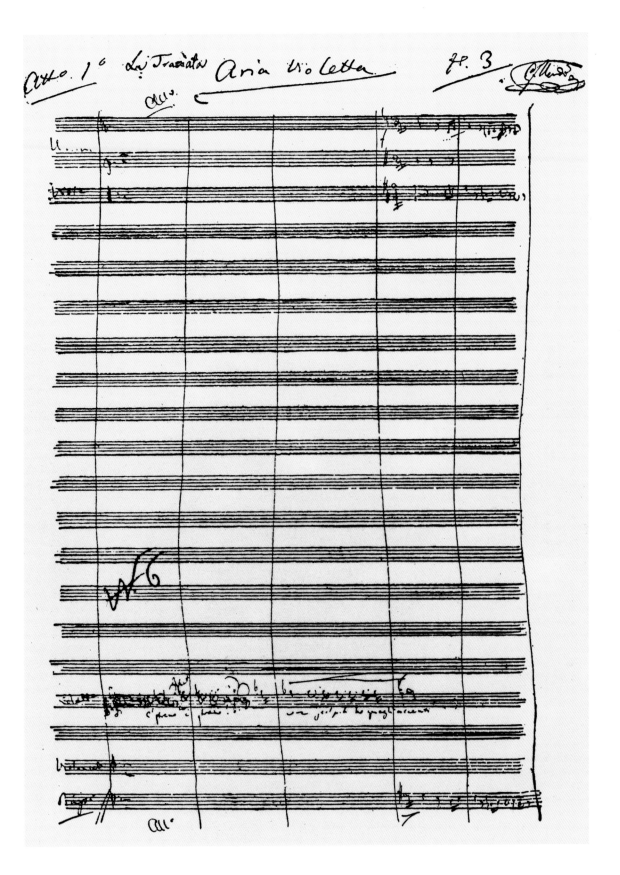

An aria sung in the concert hall has to sound complete in itself. In the opera house it is simply a point - though very often a memorable point - in the overall progress of a developing drama. The effect of an aria, therefore, will be most direct and drastic, when you hear it in its proper context in the continuity of the opera.

The *Liebestod* from Tristan has its maximum impact whenever you hear it at the end of Wagner's five-hour music drama. But it is in the operas of Mozart above all, that a singer has the scope to convey the quite often double-edged moods of an aria, in which comedy and seriousness interact, each element intensifying the other.

The double-meaning in Mozart's works calls for great subtlety of approach, because a hint of comedy within a serious theme, or a serious touch within the framework of a comedy, strikes a very fine balance. The manner in which the words and actions of the singer are conveyed to the audience is equally important as is the tone quality and the timing. Singing these arias is a challenge. I do not find - on the whole - the comic element awkward. I am by no means a comedienne, but if the music is written to carry a relaxed air, it suits a personality like mine.

The sense of comedy I have steadily developed for Donna Elvira's music in Don Giovanni has sometimes been thought unusual. Perhaps I see more than other singers the funny side of her arias, as in *Ah chi mi dice mai* when she arrives on stage in search of Giovanni. Of course, I also realise her serious side. It appears to me that too many sopranos who portray Elvira regard themselves as budding Donna Annas, because these performers think Anna is the greater role and therefore something to aspire to. But they are quite wrong and have - in my opinion - misunderstood Elvira's personality. The musical notes for her role are characterized by tragic and comic passages and quite distinct from Donna Anna's more serious and straitforward arias. Elvira, as all her arias expound, has both funny and tragic characteristics; whereas Anna is neither - she is powerful and indomitable, with a hint of Fiordiligi in Così fan tutte about her. So a singer must convey Elvira's contradictions, her switching emotions, right from the start, respecting the serious side of her but being fully aware of the comic side.

In her pursuits of Giovanni, who had seduced and spurned her, Elvira's passionate vengefulness alternates with her overpowering desire to win him back. In many ways, he has been, however briefly, the love of her life. In portraying Elvira I have thought that perhaps she has been his only true love, too, if ever he was capable of experiencing love.

I see Elvira's character in many aspects as being the direct opposite of Don Giovanni's personality, which - to me - makes Elvira the most important of the three women in the opera. They have a curious sort of empathy, she and Giovanni, his personality being elusive and hers being intense. Their encounters, unlike Giovanni's with other women, are marked by an atmosphere of combustibility.

The Countess in Figaro is an entirely different character. Fieriness is definitely not part of her nature. At the uncertain stage of her marriage featured in the opera, she displays a tender resignation and pain, reflected in her arias, *Porgi amor* and *Dove sono*. To sing the Countess, you need to show patience. There is nothing of Elvira's impulsiveness about her.

OVERLEAF: *Verdi paints an extremely dark and dismal portrait of Venice in his opera,* Simon Boccanegra. *The main characters are caught in a web of intrigue and treachery. These pictures show Amelia Boccanegra, played by Kiri Te Kanawa, pleading for the life of her lover, Gabriele Adorno, portrayed by Michael Sylvester, who has attempted to kill the Doge of Venice, Simon Boccanegra, portrayed by Alexandru Agache, and are taken from Elijah Moshinsky's 1991 production at the Royal Opera House, Covent Garden.* TOP LEFT AND CENTRE LEFT: *Photography by Clive Barda, Performing Arts Library.* BELOW LEFT AND RIGHT: *Photography by Catherine Ashmore.*

Though still quite young, the Countess accepts her destiny, even at those moments when you might expect her to resist. Mozart knew exactly what he was doing by delaying the world-weary Countess' entry into the opera to Act Two. The aria and its position in the opera suit her personality. Only when Figaro and Susanna attack her with ideas and schemes does she begin to realise that she has options.

For a soprano, though, knowing that you do not make your first appearance until the story is well developed and singing what is considered to be a monster of an aria with a long orchestral introduction, can make you apprehensive. Some singers find *Porgi amor* for these reasons a daunting task.

The aria furthermore paints emotion in slow, deliberate strokes, reflecting all the Countess' loneliness. She makes a solo appearance after an opening act which was filled with ensemble scenes and lively action. It is no wonder that the performance of this aria can be unnerving, no matter how often you sing it.

The whole opera can be gruelling for the performers if the conductor and producer fail to get the pacing right. Since FIGARO is very long - especially if the extra arias are included in the last act, as seems to be the trend now - I like a conductor who keeps the piece moving. He must of course ensure that the pace does not get out of hand, because the arias need space to make their point.

A singer must be able to relax into the music as well as push the phrasing forward. If the tempo of the performance is kept at breakneck speed, this becomes impossible. There are some precious moments in FIGARO which conductors now are prone to rush. A prime example is the scene in which Susanna comes out of the cupboard in Act Two instead of Cherubino whom the Count is suspecting to emerge. Of course, the latter is completely taken aback. This moment, with its gently mocking minuet rhythm, is too often stripped of its beauty.

You only need to observe the little pauses between the notes of Susanna's solo. They are built into the music, and they are as important as the notes themselves. The pauses make all the difference between an impersonal performance and one which really touches the audience. The conductor should trust the singer and encourage her to embrace the pauses to deepen the sentiment of the piece.

To achieve the slow, opera-seria rhythm which *Porgi amor* demands, a tempo about which singers and conductors will forever argue, the notes should be stretched by the singer as long as she can sustain them. The speed must depend on who is singing the aria, not on the conductor or producer. It does not matter how fast or slow the piece is sung, as long as the singer is able to link the notes properly, and to maintain the phrasing.

When Cherubino comes in and sings in *Voi che sapete* about his passionate love of women to the Countess, there must be no more than the gentlest of hints that the Countess, in her loneliness, finds herself attracted to the boy. Modern producers sometimes emphasise this inclination too strongly.

If Mozart had wanted to indicate real attraction between the Countess and Cherubino, he would have written it into the opera. Since this is not explicitly stated, it should never be more than implied.

OVERLEAF: *Kiri Te Kanawa as Donna Elvira, pained by passion and despair, during Peter Wood's 1988 production of* DON GIOVANNI *for the Royal Opera House, Covent Garden. Photography Zoë Dominic.*

FIGARO is such a great ensemble opera, dependent on close interplay between the different characters, that changing the emphasis is dangerously easy. If the role of Figaro is filled with a particularly rich, dark-voiced baritone or bass-baritone, with exceptionally strong bottom notes, his first aria, *Se vuol ballare*, in which he expresses his fury and wrath at Count Almaviva for pursuing his right of the first night with Figaro's fiancee Susanna, can sound so threatening that the audience would think that a revolution were already under preparation and the Count were genuinely doomed.

Some producers cast their Figaros to appear more powerful and more manipulative than others and thereby reveal the serious contents that lie at the bottom of all Mozart's comedies. Such a Figaro makes it perfectly plausible that one day, perhaps soon, he will take over the Count's role. He is just waiting to step into Almaviva's shoes - so the Count, and perhaps even Susanna, had better look out.

In my experience, the best Figaro is a very busy character. If he is physically the same size as the Count - or even taller - he exudes as much male dominance as Almaviva if not more since he constantly tricks the Count. If the Count were not slow-witted, he would not be outmanoeuvred by Figaro and the others quite as easily or as often.

So Almaviva must act a bit inanely, if the performance is to be convincing. This is a point worth considering when a producer fills the roles of the Count and Figaro because a strong Figaro can make the audience wonder who wields more power. I like the idea of Figaro actually taking control, and suspect that Mozart did so, too.

By analogy, Leporello in Don Giovanni can also be portrayed as a servant waiting to oust a master. In many productions, Leporello tends to be on the stocky side, but when he is as tall as Giovanni himself - for example, played by Bryn Terfel - a feeling of duality is created. The master and the servant become interchangeable. Mozart plays on this theme with his deliberate use of disguise while Giovanni and Leporello swap roles to delude Elvira in Act Two. This works more convincingly - not merely farcically - when the two men are of similar size.

Disguise is an important tool in these Mozart operas and needs to be handled with flair. At the end of Figaro, the intricacies of the garden scene often seem like a fumbling muddle on stage. Yet, this masquerade, in which Susanna and the Countess swap roles and seemingly yield to the forbidden advances of the Count and Figaro respectively, must make sense for the audience. Despite the imbroglio with people in black cloaks concealing their identities in the dark, the story has to be clear.

The Count's apology to his Countess, in which the entire opera culminates, is another awkward scene to stage albeit one with beautiful music. As the Count Almaviva drops to his knees and sings *Contessa perdono*, she replies that she will forgive him through the kindness of her heart. Therefore, their reunion scene can be taken literally as in traditional productions. But the question, as usual, remains: 'What did Mozart really mean?'

Mozart's music is full of deliberate ambiguity. Knowledge of the Count's personality is enough to suggest that he will just go off philandering again, the moment the Countess' back is turned. More productions of Figaro tend to imply this turn of events to the extent of ridiculing the deeply serious and moving music.

OVERLEAF: *Kiri Te Kanawa as the suffering Countess Almaviva in Act Three of John Copley's production of* Le Nozze di Figaro *for the San Francisco Opera, 1986. Photography by Ron Scherl, San Francisco Opera.*

Whatever the future may hold in store for the Count and Countess, their reunion in the opera must be cast in a convincing manner to appear realistic. The Countess knows that she can save her husband from himself only so many times. When I sing the music, I always feel that she hopes he really can be saved this time. Maybe the next time she won't bother trying, but for the moment her feelings are real.

Mozart is telling you that there is hope - even if only for so long. The producer should respect this, just as in the previous act, he should not tamper with the Letter Scene, during which the Countess Almaviva dictates a billet-doux for the Count to Susanna, to lure him to a supposed rendezvous with Susanna.

My advice to any two performers singing the duet *Che soave zeffiretto* between the distressed Countess and the playful Susanna is to treat it truthfully. No messing around, no poking fun at the ensuing intrigue. You must believe what the music is saying in this scene as well as in the final act, when the scores are telling you about the Countess' forgiveness of her husband. If you do not forgive from the heart, then you cannot express forgiveness in the way that Mozart here so completely does.

I have been tremendously lucky, in the role of the Countess, that all the Counts who have played opposite me have been wonderful in their own individual ways. Maybe I have been a bad Countess for them, but that is a different matter.

When you are singing the Countess, you have to have a tall handsome Count who can sing beautifully and has the composure befitting an appropriately arrogant aristocrat. The Countess, after all, still loves her womanizing husband. You simply cannot have a short, fat, dumpy Almaviva. Not that I am against portly people. But if your own performance is to blossom and have any sort of credibility, you must be teamed with a tenor who looks the part.

Likewise, if you are teamed with a slender, boyishly cute Cherubino, it is difficult for you to sustain the illusion of any attraction towards him, no matter how well he sings. You must always maintain the fantasy because that is what the audience came to see.

FIGARO is an opera about the emotions, commitments and fallacies of love. As a performer, one must convince the audience that you believe in your part and all its implications, especially if, as the Countess, you are aware that you have been betrayed by your husband.

As Fiordiligi in Così FAN TUTTE, I find it hard to convince myself that I am falling in love with the disguised Ferrando instead of being true to myself and to Guglielmo. Fiordiligi's sanctimonious personality for me is summed up by her aria, *Come scoglio*, in which she claims to be standing firm as a rock. However, the rock quickly crumbles, which makes it difficult for me to portray her apparently strait-laced character concealing undiscovered or stifled desires.

I believe many singers have problems playing Fiordiligi, especially at the end of the opera, when she learns that she has been the victim of a practical joke and that her latest lover was in reality her sister's fiancé. She subsequently appears to switch her feelings back to her own original fiancé, Guglielmo.

I would find Fiordiligi's role more acceptable if I could think it possible for Fiordiligi to be utterly drawn to her sister's fiancé

Kiri Te Kanawa as Amelia in SIMON BOCCANEGRA. *BELOW,
BOTTOM AND OPPOSITE: Alexandru Agache and Michael
Sylvester as Simon Boccanegra and Gabriele Adorno
respectively in Elijah Moshinsky's production at the Lyric
Opera of Chicago, 1995. Photography by Dan Rest, Lyric
Opera of Chicago. RIGHT: A production at the Met.
Photography by Winnie Klotz, New York Metropolitan Opera.*

who is disguised as an Albanian. It is the temptation of the forbidden fruit, I suppose, that makes this infatuation possible for her. But to go back to Guglielmo, the person Fiordiligi should have been with in the first place, after spending a few hours cheating on him, must be dreadfully embarrassing.

The depth of feelings of the two sisters is only hinted at by Mozart's music. If you listen carefully to the orchestration, however, and analyse the arias and duets, the notes might tell Fiordiligi and Dorabella which of the two men they should be with. All of Mozart's operas contain these conundrums.

The sisters may just possibly decide to live together with the original partners - have a long and meaningful relationship - rather than marry them. After all, these women do seem rather emancipated by eighteenth-century standards. Perhaps they even decide to swap partners once again, after a bit of breathing space. One never knows.

IN DIE ZAUBERFLÖTE, perhaps even more than in Mozart's other works, the scope of seriousness in the dramatic scenes and the extent of fun in the comic scenes is questionable. It is difficult to strike the right balance between lightness and weightiness. We have Papageno's childlike arias, which are pure comedy, and Pamina's painful doubts that Tamino still loves her. Her aria in g minor key, *Ach ich fühls*, is one of the finest pieces of music in all opera and certainly deadly serious in its sentiment.

DIE ZAUBERFLÖTE on the surface pretends to be a fairy-tale but its light-heartedness is undermined by deep and dark mysteries working behind the scenes, which Mozart exposes in his music as the opera proceeds. Good and evil are thoroughly mixed and never what they appear to be. The Queen of the Night starts out by seemingly pining for her lost daughter Pamina, whom, as it turns out, she only needs as a pawn in her own power-play. She is also a mother who clearly does not want to let her daughter out of her clutches.

Sarastro, the Queen's nemesis, on the other hand, is portrayed initially as the evil magician. Eventually, though, he is revealed as Pamina's and Tamino's benefactor. However, Sarastro also personifies cold patriarchal power. The opera is in fact an allegory of the replacement of the ancient female goddess cults with male-dominated religions.

Much as I love the music, I have always found it difficult - even with the glorious Karl Böhm as conductor - to be part of that particular jigsaw puzzle, although singing Pamina with him was a genuine musical treat. The incredible skill of this conductor meshed the disparate elements of the opera - the naive, childlike cabaletta of Papageno, the stately cavatinas of Sarastro's realm, the powerfully dramatic coloratura of the Queen of the Night and the arias of Tamino and youthful Pamina - in a manner that at least made musical sense.

Pamina, that sweet innocent girl, could never rival Donna Elvira in my affections. The whole of DON GIOVANNI and the part of the temperamental Elvira have a leitmotif holding the opera and the individual characters together. Where COSÌ FAN TUTTE lacks plausibility, and DIE ZAUBERFLÖTE is fragmented, GIOVANNI absolutely captures the imagination.

Elvira is a very satisfying role which develops throughout the opera. It has a beginning, a middle, and an end. The opera itself

Opera can use dramatic period costumes, to evoke the illusion of the part. OVERLEAF, TOP LEFT: *Tosca pleads for her lover's life at the Wembley Arena, 1991. Photography by Mick Hutson, Redferns Music Picture Library.* TOP RIGHT: LA TRAVIATA *as interpreted by Frank Galati in 1993. Photography by John Reilly, Lyric Opera of Chicago.* BELOW LEFT: *Kiri Te Kanawa in the title role of* ARABELLA *in historic costumes. Photography by Winnie Klotz, New York Metropolitan.* CENTRE: *Kiri Te Kanawa and Jane Berbie, as Fiordiligi and Dorabella respectively, sing a duet, in the 1976 production of* COSÌ FAN TUTTE, *conducted by Julius Rudel at the Paris Opera House. Photography by Agence de Presse Bernand.* BELOW RIGHT: *Kiri Te Kanawa as The Marschallin, advices Sophie, played by Barbara Bonney in John Schlesinger's 1984 production of* DER ROSENKAVALIER *at the Royal Opera House. Photography by Clive Barda, Performing Arts Library.*

has a structure and a length that never make you wonder if you are losing the audience's attention. Despite that fact, I often wish Donna Elvira had more scope at the end of DON GIOVANNI. There are times - though it may seem a shocking comment to make - when I believe that Mozart had some sort of mental blitz at the close of that opera. I feel that he forgot a final piece of music for Elvira. The fact that he added the big aria, *Mi tradì*, for her at a later date does suggest that Mozart was aware that something was missing. Yet, it seems to me that Elvira needs to bare the depth of her character more than in her earlier scenes.

In one production, I kept trying - unsuccessfully - to persuade the producer to let me keep coming onto the stage silently, getting in everybody's way, and generally being a nuisance, because that is the sort of character she seems to be. She is a disruptive personality, as Giovanni himself knows well, but this side of her needs more opportunity to show itself.

Centring around passion, pain, sensuality and death, DON GIOVANNI leaves little room for misinterpretations. Yet some performances of Mozart's opera are noticeably less convincing than others. I once sang in a production in Cologne in which Elvira was cast as a nun at the end of the last act. Though the libretto says that she intends to join a convent, I never feel she means it. Giovanni's death has left her stricken and stunned and she, in her impulsiveness, reacts to this particular situation.

BACKSTAGE

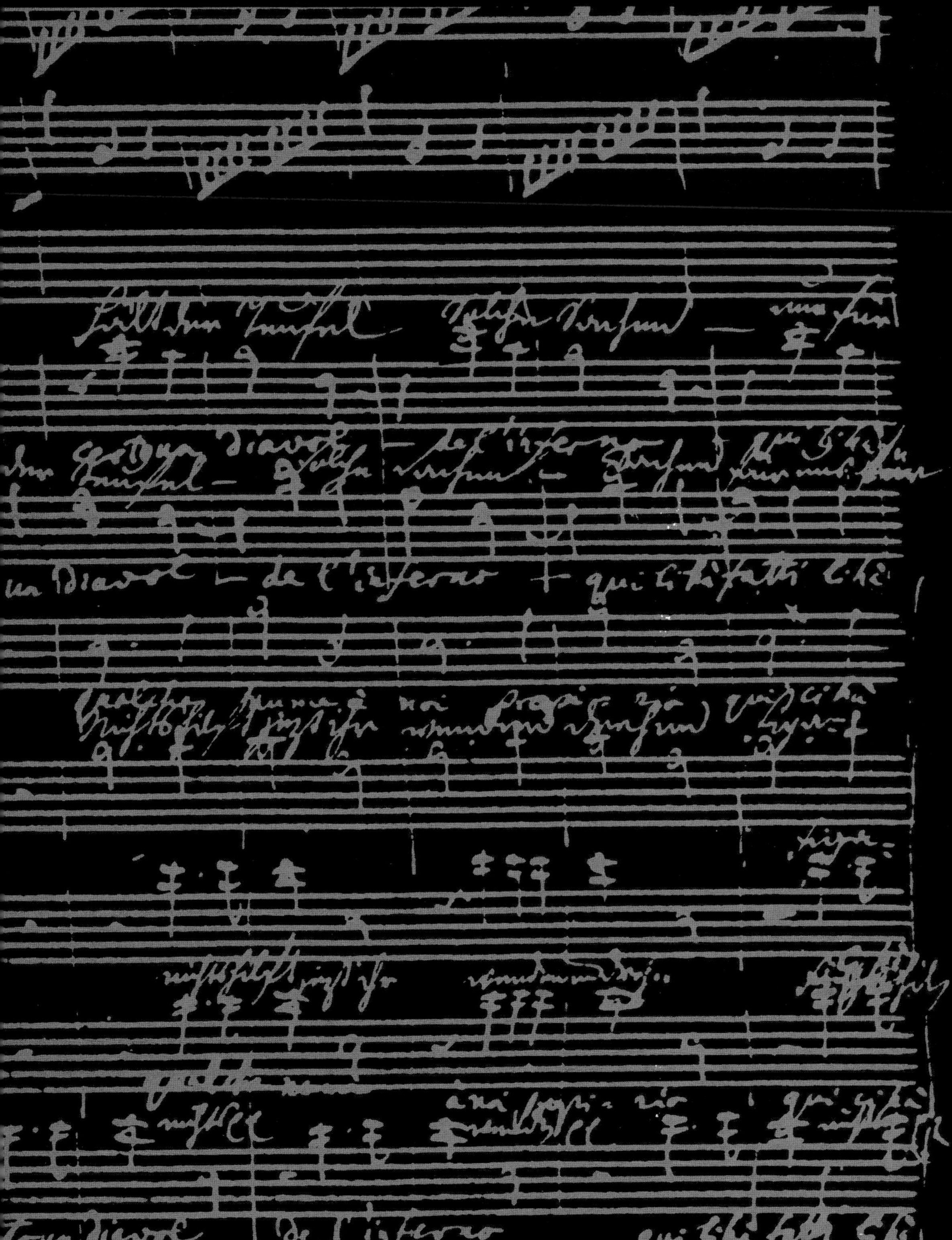

The Architecture of Opera

In opera - and particularly classical opera - the requirements on the stage settings were complex. No early opera could do without magic or mystery. The deus ex machina, the 'god from the machine' is someone who, when fortunes have turned for the worse and the future looks bleak, arrives in the nick of time to save the situation. He can bring Alceste in Christoph Willibald Gluck's opera of the same name back from the realm of death or rescue Euridice from Hades after Orfeo has foolishly lost her for the second time.

Even the everlasting magic flute in Die Zauberflöte is an ambulant deus ex machina. It charms and weakens the potential evil forces that threaten Pamina and Tamino on their way through the magic forest during their test of fortitude. Throughout the history of opera, mythological figures, electromagnetic fields, magic potions, hocus pocus and a bag of tricks were employed as symbols of supernatural forces to explain the inexplicable.

From the seventeenth century onwards, the deus ex machina was expected to play a visible or at least vocal role in the performance. He was the character who, in the days of Henry Purcell, Georg Friedrich Händel and Gluck, might fly or float onto the stage, or appear in a thunderous cloud of smoke like Mephistopheles does in Charles Gounod's opera Faust, and turn the imminent, tragic ending of a scene or the entire opera into a drastically different, often happier, event.

This heavenly helper, who may seem a ridiculous relic of the past, was an important implement to propel the story-line of pre-classical and classical opera. The appearances of the mythological Greek gods Hercules and Apollo in ALCESTE are in many modern productions good for a laugh today, while in traditional performances they are cast in the seriousness which the original librettists intended.

Throughout the ages, figures of Greek mythology were eventually supplanted by spiritual forces borrowed from Christianity, such as the Commendatore in DON GIOVANNI, or Mephistopheles in FAUST.

The omnipotent deity from above features less in newly created stories, but remains a power which we performers all trust to be watching over us when the curtain refuses to rise or fall, the scenery collapses. In reality, every single performance of every single opera appears in need of its own deus ex machina because, invariably, unexpected mishaps occur on stage.

The numerous people whose names are listed in the programme as contributors to the success of the show more often than not double up as deus ex machina for the production. The staff are vital trouble-shooters in times of necessity. A good lighting engineer can perform magic and save a performance in which part of the scenery has collapsed, and a seamstress can repair potentially disastrous tears in costumes.

From this point of view, there are particular opera houses a singer dreads appearing in because they seem jinxed, while other theatres are so well-run and efficient that they seem inhabited by various dei ex machina and the performer wishes he could sing in them all the time.

The old Paris Opera House in the middle of the city was my favourite opera house, not least because Rolf Liebermann was running it at the time together with Joan Ingpen. Between the two of them, these managers embodied the very best of operatic administration I have ever witnessed. Every performance was planned in great detail and the execution was organised and disciplined. Liebermann and Ingpen had gathered around them all the singers that I knew and loved. I would be working with them still if I could.

I always wish Joan Ingpen could have passed down her incredible knowledge of planning and of putting singers together, so that someone would have been able to carry on. She was a pillar of Covent Garden in the days when Sir David Webster was in control. I only met Webster once, with Solti at Covent Garden, but was glad to have caught a taste of that special era.

In Paris in those days, the audiences were glorious and, of course, Solti was there - it was a golden age. I savoured these moments more than any others. I felt I was at the heart of cultural life being created by great people and I was under the tutelage of true masters.

I worked in Paris for about five years on and off, from 1976 until 1981. Those were the days of grêves sauvages, the wildcat strikes. I would arrive at the theatre only to find no scenery on the stage, but the performance would nevertheless take place somehow. I also remember once coming to the opera house and finding it completely deserted. I could not handle it. Each department found its own reasons for not working on a specific day which used to drive me crazy. The perennial threat of strike-induced backstage mishaps disrupted our work schedule and furthermore, seemed to require the helping hand of a deus ex machina regularly.

I have the happiest memories of singing DIE ZAUBERFLÖTE in Paris. The large auditorium, decorated entirely in red and gold, was located in a marvellous structure dating from the middle of the nineteenth century. I remember looking up from the stage at the poetic Marc Chagall painting in the dome. My eyes would keep wandering up while I was singing, and I would lose myself - though luckily, not the music - in the sight. I rented a house in the Avenue Ternes, near the Place de l'Etoile, and seemed to find inspiration in everything I saw and everything I did in a city I absolutely adored.

Above all, it was the chance to sing in that great building with its superb acoustics. There was a prime position on stage - opportunely quite near the prompt box - which every singer tried to occupy. You knew that your voice would soar from this place, more than anywhere else on stage. So everybody made for that spot on the stage and would do his utmost to hang on to it, protecting his territory against all invaders.

The neo-baroque building was a marvel. Statues, gilded pillars and wall paintings gave the entire house a playful atmosphere. I had never looked so intently at a theatre foyer before I saw the one in Paris. People would come to attend performances simply to see the vestibule.

Every inch of the Paris theatre was stunning, a rich, harmonious, elegant structure, both inside and out. I once went up to the green copper cupola and was amazed by the spectacular panorama of the rooftops of Paris.

ABOVE: *Kiri Te Kanawa
and Jane Berbie as
Fiordiligi and Dorabella
in the exquisitely
monochrome first act of*
Così fan tutte, *conducted
by Julius Rudel and
staged for the Paris
Opera, 1976.
Photography by Agence
de Presse Bernand.* LEFT:
*Kiri Te Kanawa in the
title role of* Arabella *for
the 1981 Paris
production conducted by
Silvio Varviso.
Photography by Agence
de Presse Bernand.*

The vast backstage area and the bird's-eye view of the stage itself opened an entirely new perspective of the building to me. I could not understand how it was possible for the ballerinas to dance on a floor so steeply raked but they managed. Nureyev was rehearsing at the time. Ballet always formed a special part of the Paris Opera's tradition.

Behind the stage was a second stage, which extended the other way. Occasionally during performances, a singer would start miles back on the second stage and advance towards the spectacular staircase of different shades of marble at the far end. The Paris Opera House was the epitome of an old-style grand theatre, an opera house geared for the most sumptuous and luxurious of productions. When you came off the stage at the end of the performance, when the curtain had come down for the last time, you could see squads of firemen standing in readiness. There were not just two or three firemen, but dozens of them, lines of them, waiting there. Although this incredible number may seem an extravagance, this great historic building, constructed with an abundance of timber, requires genuine care and attention. Think what happened in Venice.

There was the intricate array of dressing rooms. People who had retired years before still had rights of occupancy to the rooms they had once used. As a conductor, John Pritchard had a wonderful little boudoir, all curtains and curlicues. Like any great opera house, the Paris theatre had a 'star' dressing room, with its own special number. But I stuck to the small dressing room I was given the first time I performed.

My first appearance at the Paris Opera was in DON GIOVANNI with Solti as conductor, Ruggero Raimondi as the Don, Margaret

Prince as Donna Anna, Jane Berbie as Zerlina, Gabriel Bacquier as Leporello, Stuart Burrowes as Don Ottavio - it was a wonderfully wicked production of this demonic drama of sensuality, with the dream cast you could expect in those days.

All opera houses have their special magic. You do not have to be Australian to understand what the Sydney Opera House means to the continent. As a New Zealander, I certainly do. It is one of the wonders of the world. There are not many theatres which everyone, whether or not they have ever seen an opera, would immediately recognise. That is not something that can be said of Covent Garden or of the New York Metropolitan, or even the Paris Opera. Despite its uncontested magic, the Sydney Opera House, too, needs its own resident deus ex machina - one trained in the ways of the Southern Hemisphere.

The Australians, with the help of a single-minded Dane, managed to create a structure of extraordinary elegance perched in an idyllic position on the harbour. Yet there is a price to be paid for that amazing shell, as has become increasingly apparent, and it has not been just a question of money.

Behind the smashing facade, the Sydney Opera House is just another theatre with a lot of problems. The magic does not extend to the interior. There is a famous saying nowadays in Australia, which is: 'We have one opera house in this country. The outside is in Sydney; the inside is in Melbourne.' That basically reflects the reality.

The big blunder in Sydney was that all initial thinking went into the exterior of the building. Of the two auditoriums beneath that wonderful roof, the one that was meant to be the opera house

OVERLEAF: *Marilyn Richardson and Heather Begg in their roles as Desdemona and Emilia, Iago's wife in John Copley's production of* OTELLO *for the Australian Opera, 1991. Photography by Branco Gaica, The Australian Opera.*

became a concert hall, and vice versa. It was wrong from the very start.

The concert hall functions well, but the opera house is far too cramped. As at the Lincoln Center in New York, there have also been a myriad of acoustical problems.

I always loved performing in the Sydney Opera House despite all its inadequacies, as the productions often have an Australian flair and freshness, an uninhibited Australian magic, which is probably furthered by being so far removed from the traditions of Europe.

Modern opera houses do not have the charm and warmth of old, they often have no more character than any other new building. The trouble is that these recent structures are not built by the people who must occupy them. The architects and interior designers who throw these buildings up, install air conditioning and central heating, and think they have created a brilliant environment. The acoustics are often a problem, as the walls are not insulated properly, or the building materials cause echoes or the shape of the hall does not amplify the sound.

Modern opera houses often feel like hotels. The builders have installed devices that hum, grind, thump and buzz all the time, which become particularly disturbing during the night. The hotel's generator is audible from every room. You hear the elevator going up and down. You hear other guests' toilets flushing. The next room's TV goes on all night long, and the management of the hotel has the audacity to charge you astronomical sums for the privilege. Leonard Bernstein, they say, used to insist on having a whole floor of a hotel to himself; I can see why.

Old opera houses - the ones that survived World War II - have their own special charm, which you feel the moment you enter them. They may be old-fashioned in many respects, but you sense that with your performance you are contributing to an operatic history dating back centuries. You are standing on the stage, perhaps the very spot, where Maria Callas once sang, or Ljuba Welitsch, or Enrico Caruso, or Jenny Lind. In that pit, Toscanini once raised his baton. In that seat, Verdi sat. Here OTELLO was first staged. There Gounod's FAUST was first sung. The walls of these old theatres carry the echoes of all past performances. You feel it all the time. New theatres will never have this special atmosphere. There seems to be a definite shortage of craftsmanship in theatre architecture.

A Mozart opera staged within the ornate proscenium arch of a rococo theatre is a harmonious event that cannot be equalled in any modern theatre. Buildings contemporary to Mozart do not feature jarring edges, and the acoustical quality in these old opera houses is in keeping with the performance.

The scientific acoustics in many modern buildings often sound technical, and thus uninspiring, at least to me. One day, perhaps, they will gain the warmth of sound, but not in my time. The new house may have better sight-lines and more comfortable seats for the audience, a restaurant and fine backstage space, but the operatic magic is often decidedly lacking. It is not in the bones of the building.

In the old days, composers and opera houses did not have to be taught to create the operatic enchantment. The magic was already there, built into the music and into the design, the decor and the facilities of the building, with its trap doors, revolving stages and sound mechanics, which were far from primitive.

Though DIE ZAUBERFLÖTE was first performed in what seemed to have been a quaint little playhouse on the outskirts of Vienna, the stage directions were amazingly intricate. Scene changes were obviously swift. Trap doors were needed. The Three Boys had to be floated in. Despite modern electronic facilities, there are many new theatres quite incapable of staging DIE ZAUBERFLÖTE today, charmingly or otherwise.

Although old works do not need new scenery just to satisfy a producer's whim, opera as an art form must progress and embrace new ideas. A good new production, imaginatively using the facilities of today, continues the magic of centuries ago, and in its own way sustains the composer's original aims.

Great conducting and singing are part of the enchantment of opera as well. It was when Karl Böhm conducted DIE ZAUBERFLÖTE in Paris that I first realised just what is possible in a theatre that combines history with present-day technology. In these performances, the entire ensemble - a conductor who knew the music through and through; a hand-picked cast; a production that never interfered with the opera; and a marvellous building - formed one harmonious unit.

We all knew that by the standards of modern Mozart conducting, the beat was very slow. But it had its own pulse, the pulse of the magical flow of the whole fairy-tale allegory. Böhm exercised a very human, relaxed control that never became slack. You were never locked into Böhm the way you are into some conductors, but you were never adrift either. If things went wrong - and they did - you learned to adjust. The Three Boys - genies who guided Tamino to the abducted Pamina in Sarastro's realm - were real boys, from a special singing school, and not three women dressed up as boys, which is what you usually get.

Their treble elfin voices wove a fabric of enchantment showing the varying hues of the Queen of the Night. One night, as the three were descending the hidden ladder to rescue the desperate Papageno from the attempt at ending his own life, they got caught in the curtain. The scene had to be recast. The ladder was pulled down, and the boys were unable to make their fairy-tale entry and ended up unceremoniously walking onto the stage. Despite the failing props and compromised theatrics, the music never failed them. Perhaps a deus ex machina had saved them from faltering in their notes.

The theatre with the best physical amenities is undoubtedly the New York Metropolitan. I love the Met. I criticise it, saying it's too big, too wide, too packed with people. With an auditorium seating more than four thousand, you cannot get the intimacy you want. I always think that three thousand is the absolute maximum for any opera house to provide at least a semblance of the cosiness you need. But the New York Metropolitan is truly an outstanding house.

As a company, the Met is hellbent on excellence and on achieving quality in every aspect of its activities. James Levine, the musical director, is always around and knows exactly what is going on. This provides a vital feeling of continuity, especially as he is a fine and perceptive conductor and has been there for a quarter of a century.

People say that if you cannot see the eyes of the singers in an opera house - as is the case in the Met - the venue is too large.

Yet, when I sang Così FAN TUTTE there with Levine conducting, I felt in surprisingly close contact with the audience. All the components of the performance came together beautifully and a harmonious balance was achieved between the scenes on stage and the audience in the house. The tasteful decor did not seem dwarfed by the building. The costumes felt right. The attention to every detail and the thoughtful organisation of the production ensured its success. This approach of the management inspires trust in a performer.

None of the directors or the cast was trying to be too clever, or to turn Mozart's opera into a personal statement. The impression I had was that producer, the performers, the conductor, the orchestra players and the stage personnel were intent on staging Così in a well-choreographed cooperation of professionals of the very highest standard. When people are working extremely hard to produce an opera without flaws, they make you want to go along with them and that is what I like so much about the Met.

However, my fondest memories will always be of The Royal Opera House, Covent Garden.

My first opera in a major opera house was performed here, albeit in the minor role of the Flower Maiden in PARSIFAL. It was thanks to Covent Garden that I was given my first big chance to perform a major role, that of the Countess in LE NOZZE DI FIGARO. They gave me time and space, enough to allow me a whole year in preparation for this part. No other house could ever have shown such support and consideration.

Many of my other major roles, including those in SIMON BOCCANEGRA, DON GIOVANNI, ARABELLA and CARMEN, were also first performed there. The remarkable aspect is that Covent Garden was always willing to provide coaching for learning all these roles. They had faith in you. Such an investment of time and effort is invaluable to a young singer.

I owe a great debt to Covent Garden, greater than that owed to all the other opera houses put together.

Fourth Act

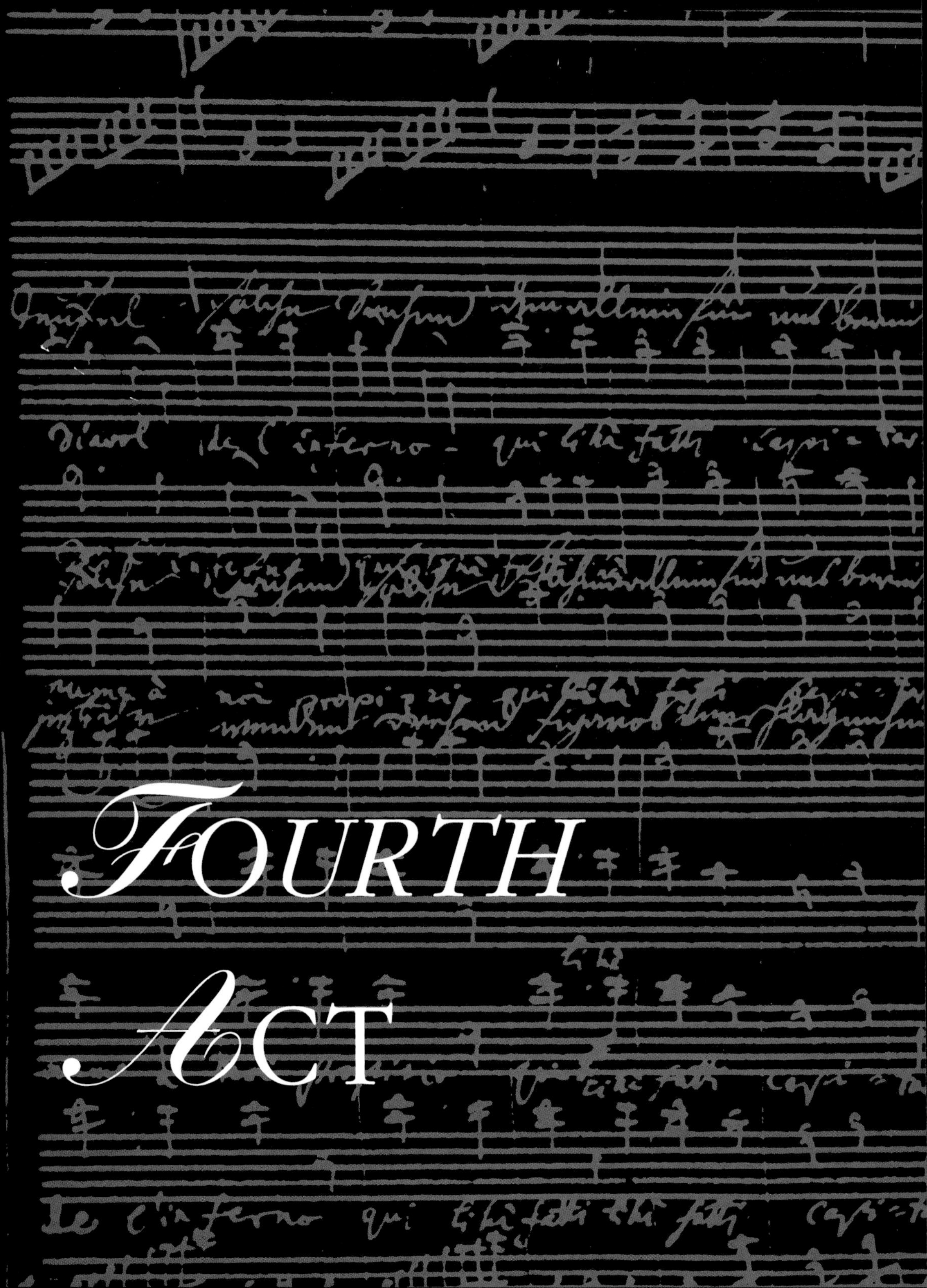

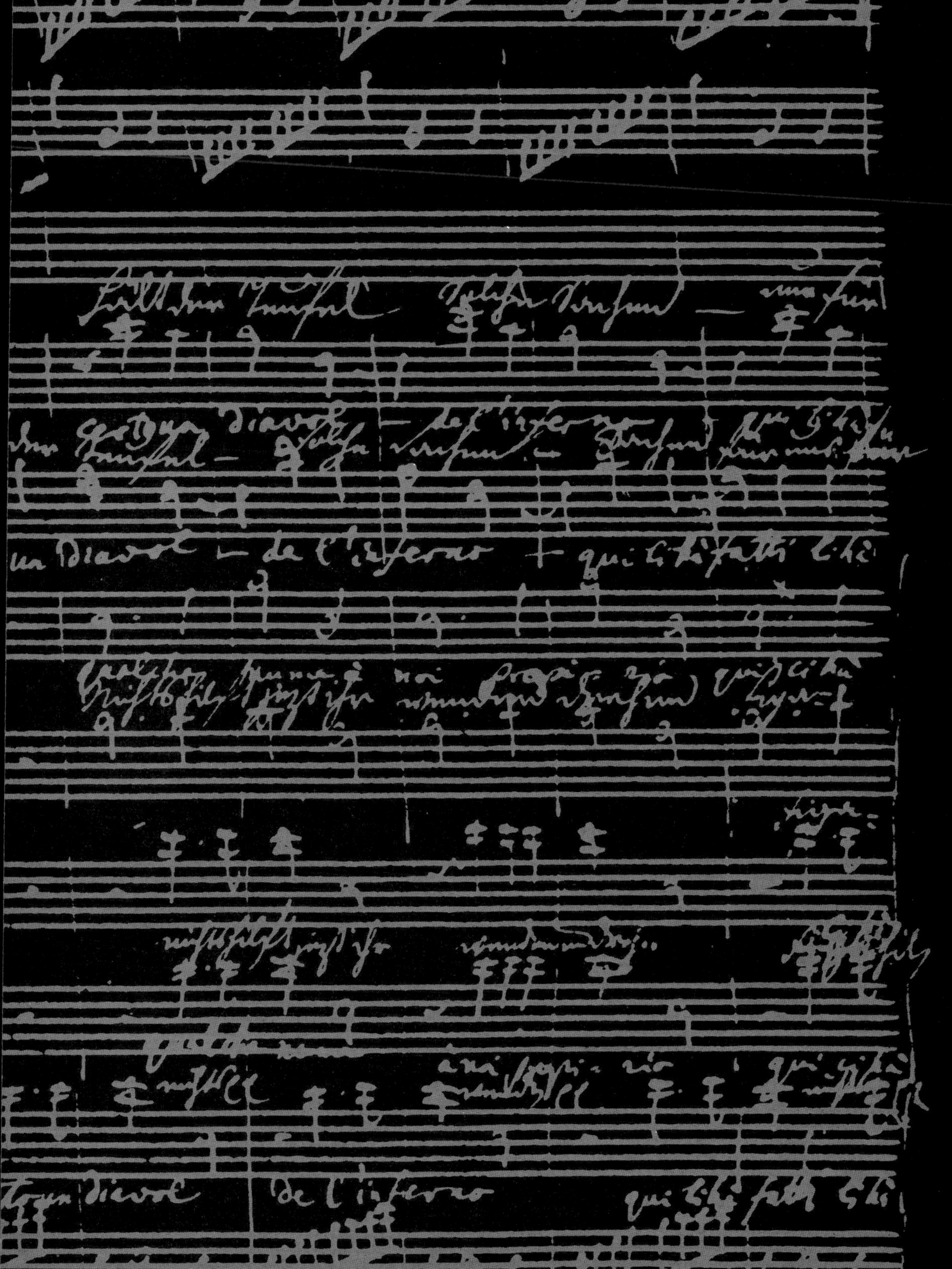

THE (UN)HAPPY ENDING

*S*low death is one of opera's traditions. The hero or heroine who has been stabbed or poisoned but still takes for ever to die - long enough at least to sing a loud and taxing aria or duet - always seems a ludicrous convention to people who get impatient with the time-scale of opera and are unresponsive to the ways in which it differs from films or from spoken drama.

How is it possible, such people ask, that Violetta can keep singing for half an hour at the end of TRAVIATA, displaying tremendous lung power, when she is meant to be in her death throes from consumption? But these people forget that an aria is principally an expression of what is passing through a person's mind, rather than a brave act of keeping death at bay while singing at full volume. The closest thing to spoken drama might be a Shakespearean soliloquy, which is likewise the evocation of what is within a character's head.

Alfredo, at the end of Act Two of TRAVIATA, sings the aria *O mio rimorso* plus two verses of lusty cabaletta simply to tell us that he has to dash off to Paris. This may seem the height of absurdity, but if we persuade ourselves that he has just learned of Violetta's impending insolvency and the thought of rushing to Paris to come to her financial rescue flashes through his mind, this sequence of events becomes plausible. If we recognise that music is able to describe a person's thoughts and emotions by expressing them at a different level of intensity and in another tempo, then it should be easy to accept what he is doing.

From this perspective, it does not matter how long a character takes for his monologues if the music is eloquent and the performance convincing enough to sustain the person's thoughts and feelings of a given moment. That is what happens in Act Three of Wagner's TRISTAN UND ISOLDE. When the unhappy couple, bound together through a misdirected love potion, discover that they cannot live apart nor live honourably together, and die - finally united - they require an hour and a half to share and experience their death scene. Tristan has been called the slowest dying hero of all time, but it has to be considered that Richard Wagner's opera is a poetic, sensitive and rousing portrayal of unconditional love.

Opera is a moulding of fantasy and illusion. As a singer, I have no problems coming to terms with its specific language and rhythm, as long as the music is good. However, in all honesty, I admit that I have never had the slightest desire to sing Isolde. Occasionally, I dream of being Otello, so that I could sing his death scene.

Though I am well aware that death scenes are one of the great elements of opera seria, not many of the works in which I appear actually involve my own death. None of the Mozart or Strauss operas ends with me lying dead on the stage or behind the scenes. Though my three Puccini roles in MANON LESCAUT, BOHÈME, and TOSCA incorporate lengthy and painful death arias, my two final scenes in the Verdi operas, TRAVIATA and OTELLO, are the ones that are particularly significant to me. In TRAVIATA, Violetta is dying slowly and alone, having given up the one and

Kiri Te Kanawa as a distraught Desdemona in Elijah Moshinsky's production of OTELLO *at the Royal Opera House, Covent Garden, 1983. Photography by Clive Barda, Performing Arts Library.*

only love in her life for the sake of his welfare. Her death scene with the ethereal aria, *Addio del passato,* is especially moving. It was written with feeling for the plight of the heroine.

Violetta's death in TRAVIATA is more interesting to me than Mimi's in BOHÈME. Though in some aspects, the two heroines are comparable, both die of consumption, Violetta's death to me to have the better music. Violetta's death ennobles her, emphasised in the composition of the varied and multifaceted notes and the complex structure of the scores. On the other hand, Mimi just fades away and her lover Rodolfo does not even notice. A typical tenor, you might say, though Alfredo's behaviour in TRAVIATA is not all that much better. Mimi's death, I always think, should be more spine-chilling and moving than Puccini actually makes it.

One of the most powerful of all death scenes, belonging to a much earlier period in operatic history, is Dido's death aria, *When I am laid in earth*, from Purcell's DIDO AND AENEAS, in which the queen laments the departure of her lover. I enjoyed singing the part when my voice still had mezzo qualities.

Desdemona's death at the hand of her husband is one of my favourite death scenes. Several producers have asked me to play Desdemona in OTELLO in a very passive and languishing manner. However, I always picture her as the young, independent aristocrat who ran off to marry the foreigner she loved against her father's wishes. She has thrown in her lot entirely with Otello's. He is the only life she has left now.

Desdemona is always in a state of panic, because of who she is and who Otello is. She tends to be overly subservient in everything she does. Desdemona is constantly rushing to please, rushing, rushing, because she knows her husband's impatience. That is my Desdemona. Her music before Otello creeps into her bedroom to kill her is some of the most haunting in all Verdi. Plagued by dark premonitions, Otello's wife remembers, with yearning, her childhood and resigns herself to her fate with *Mia madre aveva una povera ancella* and the prayer *Ave Maria*. They are very beautiful, filled with longing and loneliness and a willingness to give her life to him. She senses that her beloved Otello will murder her, but even as she is dying, she caresses the hand that is killing her.

If I had sung more Verdi, I might have had more death scenes in my repertoire, but I never performed AIDA or LA FORZA DEL DESTINO or RIGOLETTO or LUISA MILLER. I once had a brief flirtation with DON CARLOS, in which I sang Elisabetta five or six years ago in Chicago, but I had mixed feelings about the performance. I added the role to my schedule because I felt the time had come to sing this exceedingly grand opera. By the time I became uncertain about the opera, it was too late for me to withdraw.

DON CARLOS, Giuseppe Verdi's most ambitious and complex opera of which he originally composed seven variations, explores the historic confrontation between the church and the secular powers at the time during the occupation of the Calvinist Netherlands by Catholic Spain. Suspected witches, wise women and heretics were then burning on stakes throughout Spain as dictated by the Inquisition. Torture and terror ruled the lands during that time.

In this tragedy, Don Carlos of Spain loves Elisabetta, who is forced by political considerations to marry King Philipp II, Don

OVERLEAF, TOP LEFT: *The evil Scarpia, played by Sherill Milnes enjoys his supper while watching Tosca, played by Renata Scotto, comfort Cavaradossi, played by Giuliano Ciannella, who has been tortured. A scene taken from Beppe de Tomasi's 1988 production of* TOSCA, *performed at the Lyric Opera of Chicago. Photography by Dan Rest, Lyric Opera of Chicago.* BELOW LEFT: *Scarpia meets his death through the hands of Tosca in this scene taken from Puccini's opera,* TOSCA *staged at the Wembley Arena, 1991. Photography by Mick Hutson, Redferns Music Picture Library.* RIGHT: *Giuseppe Sabbatini's Alfredo, June Anderson's Violetta, Terese Fedea's Flora Bevoix and Dmitri Hvorostovsky's Germont during the party scene at Flora's mansion, taken from the Frank Galati production of* LA TRAVIATA, *performed at the Lyric Opera of Chicago, 1993. Photography by Dan Rest, Lyric Opera of Chicago.*

Carlos' father. The dark and desperate production deeply depressed me. Set in mausoleums, churches and prisons, the opera appeared to me to be one succession of grim songs and duets from the funeral march *Dies irae* to the aria *Tu che le vanità*. The members of the cast I worked with, which included Samuel Ramey, were terrific, but I decided it was one opera I would have no difficulty avoiding henceforth.

Some notable critics consider DON CARLOS the best of Verdi's operas because of the richness of the character's portrayals and the orchestration evoking powerful sentiments through the masterly composition, especially the woodwind instrumentation before the Queen's last aria in Act Four. To its credit it has tremendous masculine confrontation scenes, especially the one in which Don Carlos draws his rapier against his father, the King, and the true depiction of the agony suffered during this period of history.

My character, Elisabetta, however, bored me. She loves Don Carlos, but is bound by duty to Philipp. That role does not leave much scope for interpretation. She has no outstanding character traits about her. It did not help either that the black Spanish court costumes of the period were heavier than any I had ever worn before. They literally had to lift those costumes on to me, then lift them off again. Costumes can seriously affect a performer's attitude to a production and leave perhaps undeservedly bad feelings about certain works.

I have an antipathy to the tragic bel canto operas of Vincenzo Bellini and Gaetano Donizetti, although while a student, I did Donizetti's ANNA BOLENA, the unhappy story of Henry VIII's second wife. This silently suffering character never inspired me.

But I enjoyed doing Rossini's LA DONNA DEL LAGO, though admittedly it feels like a century since I sang it. This legendary tale of King Arthur's realm is a fine but underrated piece.

I wish now that I had developed my portrayal of Tosca more thoroughly, and perhaps spent a year or more with that role regularly in my repertoire. I loved the character of Tosca - such glamour, such bravery.

Tosca is the only opera in which I have wielded the knife. The character I play kills Scarpia, the torturer of her lover, after having pretended to agree on a bargain with the brute. Tosca appears to be offering her body in return for the life of Cavaradossi. However, when Scarpia approaches to embrace her, he is stabbed to death. Tosca was, I thought, well within my range of characterisation. What prevented me from playing the part more often was my worry that I might strain my voice.

People often criticise the melodramatic plot of TOSCA - the interrogation, torture, rape attempt and death by firing squad - but Puccini certainly knew how to depict this historical plot of politics, art, sex and crime. The composer tightens the screw relentlessly as it proceeds. Without a doubt, Tosca had the swiftest and most spectacular death scene of all - she throws herself down from the battlements of the Castel Sant' Angelo in Rome after she discovers that her lover was killed in the supposed mock-execution.

I felt unable to identify in any way with Manon Lescaut, that flighty young Frenchwoman who comes to a bad end. Yet that did not necessarily make the piece harder for me to play. As a matter of fact, I am able to enjoy singing Manon, without feeling close to her. Throughout her slow, almost Wagnerian, death in the desert with her lover, I never lose interest in the heart-rendering music.

The entire opera, MANON LESCAUT, evokes in me the image of a stormy flood of music, overflowing with impulsiveness and passionate melodies of such glowing abandon. In retrospect, I think I gave Manon a creditable death scene, maybe better than she deserved after having abandoned her lover the first time around and having led him to his death through her greed.

With Verdi, however, the relationship between plot, character and music is much more complex, to the extent that you really have to come very slowly and closely to terms with a work like SIMON BOCCANEGRA, a drama of human passion before an historic background of political conspiracy in Venice, a Verdi opera which I hold among my favourites. One of the most beautiful pieces of music ever written is the crashing of the ocean waves during Simon Boccanegra's death scene.

The audience should work on understanding the socio-cultural context of the story-line and the emotions displayed by the personalities. Everybody, be they singers or listeners, must read the story to appreciate thoroughly the intricacies of the strategic schemings behind the scenes.

This opera captures the unravelling of the political entanglements over a period of twenty years. It is therefore important to know who is related to whom, who is dead and who is alive, and which generation is which. Once you have dedicated yourself to an understanding of the libretto, you can let the music carry you through the work of black melancholic and sinister male power play.

ABOVE: *Marguérite and Faust, performed here by Renée Fleming and Richard Leech, in their last scene together. This scene is taken from Frank Corsaro's production of Gounod's* FAUST, *at Lyric Opera of Chicago, 1996. Photography by Dan Rest, Lyric Opera of Chicago.*
LEFT: *Susan Bullock portrays the dying Mimi in Act Four, with Arthur Davis as Rodolfo by her side, in a performance of* LA BOHÈME *at the Royal Albert Hall, 1996. Photography by Henrietta Butler, Redferns Music Picture Library.*

Surtitles have been a great boon to audiences. Nevertheless, Boccanegra requires more than that to explain that Fiesco is Amelia's grandfather and Boccanegra, her father; or to show how the opening scene relates to the rest of the work. The masterpiece is one of Verdi's most touching studies of a father-daughter relationship. I find the role irresistible to perform - even if you cannot take the story at face value.

Opera has quite an arsenal of deadly weapons at its disposal, ranging from poison, swords, vipers to executioner's axes and torture chambers. The closest poetic brush with death off stage for me is my brief encounter as Donna Elvira with the marble statue of the Commendatore on its way to deal with Don Giovanni. I flee screaming, of course. Just think if I were to try to protect him by standing in the apparition's path!

But even before death knocks at the door in an opera, it is announced by many mysterious portents, ill omens and fateful symbols like the card scene in Carmen, in which the cards foretell her violent death. The voice of the oracle in Alceste, the terrible maledictions in Rigoletto and La Forza Del Destino, the witches in Macbeth, the ravens in Götterdämmerung serve to prepare the viewer for impending doom. But not all omens are bad, and not all potentially tragic operas end tragically.

As I am of Maori origin, I do not find the symbols and superstitions associated with opera to be in any way unusual, and there is no way I can get away from them in my private life. Although I was raised differently from other Maori kids - I was brought up white - I am Maori in every other sense. Everything I am - my superstitions, my instincts, my values - relates to my Maori belief that there is a guardian spirit eternally watching over me. That is why I tell my children: 'Try very hard never to hurt anybody, never to destroy anybody, never to think evil of anybody, because if you do, it will come back to you.'

Even if I dislike someone immensely, I do my best not to think bad thoughts about them. Sometimes when I am angered, I unintentionally begin to wish ill of them, then I think: 'No, I can't do that.' I try hard not to poison anyone's mind against anyone else's, because I fear that my ill will could revert back to me. When I see my family after some time, I always feel it should rain. Rain, for Maoris, symbolises the tears of the gods, but it is nevertheless considered a good omen.

My whole life has been based on instincts, intuitively knowing whether or not to take a job, sing a song, or travel somewhere. For a period, I worked as a stenographer in New Zealand, because my parents had no money and I felt I needed to acquire a skill although I sensed that my role would be to promote music.

My mother used to make up bedtime stories which were full of symbols. So I do not put new shoes on the table or chair and I dislike people whistling in the dressing room. If anybody does so, he has to go out the door and turn around three times before re-entering.

For a time, I felt I needed for every premiere a sharp new knife, a special knife - one with a black handle. I still do. I have quite a collection of them now. The knife superstition seems to be peculiar to me, though it began for quite practical reasons. I just happened to need a sharp knife in order to peel an orange during a performance. After that I felt it was one of the things I had to have, to bring me luck. Each time I had fruit in my dressing room, I thought I had better go out and get another sharp knife. And so it went on until I did it as a matter of course, a little private tradition.

The need to eat fruit before and during a performance is purely a practical matter. We all have our little tricks to replenish our saliva. Some of us drink water, some use throat sprays. Others suck lemons or oranges, and some of us eat apples. Before singing, you can get very preoccupied with the state of your throat. It probably results from an excess of nervous energy. Any form of lubrication helps.

OPPOSITE: *Placido Domingo as the brooding and distrustful Moor in Elijah Moshinsky's 1992 production of* OTELLO, *staged at the Royal Opera House, Covent Garden. Photography by Henrietta Butler, Redferns Music Picture Library.*

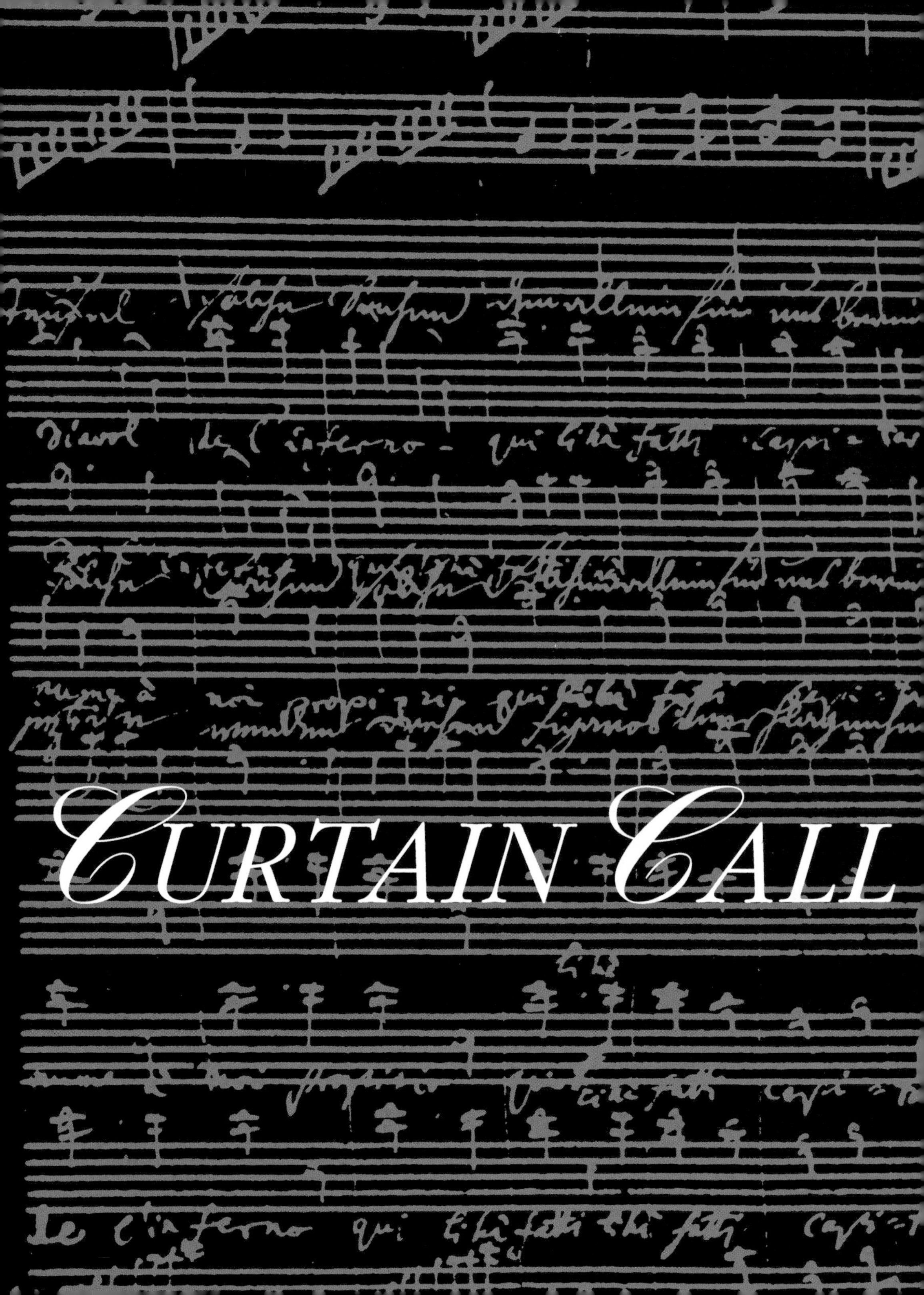

CURTAIN CALL

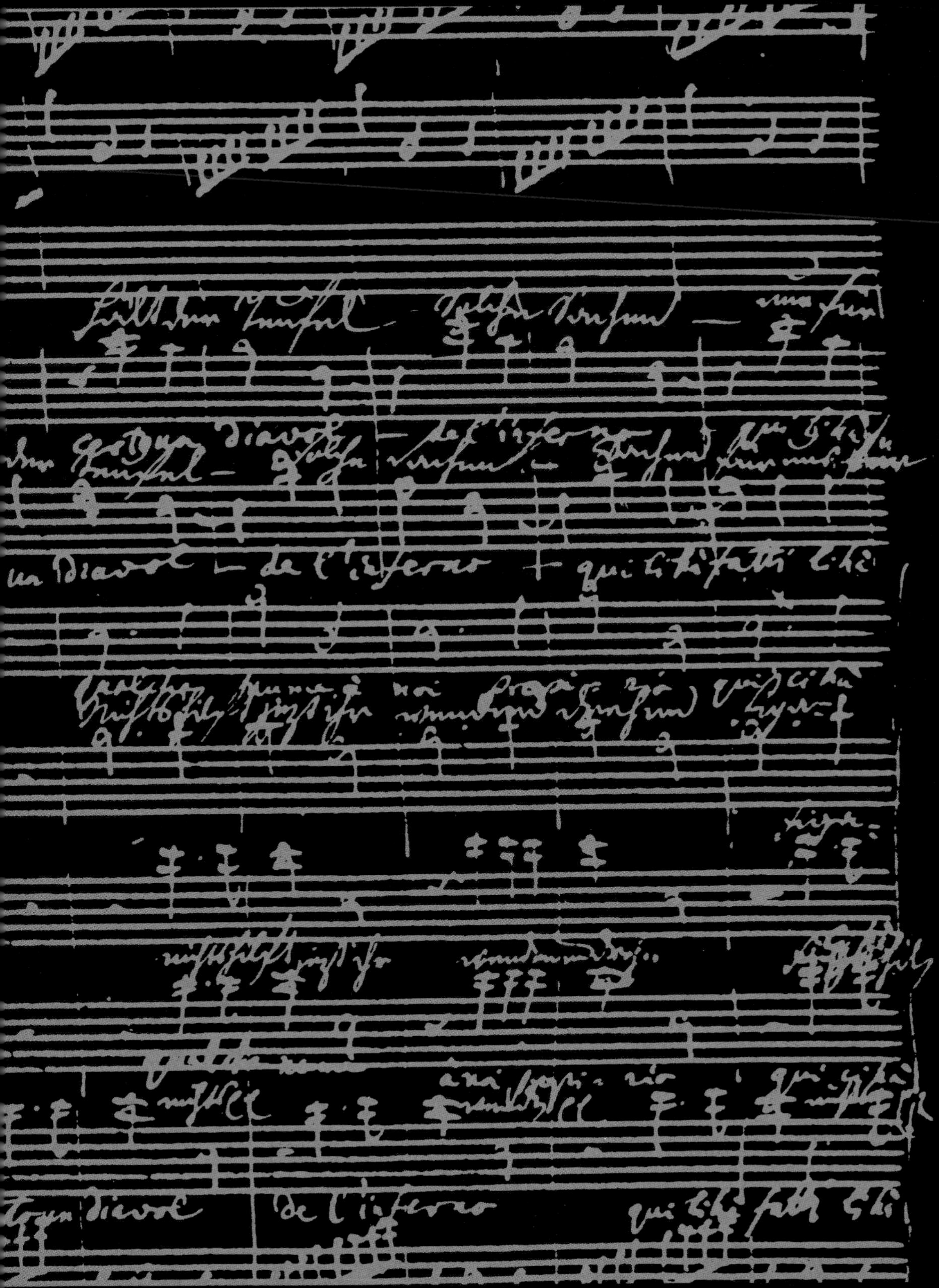

THE FINAL BOW

*S*o many curtain calls for me have seemed much the same. The tenor is always standing on the back of my dress. The baritone stays out longer than he should to get more applause. The curtain stays up when it should come down, and down when it should stay up. Then there is a singer who gets left out on the wrong side of it. Sometimes someone trips over a chair or crashes into a table or - very rarely - falls into the pit. Occasionally the conductor gets lost on his way to the stage.

The producer either has or has not rehearsed the curtain call properly - and it is worth taking time over this. When the grand assembly is not properly rehearsed, it can fall deadly foul. There is nothing like an uncertain, sloppy curtain call to make a good performance look unprofessional. A well-choreographed curtain call becomes a little performance in itself and a pleasure to take part in.

Stories abound of people being booed off the stage during curtain calls. Unfortunately, the sound of a single person booing can cut its way through the loudest applause, and a full-throated roar of disapproval can be a terrible noise. Kindlier people, if they have not enjoyed themselves, usually just sit on their hands. Not to clap, or to clap very quietly, is quite a sufficient statement of unhappiness.

It is usually the producer and designer who are the victims. They have become the controversial figures of opera, the ones who arouse public wrath, whereas at one time they scarcely existed as actual personalities. But since they are now of prime importance to any opera, they must carry the blame when the public does not like what they see.

If a producer is allowed, even encouraged, by an opera company to drag a masterpiece out of its context or period, then it is right that he must bear the consequences if the audience hates what has been done. The public does not owe him a living, and if it thinks that the efforts of the singers and of the conductor are being undermined by the producer, it is increasingly likely to object.

Singers, too, seem increasingly vulnerable because audiences expect nothing but the best at the prices they are being charged today. If there is a seriously weak link in the cast, the singer in question may pay the penalty when the time comes for the curtain call.

Picking on a single singer can be cruel. When a performer seems likely to be singled out as the culprit for the failure, curtain calls may be so arranged that no singer is ever left standing on the stage alone. They take their calls in a line-up, so that the strong members of the cast are able to protect the weak. The stars, if they are feeling confident enough to do so, can always risk taking solo bows. Usually they are experienced enough to be able to test the temperature of the house beforehand to avoid any embarassing situation.

Prima donne and leading men often regard the final solo bow as their privilege and predestined right, though the effect is not always edifying. One star soprano - whom I shall refrain from naming - demanded a solo curtain call after appearing with a tenor whom she considered below her standard. She was denied this public display of vanity. It was not the house policy, she was told.

The diva then demanded the privilege a second time, again without success. So she took matters into her own hands and went out for her lone appearance anyway. Some versions of the story say that the curtain, having been lowered behind her, was not raised again and she had to force her way back beneath it; others say that she started shouting at the director of the company. Either way, it was not the most dignified behaviour.

At times you can be pleasantly surprised, or baffled, by the applause because a performance may be perceived differently by opposite sides of the orchestra pit. Usually, the success or failure of a performance is decided long before the final curtain is reached. Failure can be sniffed even before the first interval, and the smell does not go away. If anything, it gets worse.

It is during rehearsals that we get our first inkling if a production is likely to be acceptable to the audience. Of course, the success not only depends on the director, but also on the man who is leading the orchestra. Singers always know a bad conductor when they see one. Opera is a team effort from the producer and the cast all the way to the carpenter of stage props and make-up artists and theatrical costumier, and if one member is weak, much can go wrong.

Suggested interesting prospects come and go, but never at times that suit me. My family life is precious to me, and frequently I give my husband and children full priority, which means that I have to turn down potentially enticing musical invitations. No matter how distinguished the conductor or director, I am simply not prepared to go on singing, singing, singing, with no light at the end of the tunnel.

Time is running out. I do not want to be like so many singers who have left the stages and concert halls of this world too late. A performer must quit earlier rather than later. When I decide to stop singing, the decision will be final. Janet Baker did it that way, and she was right. There will not be an eternal series of farewell appearances. This approach would lack dignity, much like taking one last curtain call on a stage, which is already empty, with only three people left in the audience.

LEFT: *Kiri Te Kanawa and Placido Domingo have appeared together as Desdemona and Otello in so many different productions of Verdi's opera,* OTELLO, *that nowadays, all they need to work out beforehand is how the jealous Moor is going to kill his devoted wife. In this scene, they are taking their curtain call after a triumphant performance in Elijah Moshinsky's 1983 production at the Royal Opera House, Covent Garden. Photography by Clive Barda, Performing Arts Library.*

 $\mathscr{S}$UMMARY OF $\mathscr{W}$ORKS

Cast:

COUNT WALDNER *(bass)*
ADELAIDE, HIS WIFE *(mezzo-soprano)*
ARABELLA, THEIR DAUGHTER *(soprano)*
ZDENKA, HER SISTER *(soprano)*
MANDRYKA *(baritone)*
MATTEO *(tenor)*
COUNT ELEMER *(tenor)*
COUNT DOMINIK *(baritone)*
COUNT LAMORAL *(bass)*
FIAKERMILLI *(coloratura soprano)*
FORTUNE TELLER *(soprano)*
WELKO *(speaking role)*
DJURA AND JANKEL,
MANDRYKA'S SERVANTS
(speaking roles)
WAITER *(speaking role)*
ARABELLAS'S COMPANION, 3
GAMBLERS, A GROOM, A
COACHMAN, GUESTS AT THE
BALL, HOTEL GUESTS, WAITERS

ARABELLA
Lyrical comedy in three acts in German

Music: Richard Strauss (1864-1949)
Libretto: Hugo von Hofmannsthal
First performance: July 1, 1933, Dresden, Germany
Duration: 2 1/2 hours
Setting: Vienna, 1860

ACT ONE
Count Waldner has gambled away his fortune and lives with his wife and two daughters in a cheap hotel. Since he cannot afford to educate both his daughters adequately, the younger, Zdenka, passes as a son, Zdenko. The family hopes that Arabella will salvage their fortune through a good marriage. Adelaide consults a fortune teller who predicts that Arabella will marry a stranger. Meanwhile, Zdenka will cause complications.

Zdenka would like Arabella to marry Matteo, whom Zdenka adores. Matteo appears and tells his friend, Zdenko, that he will kill himself if Arabella refuses him. Against the three Counts, who are courting Arabella, Matteo has no chance. However, Arabella is certain that Matteo is not her Mr. Right. She tells Zdenka of a stranger whose glance she cannot forget.

Waldner returns from gambling with further losses. All the jewellery is pawned, and the creditors are demanding their money. When a waiter announces a visitor, Waldner recognises with delight the calling card of his wealthy friend Mandryka to whom he has sent Arabella's picture hoping to lure him into marriage. Instead of his old friend, an elegant young man appears, his old friend's nephew and heir. Mandryka asks for Arabella's hand.

ACT TWO
At a ball, Waldner presents Mandryka to his wife and Arabella, who recognises him as the stranger she cannot forget. He tells her of a custom in his country in which a girl brings her lover a glass of clear water as a sign of eternal loyalty. Arabella declares her love, but begs to be alone that evening to bid farewell to her childhood. After the ball, Arabella parts company with the three Counts and returns to the hotel, leaving a billet-doux for Mandryka.

Zdenka passes an envelope to Matteo, supposedly containing Arabella's room key, but in actuality it contains hers. Mandryka overhears their conversation and feels betrayed. He scoffs at Arabella's letter. Angry and jealous, he joins the ball, flirts with Fiakermilli and insults the Countess Adelaide. Waldner challenges him to a duel.

ACT THREE

Arabella enters the hotel, baffling Matteo who thought he had just enjoyed her love. Her parents arrive with Mandryka, who recognises Matteo as the recipient of the key. He causes a scene, awakening Zdenka who descends in her nightgown, and confesses it was she who had received Matteo. Mandryka asks for Zdenka's hand on Matteo's behalf. Everyone retires contentedly, leaving Mandryka alone and unhappy in the hall. Then Arabella appears with a glass of water and offers it to Mandryka who, overjoyed, empties the glass and smashes it on to the floor.

LA BOHÈME
Opera in four acts in Italian

Music: Giacomo Puccini (1858-1924)
Libretto: Giuseppe Giacosa and Luigi Illiaca
First performance: February 1, 1896, Turin, Italy
Duration: 2 hours
Setting: Paris, about 1830

ACT ONE

On Christmas Eve, Rodolfo and Marcello work in their icy cold attic in the Parisian Quartier Latin. To heat up the room, Rodolfo burns pages of his drama. Colline returns, followed by Schaunard who brings victuals, wine, cigars and firewood because he has played for a crazy lord. Schaunard invites his starving friends to dine but is interrupted by the landlord asking for the rent. Benoit drinks their wine and boasts of his sins. The four friends seize the chance to throw this immoral visitor out, without paying their rent.

Rodolfo remains behind to finish an article. Suddenly, Mimi, a new neighbour, appears at his door asking for a light. The beautiful and obviously ill lady leaves after a sip of wine but returns to retrieve her key. A gust of wind extinguishes her candle and Rodolfo's light as well. Both look for the door key in the dark and their hands touch. His friends call from downstairs and he promises to return with company. Mimi is lit by the moon and he embraces her.

ACT TWO

Salesmen, shoppers and children mill around outside the cafe. Rodolfo buys Mimi a bonnet before introducing her to his friends. In the cafe, the flighty Musette tries to seduce Marcello once again, singing a waltz for him. She sends her old and wealthy benefactor, Alcindoro, to get her shoes fixed. As soon as he departs, the two lovers embrace. When the cafe closes, everyone departs, leaving the bill for Alcindoro.

ACT THREE

Rodolfo has left Mimi because of his unfounded jealousy, so she goes to the bar in search of Marcello and Musette. However, Rodolfo appears instead. Mimi hides behind a tree and discovers that her lover's jealousy is just a pretext. He loves her but feels helpless in the face of her impending death. Mimi weeps copiously upon learning of her condition and the extent of his love. Rodolfo takes Mimi in his arms.

Cast:

RODOLFO, POET *(tenor)*
MARCELLO, PAINTER *(baritone)*
SCHAUNARD, MUSICIAN *(baritone)*
COLLINE, PHILOSOPHER *(bass)*
MIMI, SEAMSTRESS *(soprano)*
MUSETTE *(soprano)*
BENOIT, LANDLORD *(bass)*
ALCINDORO, MAGISTRATE *(bass)*
PARPIGNOL, TOY SELLER *(tenor)*
CUSTOMS SERGEANT *(bass)*
CUSTOMS OFFICIAL *(bass)*
STUDENTS, CITIZENS, SALESMEN, SEAMSTRESSES, SOLDIERS, WAITERS, BOYS AND GIRLS

ACT FOUR

In their room, Marcello and Rodolfo try to forget their lovers, to no avail - Rodolfo has seen Musette with a rich admirer while Marcello has spotted Mimi in an elegant coach. When Colline and Schaunard bring food, they share a meagre meal. Musette interrupts them, saying that Mimi is dying and wants to see Rodolfo one last time, but is unable to climb the stairs. They carry her into the room. Rodolfo and Mimi swear eternal love, before she dies after a coughing fit. Rodolfo hurls himself onto the corpse of his beloved.

Cast:

COUNTESS MADELEINE
(soprano)
THE COUNT, HER BROTHER
(baritone)
FLAMAND, MUSICIAN (tenor)
OLIVIER, POET (baritone)
LA ROCHE, THEATRE DIRECTOR
(bass)
CLAIRON, ACTRESS
(contralto)
MONSIEUR TAUPE (tenor)
MAJORDOMUS (bass)
8 SERVANTS (4 tenors, 4 basses), 1 YOUNG DANCER, 3 MUSICIANS

CAPRICCIO

A conversation piece in one act in German

Music: Richard Strauss (1864-1949)
Libretto: Clemens Krauss and Richard Strauss
First performance: October 28, 1942, Munich, Germany
Duration: 2 1/4 hours
Setting: A castle near Paris, around 1775

Before the curtain rises, a concerto is played, which Flamand has composed as a gift for Countess Madeleine. The poet, Olivier, and the theatre director, La Roche, are preparing for the birthday of the Countess. Olivier and Flamand are both interested in the young widow. The question is if the sophisticated lady prefers music or poetry. The brother of the Countess, who is in love with the actress Clairon, is not moved by music but the Countess is.

The actress arrives and rehearses with the Count a love scene from a drama which ends in a fiery sonnet. Olivier repeats the sonnet to the Countess while Flamand sets out to put the poem to music. His composition charms the Countess no less than Olivier's words. For her, words are inseparable from the music. Pressed for a decision between her two admirers, Madeleine asks the composer to come to the library at eleven the next morning.

The Countess asks Flamand and Olivier to produce an opera for the celebration. The Count suggests they take the events of the day and the persons involved as material for the opera. After the guests leave, the servants mock their masters whose lives are nothing but theatre to them. The prompter, Monsieur Taupe, emerges from his box, feeling that he is the actual ruler of the theatrical world.

The Countess appears for supper and her Majordomus lets her know that Olivier will come by tomorrow at eleven to learn of her decision and the ending of the opera. The Countess remembers that she has asked Flamand to come at the same time. Poet and musician seem constantly tied together. She cannot choose between them. The Majordomus announces that supper is being served.

CARMEN
Opera in four acts in French

Music: Georges Bizet (1838 - 1875)
Libretto: Henri Meilhac and Ludovic Halévy
First Performance: March 3, 1875, Paris
Duration: 2 3/4 hours
Setting: Seville and environs, about 1820

ACT ONE
Micaela hesitantly approaches the soldiers on duty at the plaza and enquires about Sergeant José. The girls working for the cigar factory leave the building to take their lunch, much to Lieutenant Zuniga's interest. The last one to emerge is Carmen who sings a Habanera and tosses José a flower. He is mesmerized. When Micaela, his childhood sweetheart, brings a letter from his mother, he feels released from Carmen's spell. José decides to follow his mother's wishes and marry Micaela.

Suddenly, cries for help emerge from the factory and the female workers run out. Carmen has wounded a colleague with a knife. The soldiers disperse the fighting women and José fetches Carmen on orders of his lieutenant. When Carmen mocks Zuniga's interrogative attempt, José handcuffs and arrests her. Carmen uses her feminine wiles on José, promising him the fulfilment of his dreams if he lets her go. He cannot resist, Carmen escapes and José is arrested in her stead.

ACT TWO
In the Inn of Lillas Pastia, Carmen and other gypsies are singing and dancing with the soldiers. The torero Escamillo joins them and is immediately fascinated by Carmen, who first mocks him, only to throw him a languishing glance when the inn closes. The innkeeper asks the gypsies to stay behind and distract the custom officers from the smugglers who suddenly appear. Carmen, however, admits that she expects José, who has just been released from jail.

When he comes, she dances for him alone, but the trumpet sounds to call the soldiers back to barracks and he makes ready to leave. She is infuriated despite his avowals of love for her. She asks him to take her away, but as he forces himself from her arms, the jealous Zuniga bursts into the inn. When Carmen cries for help, the gypsies and smugglers return and disarm Zuniga. José now has no choice but to join the smugglers.

ACT THREE
José is with the band of smugglers that night in the mountains. Tired of him by now, Carmen asks if he would kill her if she leaves him. She claims not to fear a violent death which the cards have foretold. The gypsies lay the cards again and although they predict a prosperous future for them, Carmen draws the ace of spades, the death card, once more.

José remains in the camp. Micaela searches for him to take him back to his dying mother. She sees him when José fires a gun at a man - it is Escamillo, who is looking for Carmen. When Escamillo and José

Cast:

CARMEN, GYPSY *(mezzo-soprano)*
DON JOSÉ, SERGEANT *(tenor)*
ESCAMILLO, TORRERO *(bass or baritone)*
MICAELA, PEASANT GIRL *(soprano or mezzo-soprano)*
ZUNIGA, LIEUTENANT *(bass)*
MORALES, SERGEANT *(baritone)*
DANCAIRO AND REMENDADO, SMUGGLERS *(tenor)*
ANDRES, SERGEANT *(tenor)*
LILLAS PASTIA, INNKEEPER *(speaking role)*
MOUNTAIN GUIDE *(speaking role)*
ORANGE SELLER *(contralto)*
SOLDIERS, YOUNG MEN, WORKERS IN A CIGARETTE FACTORY, GIPSIES, SMUGGLERS, POLICEMEN, TORREROS, CITIZENS, STREET KIDS

recognise each other, they have a knife fight. The smugglers return just as José is ready to make his deadly lunge. Escamillo, saved by the smugglers, invites everybody to his next bullfight, while José joins Micaela, not without threatening Carmen with his return.

ACT FOUR
On the day of the great bullfight, Escamillo approaches the arena with Carmen who is warned by her friends that José has been seen in the vicinity. José confronts her, asking her to start a new life with him. Carmen declares that she no longer loves him and that she wants to be free to live or die. When Escamillo returns victorious from the bullfight, Carmen makes to greet him, but José blocks her way. She shouts that she belongs to Escamillo and throw José's ring into the dust. Jose stabs her to death.

Cast:

FERRANDO, DORABELLA'S LOVER *(tenor)*
GUGLIELMO, FIORDILIGI'S LOVER *(baritone)*
DON ALFONSO, PHILOSOPHER *(bass)*
FIORDILIGI *(soprano)*
DORABELLA, HER SISTER *(soprano or mezzo-soprano)*
DESPINA, CHAMBERMAID OF THE TWO SISTERS *(soprano)*
SOLDIERS, SERVANTS, SAILORS

COSÌ FAN TUTTE
Opera buffa in two acts in Italian

Music: Wolfgang Amadeus Mozart (1756-1791)
Libretto: Lorenzo da Ponte
First performance: January 26, 1790, Vienna, Austria
Duration: 3 hours
Setting: Naples, around 1790

ACT ONE
Two officers, Ferrando and Guglielmo, argue with their friend, Don Alfonso, about the fidelity of women. The officers praise the loyalty of their respective beloved ones, Fiordiligi and Dorabella, but Don Alfonso scoffs at their naivety. The two men agree to a wager of a hundred guineas with their friend. Alfonso vows that he will prove that their fiancées are no different from any other woman in their fickle loyalties, provided that the two men do exactly as he tells them.

In their room, Fiordiligi and Dorabella admire each other's lockets, with portraits of their lovers. Alfonso dashes in with news that the two officers are being sent to war and must depart immediately. When Ferrando and Guglielmo enter, the lovers bid each other an emotional farewell.

Fiordiligi and Dorabella are found distraught by their maid, Despina. She scolds them for wasting so much emotion on useless menfolk, of which one is as false as the next. She counsels them to make the best of this opportunity and seek solace elsewhere. The two sisters are disgusted by her suggestion and storm out of her presence.

As if on cue, Alfonso turns up to enlist Despina's help. He wants to introduce two of his friends from Albania, who follow close on his shirt tails, to Fiordiligi and Dorabella. Unbeknown to Despina, the two Albanians are, in fact, Ferrando and Guglielmo in disguise. When the two damsels turn up, they too are unable to recognise the men close to their hearts and promptly throw them out of the house.

Alfonso forestalls their action and introduces the men as two of his closest and dearest friends. The Albanians lavish their attention on the ladies, each trying to seduce the other's fiancée, inciting Fiordiligi to declare that she is 'Firm as a rock'. The two women depart in a huff, with Despina in tow, leaving the men in laughter.

Alfonso reminds his friends that it is still early in the game. Alfonso leaves it to Despina to continue the ploy who convinces Ferrando and Guglielmo to pretend to have swallowed poison because the damsels rejected them. Despina appears masked as a physician whom the ladies have called and cures the two Albanians with magnetism. But the two cured patients are denied the kiss they languish for.

ACT TWO
The sisters begin to enjoy the game. Dorabella falls prey to Guglielmo's pressing, but Ferrando is not so lucky with Fiordiligi. She renews her vow of steadfastness. Guglielmo learns with pride of the constancy of his fiancée, but when he shows Ferrando the locket he has won from Dorabella, the game begins to turn into a tragedy.

Dorabella and Despina try their best to change Fiordiligi's mind. The latter, however, makes ready to join her fiancé in battle. Suddenly, Ferrando rushes in and threatens to kill himself if she will not have him. Fiordiligi's heart is finally won. Guglielmo is shocked. Don Alfonso comforts the friends - women are all alike and fickle. He promises to see things right by means of a double wedding.

Despina, this time clad as a notary public, brings the marriage contracts for the ladies to sign. Alfonso announces the return of the officers. The two Albanians are quickly hidden in another room, only to emerge as homecoming soldiers. When they notice the lavish banquet on the table and the embarrassment of the ladies, they feign suspicion. The ladies admit to their infidelities. The men then disclose their masquerade, causing the ladies to almost lose their minds. Alfonso leads each of the ladies back to her original partner for the wedding.

DON GIOVANNI
Dramma giacoso in two acts in Italian

Music: Wolfgang Amadeus Mozart (1756-1791)
Libretto: Lorenzo da Ponte
First performance: October 29, 1787, Prague, Czech Republic
Duration: 3 hours
Setting: A city in Spain, about 1700

ACT ONE
In front of the Commendatore's house, a foul-tempered Leporello is left on guard. Suddenly, Don Giovanni rushes out of the house, pursued by an enraged Donna Anna who wants to prevent the unknown trespasser from escaping. Upon her cries, the Commendatore rushes to her aid and challenges Don Giovanni to a duel, during which Giovanni kills him. Anna who had run into the house to fetch her fiancé Don Ottavio, finds her dead father and makes Ottavio swear revenge.

Giovanni goes in search of new love adventures. He encounters another woman, who laments of being abandoned by her lover. She

Cast:

DON GIOVANNI, YOUNG AND RECKLESS ARISTOCRAT *(baritone)*
IL COMMENDATORE *(bass)*
DONNA ANNA, HIS DAUGHTER *(soprano)*
DON OTTAVIO, HER FIANCÉ *(tenor)*
DONNA ELVIRA, ARISTOCRAT FROM BURGOS, DISCARDED BY GIOVANNI *(soprano)*
LEPORELLO, GIOVANNI'S SERVANT *(bass)*
MASETTO, YOUNG PEASANT *(bass)*
ZERLINA, HIS FIANCÉ *(soprano)*

wants him back. Giovanni approaches her and is taken aback: it is Donna Elvira. He leaves it to Leporello to explain that she is only one of many women whom Giovanni has seduced and abandoned afterwards.

Giovanni is interested in the bride-to-be, Zerlina, and invites her wedding party to his castle. He promises Zerlina marriage, but Elvira interferes and takes her under her protection. Still looking for the murderer of her father, Anna and Don Ottavio meet Giovanni, but fail to recognise him and enlist his help. Donna Elvira warns them that Giovanni is a traitor. Giovanni tries in vain to convince the couple that Elvira is mad. Donna Anna is finally certain that Giovanni was the one who had entered her bedroom on that fateful night.

Giovanni prepares a feast in his castle. Zerlina succeeds in alleviating Masetto's jealousy and survives another potentially damaging scene with Giovanni and Masetto. Three masked persons also attend the wedding: Donna Elvira, Donna Anna and Don Ottavio who have come to confront Giovanni. The latter manoeuvres Zerlina into another room from which shortly thereafter her cries for help emerge. The guests come to her help. Giovanni presents Leporello as the culprit but he is not believed. The three masked guests identify themselves and prophesy Giovanni's approaching death.

ACT TWO
Leporello has had enough and decides to leave Giovanni's service, but a purse of money lures him back. Giovanni now targets Elvira's chambermaid. To this purpose, he changes his outfit with Leporello's in front of Elvira's house at night. When Elvira appears on the balcony, Leporello pretends to be Giovanni who is hiding behind him and prompts him to flatter Elvira to lure her out of the house. Elvira exchanges endearments with the wrong Giovanni and comes into the garden. The real Giovanni suddenly causes a lot of noise and chases both Elvira and Leporello away to have the house and the maid to himself. While he is playing a serenade for her, the peasants come, led by Masetto, to kill Giovanni who, still in Leporello's outfit, succeeds in misleading them. He gives Masetto a good bashing in the bargain. Zerlina comforts the beaten Masetto.

Leporello, still disguised as Giovanni, and accompanied by Elvira is confronted by Zerlina and Masetto, then by Donna Anna and the armed Ottavio. Donna Elvira begs for mercy for her supposed lover when Leporello discards Giovanni's cloak and escapes. Don Ottavio continues to search for Giovanni alone, leaving his fiancée in the care of the others.

At a cemetery, Giovanni and Leporello meet again. In an exuberant mood, Giovanni tells of his adventures when he is interrupted by a ghostly voice warning him that his laughter will not outlive the next morning. Giovanni forces the trembling Leporello to invite the statue on the grave of the killed Commendatore, from which the voice had emerged, to dinner at Giovanni's castle. The statue replies 'yes'.

In his castle, Giovanni has Leporello set a luxurious meal. Desperately, Elvira counsels Giovanni to mend his ways, to no avail. Giovanni praises women and wine and mocks her. Leaving, Elvira stops dead in her tracks with a cry and flees through another exit. The statue from the cemetery has arrived. Refusing the offer of food, it asks Giovanni to accept another invitation, which Giovanni does, offering his hand. The statue grips his hand with increasing pressure and demands that Giovanni repent, each time more and more threateningly. Giovanni denies the requests with a resounding 'no'. Thereupon, the earth begins to tremble and opens. Flames emerge and swallow Giovanni.

MANON LESCAUT
Lyrical drama in four acts in Italian

Music: Giacomo Puccini (1858-1924)
Libretto: Ruggero Leoncavallo, Marco Praga, Domenico Oliva, Giulio Ricordi, Luigi Illica, Giuseppe Giacosa
First Performance: February 1, 1893, Turin, Italy
Duration: 2 hours
Setting: France and North America, 2nd half of the eighteenth century

Cast:

MANON LESCAUT *(soprano)*
LESCAUT, SERGEANT OF THE ROYAL GUARD, HER BROTHER *(baritone)*
CHEVALIER RENATO DES GRIEUX, STUDENT *(tenor)*
GERONTE DE RAVOIR, ROYAL TAX INSPECTOR *(bass)*
EDMONDO, STUDENT *(tenor)*
INNKEEPER *(bass)*
MUSICIAN *(mezzo-soprano)*
DANCE INSTRUCTOR *(tenor)*
LAMP LIGHTER *(tenor)*
SERGEANT OF ARCHERS *(bass)*
CAPTAIN OF A SHIP *(bass)*
WIG MAKER *(silent role)*
GIRLS, CITIZENS, STUDENTS, MUSICIANS, OLD GENTLEMEN AND ABBOTS, COURTESANS, ARCHERS, SAILORS, SEAMEN

ACT ONE
In Amiens, the students Edmondo and de Grieux are singing ironic adulations of women. The post coach arrives from Arras with Manon Lescaut, her brother and tax inspector Ravoir. De Grieux is immediately taken by Manon. While her companions go into the inn, he learns from her that her brother is bringing her on orders of her father to a convent. He replies that this cannot be the fate of so much beauty and receives a promise of a rendezvous for the evening.

In the meantime, Ravoir who has loved Manon secretly for some time, plans to elope with her that night. Edmondo witnesses his orders to the innkeeper to prepare a coach and horses and tells de Grieux about it. When he meets Manon again, de Grieux tells her about Ravoir's plans, but instead of Ravoir she allows de Grieux to take her to Paris in Ravoir's coach. When Ravoir wants to pursue the couple, Lescaut calms him. A poor student will not be able to keep his sister's affections for long.

ACT TWO
Lescaut was right. Manon has deserted de Grieux and is the mistress of the old Ravoir, leading a life of luxury in his palace. While she is getting ready for the day, she admits to her brother how she is missing the humble abode she shared with de Grieux compared to this gilded and cold cage. Lescaut tells her that her former lover still misses her and tries to win at the gambling table so that he may be able to reconquer her.

De Grieux has been told by Lescaut that Manon still loves him and suddenly appears at her doorstep after the guests have left. The lovers embrace and are surprised by Ravoir. When he starts to scold Manon, she passes him a mirror to compare himself to de Grieux. Ravoir threatens them and the lovers prepare for their escape. Manon loses precious time amassing her jewellery and is caught by Ravoir who has returned with armed guards. Manon is arrested and de Grieux disarmed.

ACT THREE

The port of Le Havre. De Grieux did not succeed in obtaining Manon's release. He and Lescaut have followed the train of prisoners to Le Havre where Manon is scheduled to be deported alongside whores and courtesans to a penal colony in North America. Lescaut has managed to bribe a soldier who allows de Grieux to speak to Manon, but an escape plot by Lescaut is foiled.

When the morning dawns, the women are called individually and brought on board. De Grieux begs the captain to allow him to sail with the ship and permission is granted.

ACT FOUR

Manon and de Grieux have fled from the penal colony. They drag themselves through an arid area near New Orleans. Manon collapses with fever and half loses consciousness. De Grieux pulls himself together to search water for his beloved who finally realises that there is no more hope. De Grieux returns without water. With the words 'my guilt will be forgotten, but my love does not die', Manon dies. De Grieux collapses over her corpse.

Cast:

FIGARO, STEWARD OF THE COUNT *(baritone)*
SUSANNA, CHAMBERMAID OF THE COUNTESS *(soprano)*
COUNT ALMAVIVA *(baritone)*
COUNTESS ALMAVIVA *(soprano)*
CHERUBINO, PAGE BOY OF THE COUNT *(soprano)*
MARCELLINA *(contralto)*
DR. BARTOLO, PHYSICIAN FROM SEVILLE *(bass)*
DON BASILIO, MUSIC MASTER *(tenor)*
ANTONIO, THE COUNT'S GARDENER AND SUSANNA'S UNCLE *(bass)*
DON CURZIO, JUDGE *(tenor)*
BARBARINA, DAUGHTER OF ANTONIO *(soprano)*
PEASANTS ON ALMAVIVA'S ESTATE, SERVANTS

LE NOZZE DI FIGARO
Opera buffa in four acts in Italian

Music: Wolfgang Amadeus Mozart (1756 - 1791)
Libretto: Lorenzo da Ponte
First performance: May 1, 1786, Vienna, Austria
Duration: 3 hours
Setting: Castle of Count Almaviva near Seville, Spain

ACT ONE

A rousing overture raises the curtain on a semi-furnished room in Count Almaviva's castle. Figaro is measuring the floor with his fiancée, Susanna who tells him that their master intends to reinstate the right of the first night, under which a landlord can bed any newly-wed woman on his estate before her husband, a feudal custom he had previously abolished. As she goes off in response to her mistress' bell, the furious Figaro swears to teach the Count a lesson.

Dr. Bartolo, formerly the guardian of Countess Almaviva, enters with his housekeeper, Marcellina, whom Figaro once borrowed money from against a promise of marriage. The doctor has not forgiven Figaro for assisting the Countess Almaviva's elopement with the Count from under his guardianship. He urges Marcellina to bring legal proceedings against Figaro for not making good on his promise of paying back the loan or marrying her.

Cherubino begs Susanna for help. The Count has recently dismissed him for flirting with the gardener's daughter, Barbarina, and he needs her aid to get his job back. They hear male voices and Susanna has only just enough time to conceal Cherubino before the Count enters. Almaviva, a philanderer, flirts with Figaro's fiancée but stops when he hears Basilio approaching and also hides.

Basilio teases Susanna about her supposed affair with Cherubino, but when Basilio mentions that the page boy is infatuated with the Countess, Almaviva is unable to contain himself and breaks out of his hiding place in indignation. Susanna defends Cherubino, insisting that he is just a boy and knows no better. The Count disagrees and expounds upon how he discovered the boy in Barbarina's room. He inadvertently discovers the culprit behind the chair. The incensed Count orders Basilio to fetch Figaro but suddenly realises that his position is precarious as the page boy has overheard his conversation with Susanna.

Figaro enters with a group of peasants who live on the Almaviva estate to solemnly thank the Count for abolishing the right of the first night. The Count rids himself of Cherubino, the witness of his propositions to Susanna, by commissioning him as an officer to his regiment and urges him to depart immediately. Figaro hastens the reluctant boy on his way with a colourful description of the life that awaits him.

ACT TWO
In her boudoir, the sad Countess, her maid Susanna and Figaro plot their intrigue. A billet-doux will be passed to the Count, indicating that the Countess is seeing a lover. At the same time, Susanna will arrange to rendezvous with the Count but instead of Susanna, Cherubino, dressed as a girl, will await the Count. Figaro will then surprise the two.

The Countess and Susanna have fun dressing Cherubino up in a ladies' clothes, and all three are thrown into a panic when a knock is heard on the door. It is the Count, who has received the billet-doux. Cherubino locks himself in the bedroom while Susanna hides behind a curtain. The Count searches the boudoir and demands that the locked door be opened, which the Countess refuses to do. Almaviva takes the Countess with him as he goes to look for tools to break down the door. The remaining two take this opportunity to emerge from their hiding places. As soon as they hear the Count returning, Cherubino jumps out the window and Susanna takes his place in the bedroom.

To appease the Count, his wife confesses that Cherubino is hiding in the bedroom. This only serves to infuriate him further and his anger escalates when the Countess pleads for mercy. Much to the surprise and amazement of both, Susanna unlocks the door and emerges. The Count then asks for his wife's forgiveness. The ladies explain that the note was written by Figaro, who chooses that inopportune time to appear and deny all knowledge of the billet-doux.

At that moment the gardener, Antonio, enters with a broken flower pot and complains that he will not tolerate people jumping out of windows. Figaro quickly takes the blame and apologises to Antonio. Although the gardener says that the figure he saw looked more like Cherubino than Figaro, he nonetheless returns to Figaro a letter that was dropped. The Count snatches it away from Antonio and dares Figaro to tell him which letter it is. The Countess recognises it as Cherubino's commission and prompts Figaro just in time.

Just when it seems that the Count is pacified and things can get back to normal, Bartolo, Marcellina and their lawyer, Don Curzio enter, demanding justice from the Count.

ACT THREE

Susanna interrupts the Count, saying that she wishes to meet him in the castle gardens that night, always provided that the Count pays her a dowry with which Figaro would then be able to pay back Marcellina instead of having to marry the old hag. The Count overhears her telling Figaro that his court case is as good as won and realises that if Figaro is free to marry Susanna, Almaviva may never have his chance with her. So the Count decides that Figaro is to pay Marcellina or marry her. Figaro thereupon claims that, though a foundling, he cannot marry without the consent of his parents. When he tells of a strawberry-coloured birthmark, Marcellina realises that he is her long-lost illegitimate son, whose father is Bartolo. The three embrace in happy reunion while the Count fumes with frustration at having his plans disrupted.

The Countess and Susanna contrive to write a letter to the Count to arrange for the rendezvous in the garden that night, at which the Countess, dressed as Susanna, will meet her husband. The letter is sealed with a pin which the Count is asked to return to Susanna as a sign of his consent.

A group of peasant girls enter to present the Countess. The Count discovers Cherubino, disguised as a girl. Barbarina, who secretly loves Cherubino, has the Count wrapped around her little finger through past favours. She reminds Almaviva of his promise to do as she pleases and asks for Cherubino's hand in marriage. Cornered, the master of the house has no choice but to pardon the page boy. He puts on a happy face to join the two couples, Figaro and Susanna and Bartolo and Marcellina. As they dance, Susanna passes the note to the Count. The missive is secured with a pin that pricks the Count as he opens it, which is noticed by Figaro. Lulled into a sense of euphoria for the moment, the Count then declares a wonderful feast in honour of the two couples.

ACT FOUR

The Count asks Barbarina to return the pin to Susanna. Unfortunately, the gardener's daughter loses it in the garden in the presence of Figaro and Marcellina. Barbarina tells Figaro of her plight, who then believes that Susanna is betraying him. He vows that Susanna will pay for her treachery. He asks Basilio and Bartolo to remain close by as witnesses to his wife's deceit. Susanna has found Figaro out and pretends to ardently await the Count to take revenge for Figaro's distrust in her.

In the dark of the night, a magical dance of mistaken identities begins with Cherubino as an erotic pixie flitting among the different parties. In the end, the Count forces Susanna - in reality the disguised Countess - into a pavilion. Figaro, who observed them then sees the Countess and recognises in her the hooded Susanna. He pretends to make passes at the false Countess who slaps him across the face. Figaro is delighted and the bridal couple make up. They continue, however, to play the loving couple Figaro and Countess in front of Almaviva, thus infuriating the Count who comes to lay bare the infidelity of his wife. Only then does the true Countess abandon her cloak and the intrigue is unravelled. The Count asks of her what he was not prepared to grant his wife - forgiveness.

OTELLO
Lyric opera in four acts in Italian

Music: Guiseppe Verdi
Libretto: Arrigo Boito
First performance: February 5, 1887, Milan, Italy
Duration: 2 1/4 hours
Setting: Port on Cyprus, end of fifteenth century

ACT ONE
Thunder and lighting erupt into a storm upon a port in Cyprus. Anxious watchers look seawards from the harbour, awaiting Otello's safe return. Iago and Roderigo are among them. A cannon shot announces the arrival of his ship and suddenly Otello is on the scene. To the delight of the crowd, he declares his victory over the Turks, then makes his way to the citadel. The Cypriots celebrate with joyous laughter, dancing and drinking around a bonfire. Iago and Roderigo huddle together on their own. Iago harbours great hatred for Otello because the Moor has promoted Cassio instead of Iago. Roderigo is in love with Desdemona, the lady whom Otello married. The two hatch a scheme of revenge against Otello and Cassio.

When the storm dies down, Cassio returns from the citadel to the merrymaking at the bonfire. Iago puts his poisonous scheme into action when he starts up a song and intoxicates Cassio with wine. The crowd, not seeing the malice behind Iago's actions, joins in the fun and in the midst of their merriment, Roderigo taunts Cassio into a duel. The drunk Cassio accidentally injures Montano, who has attempted to intercede. The commotion brings Otello out from the citadel, and on discovering the sequence of events, strips Cassio of his rank.

ACT TWO
In the citadel, Iago suggests to Cassio that he ask the kind and naive Desdemona to appeal to Otello on his behalf. When Cassio leaves, Iago sings of his belief in a cruel god, whose image he is fashioned after. Soon after Otello approaches and Iago seizes this opportunity to infect his mind with false suspicions that Desdemona has a liking for Cassio, thus ensnaring Otello into his foul web.

Otello meets Desdemona who asks him to forgive Cassio, thus reawakening his jealousy. Otello, pretending to have a headache, turns from her and angrily snatches her handkerchief away with which she was trying to wipe his brow. Iago is quick to pick it up for future use in his scheme.

Otello is left alone with Iago and laments that he is no longer at peace with himself, now that he doubts his wife's fidelity. Iago pretends to console him while actually fanning the fire he has started. In a rage, Otello throws Iago to the ground and demands proof of his allegations. The cunning ensign is thus prompted to disclose that he has heard Cassio speaking of his love for Desdemona in his sleep and

Cast:

OTELLO, MOOR, COMMANDER OF THE VENETIAN FLEET *(tenor)*
DESDEMONA, HIS WIFE *(soprano)*
IAGO, OFFICER *(baritone)*
EMILIA, HIS WIFE *(mezzo-soprano)*
CASSIO, CAPTAIN *(tenor)*
RODERIGO, VENETIAN ARISTOCRAT *(tenor)*
MONTANO, GOVERNOR OF CYPRUS, OTELLO'S PREDECESSOR *(bass)*
A HERALD *(bass)*
LODOVICO, AMBASSADOR OF VENICE *(bass)*
SOLDIERS, SAILORS, AMBASSADORS, PEOPLE OF CYPRUS

that he has even seen Cassio in possession of the lady's handkerchief, which Otello had given to her. Infuriated, Otello vows to make Desdemona suffer for her betrayal.

ACT THREE
Desdemona appeals for Cassio's forgiveness again, and Otello responds by asking for her handkerchief, which, of course, she is unable to produce. Otello condemns her as a harlot. Iago tells the Moor to hide himself as he will soon expose Cassio for the traitor that he is. Cued by Iago, Cassio begins to speak of his lover whose name is only whispered, thus leading Otello to believe that Cassio is speaking of Desdemona, especially since he holds the handkerchief which Iago had slipped to Cassio. On Cassio's departure, Otello tells Iago that he plans to kill Desdemona that night. Iago, false friend that he is, promises to see that Cassio also suffers the same fate.

The ambassadors of the Doge arrive to the cheers of the crowd. Their leader, Lodovico, passes Otello a message from the Doge, which he reads immediately then summons Cassio. He announces that he has been requested by the Doge and Senate to return to Venice but he is unable to control his fury when he pronounces Cassio to be successor, casting hurtful remarks at his wife while he hurls her to the floor to the disgust of the Venetian delegation. Lodovico pleads with Otello to take pity on his weeping wife but his anger knows no bounds. With a wave of his hand and a sharp command, he dismisses the crowd, only to fall to the ground in a epileptic fit.

ACT FOUR
In Desdemona's bedroom, Emilia assists her mistress in getting ready for bed. As she leaves, the wronged woman sings the melancholy willow song, expressing her deep sorrow at the loss of her husband's love and trust. She ends with a prayer to the Virgin Mary as Otello enters through a secret door. He awakens his wife with three kisses then attempts to force her admission of guilt. Desdemona adamantly asserts her innocence, which inflames Otello even more till all he can do is strangle her. Even as she takes her last breath, she still revels in her love for Otello and caresses the hand that murders her.

Emilia runs in with news that Cassio has killed Roderigo but all she hears is her mistress' last gasp. She accuses Otello of murder and shrieks for help, which comes in the form of Cassio, Iago and Lodovico. Emilia who is aware of her husband's malevolent nature and his evil schemes, denounces him to those present. The company's disbelief is soon quelled when Montano enters with Roderigo's dying confession. Fearing for his life, Iago flees leaving behind a distraught Otello who mourns his dead wife and is overwrought with guilt for his lack of faith, his tainted love and his rash impulses. Taking his sword from the table, he stabs himself.

DER ROSENKAVALIER
Comedy in three acts in German

Music: Richard Strauss (1864-1949)
Libretto: Hugo von Hofmannsthal
First performance: January 26, 1911, Dresden
Duration: 3 1/2 hours
Setting: Vienna during the reign of Empress Maria Theresia

ACT ONE
The lovemaking of Octavian and the Marschallin is musically depicted in a prelude, leading into the first act. The lovers are deep in conversation in the Marschallin's bedroom. She is telling Octavian that he will soon leave her for a younger woman, though she is extremely reluctant to see him go. Suddenly, there is a noise in the anteroom. Both are frightened, thinking that her husband may be returning from a hunting trip. Octavian immediately hides behind a screen and quickly disguises himself as the Marschallin's maid, Mariandel, to sneak out of the Feldmarschallin's rooms past the newly-arrived guests.

The Marschallin's country cousin, Baron Ochs, forces his way into her bedroom, despite the protests of the servants, and is distracted along the way by the pretty maid Mariandel with whom he attempts to flirt. He then reverts to the reason for his visit and asks the Marschallin's assistance in procuring the hand of Sophie, daughter of the newly ennobled Herrn von Faninal. As is the custom, Ochs needs to nominate a suitable knight of the rose (Rosenkavalier) to present a silver rose to his chosen bride, and the Marschallin recommends Octavian.

The Marschallin recollects the time of her own arranged marriage, a fate very similar to the one threatening now Sophie von Faninal, who has to marry a lout like Ochs. Even Octavian, who came back in his ordinary clothes, cannot cheer her up. Once again, she tells Octavian that he will leave her for someone younger. Hurt by this obvious mistrust, Octavian takes a formal farewell. As soon as he leaves, the Marschallin realises that she had not even kissed him and orders her black page boy, Mahomet, to bring the silver rose to Octavian.

ACT TWO
In the lavishly decorated salon at the Faninal's home, the family waits for the knight of the rose. Sophie and her nurse, Marianne, are agitated in anticipation. Octavian enters, bearing the silver rose. He and Sophie are immediately attracted to each other. Their tête-à-tête is soon interrupted by the Baron, who presents himself as an uncouth man, shocking Sophie. The Baron's callous statements and insensitive remarks make Octavian's blood boil.

Upon the Baron's departure, Sophie begs Octavian to rescue her from this unsavoury marriage. Octavian agrees. The two fall into each other's arms but are surprised by Valzacchi and Annina, who walk in on them and raise an alarm. Ochs rushes in, but before he can react, Octavian swears that Sophie will never marry him. He challenges the Baron to a duel on the spot. Ochs reluctantly agrees and in the

Cast:

THE FELDMARSCHALLIN
PRINCESS WERDENBERG
(soprano)
BARON OCHS AUF LERCHENAU
(bass)
OCTAVIAN COUNT ROFRANO,
AGED SEVENTEEN *(mezzo-soprano)*
MAJORDOMUS OF THE
FELDMARSCHALLIN *(tenor)*
VALZACCHI, AN INTRIGANT
(tenor)
ANNINA, HIS COMPANION
(mezzo-soprano)
HERR VON FANINAL, A RICH,
NEWLY ENNOBLED GENTLEMAN
(baritone)
SOPHIE, HIS DAUGHTER
(soprano)
MARIANNE LEITMETZERIN, HER
CHAPERONE *(contralto)*
MAJORDOMUS OF HERRN VON
FANINAL *(tenor)*
A NOTARY *(bass)*
AN INNKEEPER *(tenor)*
AN ITALIAN SINGER *(tenor)*
THREE ARISTOCRATIC ORPHANS
(soprano, mezzo-soprano, contralto)
A MILLINER *(soprano)*
AN ANIMAL TRADER *(tenor)*
FOUR LAQUAIS OF THE
FELDMARSCHALLIN *(two tenors, two basses)*
COMMISSIONER OF POLICE
(bass)
FOUR WAITERS *(one tenor, three basses)*
A FLUTE PLAYER, A
HAIRDRESSER, HAIRDRESSER'S
ASSISTANT, AN ARISTOCRATIC
WIDOW, A MOOR, KITCHEN
PERSONNEL, SERVANTS,
INTRIGUERS, CHILDREN, THE
MARSCHALLIN'S PAGE

ensuing skirmish, he receives a pinprick wound from his opponent. Ever the deceitful liar, the Baron acts as if the wound is fatal and fools all those around him. Faninal, unwilling to have the Baron's wrath on his hands, issues an ultimatum to his daughter - marry Ochs or enter a convent.

Octavian is determined to protect Sophie from the Baron's clutches. When he learns that Valzacchi and Annina are on the rampage because Ochs has refused to pay them, he decides to let them into his plan to get the Baron out of his beloved's life. The intriguers agree and Annina is despatched to Ochs with a note from Mariandel in which Mariandel agrees to meet him that evening. Needless to say, the odious little man is ecstatic and dances in the salon in glee.

ACT THREE
Valzacchi and Annina own an inn, a rather disreputable one, on the outskirts on Vienna, and let Octavian use one of the rooms for Mariandel's meeting with the Baron. They let him in on a secret - the room he has hired is filled with trap doors, blind windows and other tricks. The couple leave Octavian, dressed in his role as the Marschallin's maid, when they hear Ochs approaching.

The Baron enters, and supper is served. The salacious man attempts to get Mariandel drunk so that he can possess her but the disguised Octavian manages to hold him off. Ochs soon tires of the prolonged seduction and tries to make a move on her. This is the cue Octavian needs. He stamps his foot loudly on the floor. In response, trap doors and windows fly open and spectre-like figures are seen floating through the air. Ochs, superstitious by nature, is terrified. Panicking, he yells for help.

The Commissioner of Police and some of his men soon arrive on the scene. Caught in a compromising situation, Ochs frantically claims that the woman with him is Sophie von Faninal, his fiancée. Of course, the plotters have not left anything to chance and have called Faninal to the scene. The Baron, in a desperate attempt to extricate himself from the situation he has created, pretends not to know Faninal.

The confusion reaches a climax when the Marschallin, in a resplendent court dress, enters in answer to Ochs' summons. She quickly sizes up the situation and persuades the Commissioner, whom she recognises as her husband's former orderly, that the whole affair was just a practical joke. Sophie, who has likewise been called to the scene, informs the Baron that both she and her father never want to see him again and that the wedding is cancelled.

Sophie is reassured by the Marschallin, who dismisses Ochs. The Baron leaves like a whipped dog, with Annina, children, servants and creditors in pursuit, all wanting a piece of him. When the Marschallin is left with only the two young lovers, she thrusts Octavian into Sophie's arms. She renounces any claim on Octavian and tells him to marry Sophie, then leaves to comfort the disconcerted Faninal. Mahomet runs in to fetch the handkerchief which Sophie has dropped. He picks it up from the floor, triumphantly waves it in the air and runs off after the others.

SIMON BOCCANEGRA
Melodrama in three acts in Italian

Music: Giuseppe Verdi (1813-1901)
Libretto: Arrigo Boito
First performance: March 24, 1881, Milan, Italy
Duration: 2 1/2 hours
Setting: Genoa and environs, 1364

PROLOGUE

Paolo Albiani and Pietro meet in the dark of the night in the year 1339 and plot to use their influence to get the corsair, Simon Boccanegra, elected Doge. Boccanegra himself is not inclined to become the first man in the city, but Paolo convinces him that once Simon is Doge, Jacopo Fiesco can no longer refuse Simon's request for the hand of Fiesco's daughter, Maria, who is Simon's lover and the mother of his daughter. Boccanegra does not know yet that Maria has just died of a broken heart because her father did not allow her to marry Simon. Jacopo Fiesco appears in front of the palace lamenting Maria's death and blaming her seducer Boccanegra who approaches Fiesco for a reconciliation. Fiesco agrees, provided Boccanegra grants him custody of his granddaughter. Simon reveals that his daughter has been abducted under mysterious circumstances. Subsequently, Fiesco gives him the cold shoulder. Boccanegra goes into the palace to find his beloved dead. When he leaves deeply shaken, the population of Genoa comes to honour him as the new Doge.

ACT ONE

Twenty-five years later, Maria Boccanegra, Simon's daughter, who lives as Amelia Grimaldi in the Count's palace outside of Genoa under the protection of Jacopo Fiesco, alias Andrea. He adopted her when the Grimaldis became ostracized by the community for their political activities. Amelia is waiting for her lover, Gabriele Adorno. She warns him to stay out of a conspiracy of the nobility against Boccanegra who wants to give her in marriage to his favourite, Paolo. When Andrea informs Gabriele that Amelia is a foundling, Gabriele does not waiver in his loyalty. The Doge appears and gives Amelia a document pardoning the Counts Grimaldi. To prevent Simon from mentioning Paolo's marriage proposal, she admits to him that she is an orphan and shows him a miniature portrait of her mother. Simon recognizes his beloved and embraces his newly found daughter. When the Doge tells Paolo that he would have to renounce Amelia, Paolo decides to elope with her.

In the senate, the Doge alone advocates peace with rivalling Venice. The population forces its way into the hall, demanding vengeance for a murder committed by Gabriele Adorno. Gabriele admits to having killed Lorenzino, who planned to kidnap Amelia by order of a powerful person. Gabriele believes that the order came from the Doge and wants to attack him with his sword. Unexpectedly, Amelia interferes. She separates the two enemies and asks her father for mercy for Gabriele which Boccanegra grants. He suspects that Paolo is the initiator of this bungled kidnap attempt and orders Paolo as a guarantor for public safety to publicly curse the responsible party, which Paolo does filled with terror.

Cast:

SIMON BOCCANEGRA, DOGE OF GENOA *(baritone)*
MARIA BOCCANEGRA, ALIAS AMELIA GRIMALDI, HIS DAUGHTER *(soprano)*
JACOPO FIESCO, ALIAS ANDREA *(bass)*
GABRIELE ADORNO, ARISTOCRAT FROM GENOA *(tenor)*
PAOLO ALBIANI, FAVOURITE COURTIER OF THE DOGE *(baritone)*
PIETRO, COURTIER *(baritone)*
CAPTAIN OF THE ARCHERS *(tenor)*
AMELIA'S MAID *(soprano)*
SOLDIERS, SAILORS, SENATORS, SERVANTS OF FIESCO, COURT OF THE DOGE AND PRISONERS

ACT TWO

Paolo pours a slow acting deadly poison in the Doge's drink. Then he attempts to instigate Fiesco and Gabriele to murder Simon. Fiesco declines but Gabriele is willing. He believes Paolo's lies that Amelia is the Doge's lover. In the meantime, Amelia admits her love for Gabriele to her father whereupon the Doge promises to grant his enemy amnesty. After taking a sip from the poisoned cup, Boccanegra falls asleep, thus giving Gabriele the opportunity for an assassination attempt. However, Amelia interferes again, and upon awakening, Simon explains to Gabriele that Amelia is his daughter. Immediately, he asks Simon for forgiveness and swears allegiance to Boccanegra, while the rebelling party of the nobility is already approaching the palace.

ACT THREE

The rebellion has been quelled. Boccanegra releases Fiesco but condemns Paolo to death. Paolo triumphantly announces that the Doge will die of his poison before Paolo is executed because of his poison. Fiesco rejoices. However, Simon recognizes in him the father of his beloved and again offers him a reconciliation. He can now present his long lost granddaughter. Fiesco is touched and accepts. Boccanegra's last deed is to appoint Gabriele Adorno Doge of Genoa. Fiesco announces Simon's death.

Cast:

Floria Tosca (*soprano*)
Mario Cavaradossi, painter (*tenor*)
Baron Scarpia, Chief of Police (*baritone*)
Cesare Angelotti, an escaped political prisoner (*bass*)
The Sacristan (*baritone*)
Spoletta, agent (*tenor*)
Sciarrone, a police officer (*bass*)
A shepherd boy (*alto*)
A gaoler (*bass*)
Choristers, police agents, soldiers, citizens of Rome

Tosca

Opera in three acts in Italian

Music: Giacomo Puccini
Libretto: Giuseppe Giacoso and Luigi Illica
First performance: January 14, 1900, Rome, Italy
Duration: 2 hours
Setting: Rome, June 17, 1800 and the dawn of the next day

ACT ONE

Angelotti, once a consul of the Roman Republic but now an escaped political prisoner, enters the church of Sant' Andrea della Valle in Rome. He retrieves the key to the family chapel from the base of the Madonna's statue, left there by his sister, the Marchesa Attavanti in a bid to aid in his escape. Footsteps are heard as he opens the door with the key and enters.

The Sacristan enters to perform his duties of dusting and cleaning. The sound of the Angelus brings him to his knees in prayer and heralds Cavaradossi's arrival at the church. The painter is there to continue his painting of Mary Magdalene, based on the likeness of the Marchesa. When the Sacristan finishes his prayers and leaves, Angelotti emerges from his hiding place and reveals himself to the artist. Recognising him as the Marchesa's brother, Cavaradossi agrees to help him. Suddenly he hears the voice of Flora Tosca, his lover, calling his name. Quickly he shoves the food basket lying at the foot of his easel into Angelotti's hands and pushes him back into the chapel.

Tosca overhears her lover speaking in hushed tones to someone hiding in the dark. Of an extremely jealous nature, she suspects that Cavaradossi is unfaithful to her. The painter assures her that there is no other woman in his life. They agree to meet that night in his country villa. Cavaradossi then urges her to leave so that he can continue working on his painting. She misinterprets this as an effort to get rid of her so that he can continue with his rendezvous with another lover, maybe the Marchesa, whose features she can make out in his current painting.

Tosca leaves and the painter releases Angelotti. While both men speak of their loathing for the evil Scarpia, they hear the cannon shot which signifies that the guards have discovered Angelotti's escape. Feeling that he must do something for the man, Cavaradossi promises to hide him in a disused well at his villa, and the two men make their way there.

The Sacristan announces that Napoleon has been defeated by the Austrians at Marengo and a thanksgiving cantata, with Tosca as the main soloist, will be held at the Palazzo Farnese that night. Then Scarpia enters, accompanied by Spoletta. The police chief has tracked Angelotti to the church and means to find his man.

On Scarpia's orders that church is searched. The search yield the empty food basket and a fan bearing the Attavanti coats of arms, implicating Cavaradossi. Scarpia is quick to make the connection between his prisoner's escape and the painter's abetment. Tosca has returned to tell her lover that she will be not be able to meet him that night. In place of Cavaradossi, she finds the dreaded Scarpia. The police chief, who has lusted after the singer for a long time, sees this coincidence as a wonderful opportunity to recapture his prisoner and rid himself of Cavaradossi so that Tosca can be his. He offers the fan to her as evidence of Cavaradossi's infidelity, and even goes so far as to incriminate the Marchesa as the other woman. Tosca storms off. Spoletta is told by Scarpia to follow her in the hopes that she will lead them to Cavaradossi and Angelotti in turn.

ACT TWO
After sending a message to Tosca requesting that she join him after her performance, Scarpia settles down to supper. Spoletta returns and reports that he has not been able to locate the escaped criminal but has the painter in custody. Cavaradossi is brought in and, with Tosca's voice leading the cantata in the background, Scarpia relentlessly interrogates him. The artist, however, has strong will power and does not give away Angelotti's hiding place. Unable to extract any information from him, Scarpia orders that he be tortured. As Cavaradossi is being dragged out, Tosca arrives. They pass each other and Cavaradossi warns her, under his breath, to hold her tongue.

Scarpia questions Tosca who firmly keeps quiet. To goad her into speaking, the cruel police chief opens a concealed door through which Tosca is able to hears her lover's screams of anguish as he is tortured. Despite her jealous nature, she cannot bear to hear his cries of pain. She tearfully informs Scarpia of Angelotti's hiding place.

The excruciating torment of Cavaradossi is halted and he is brought into the room. Tosca rushes to his side. He, however, is more concerned about Angelotti's safety and asks her if she has said anything. Before she can answer, Scarpia directs Spoletta to the garden well at the painter's villa, telling him to hurry before Angelotti escapes again. Cavaradossi realises that Tosca has betrayed them all. Sciarrone rushes in to report that the Austrians are not victorious after all - Napoleon is now attacking the retreating Austrians. The painter exults, whereupon Scarpia orders his immediate execution as traitor.

Once Cavaradossi has been removed, Tosca begs for his life, only to be told that it will be at a price - her body. She does not blink an eye as she agrees to Scarpia's demands. The chief tells Spoletta to arrange for a mock execution, very much like the one they did for Palmieri. As his agent leaves, Scarpia starts to write a note of safe conduct for the lovers. Tosca notices a sharp knife on the supper table, and when the loathsome man starts to embrace her, she snatches it and plunges it into his body. Tosca pries the safe conduct from his hands as he takes his final breath. Before leaving the room, she places a crucifix on his lips and lights two candles by his side.

ACT THREE
Morning is about to dawn on the battlements of Castel Sant' Angelo and its surrounding pastures where a shepherd sings of the glories of a new day. As the city bells ring in the hour, Cavaradossi is led by his gaoler to the site of his execution. The condemned man, in the last few minutes of his life, bribes the gaoler into letting him write a last farewell to the woman he loves.

Just as he scribbles his last word, Tosca enters, bearing the letter of safe conduct. She tells Cavaradossi that she has murdered Scarpia and that he has nothing to fear as the upcoming firing will be faked. They sing of their future together and rehearse the mock execution. Spoletta enters with the firing squad, and in a volley of shots the artist falls to the ground. As the soldiers leave, Tosca approaches Cavaradossi, but he is dead. Scarpia had cheated her.

As she wallows in her grief, distant shouts are heard. Scarpia's dead body has been found and she is wanted for murder. Spoletta hurries in to arrest her. Knowing that her fate is sealed, Tosca, with a cry to Scarpia that they will meet before God, throws herself down from the battlements.

Cast:

Violetta Valery, courtesan *(soprano)*
Alfredo Germont, her lover *(tenor)*
Giorgio Germont, his father *(baritone)*
Doctor Grevil *(bass)*
Baron Douphol *(baritone)*
Marchese d'Obigny *(bass)*
Flora Bervoix *(mezzo-soprano)*
Gastone, Vicomte de Letorieres *(tenor)*

La Traviata
Opera in three acts in Italian

Music: Guiseppe Verdi
Libretto: Francesco Maria Piave
First performance: March 6, 1853, Venice, Italy
Duration: 2 1/4 hours
Setting: Paris and environs, about 1700

ACT ONE
A party is in full swing at a mansion in Paris. The hostess is the courtesan Violetta Valery, who is informed by one of her guests, Gastone, that his friend, Alfredo, is in love with her. She laughs at this ludicrous idea. As Violetta prepares to follow her guests to the dance floor, she is seized by a coughing fit and collapses into a chair. Alfredo

is her only witness, and he takes this opportunity to declare his love for her in a moving serenade. Violetta warns him that it would be better for them to remain friends, but she hands him a camellia blossom and allows him to return when the flower is wilted - in other words: the next day. The guests depart for another party and take Alfredo with them, leaving their hostess behind.

Violetta, in a tumult of emotions, is moved by Alfredo's proclamations and thinks for a moment that perhaps she will be able to leave her present circumstances and start a new life with him. These thoughts are soon quelled when Violetta admits to herself that it is too late for her to change. She has lived the life of pleasure for too long and has revelled in its delights. She sings of her zest for celebration while Alfredo's plaintive song can be heard in the background.

ACT TWO
Violetta and Alfredo have set up a country house together outside Paris. Violetta's maid, Annina, informs Alfredo that their lifestyle has almost bankrupted Violetta. Alfredo leaves for Paris to raise the money to repay her.

A visitor is announced to Violetta. Alfredo's father, Giorgio Germont, has come to plead with Violetta for his son's freedom. Alfredo's association with her has resulted in dire repercussions. Germont's daughter's fiancé has broken off the engagement when the latter's family learned of Alfredo's affair. Violetta finally accedes to Germont's request.

Violetta composes a farewell letter to Alfredo, telling him of her decision to return to her former lover Baron Douphol, who will support her in the style to which she was accustomed. Alfredo interrupts her, explaining that his father is to be expected shortly. To allow them some privacy, Violetta departs, after bidding Alfredo a passionate and emotional goodbye.

While Germont is visiting his son, Violetta's note is brought in. Alfredo impatiently opens it and reads about his lover's decision. Overcome by powerful emotions, he collapses into his father's arms. Germont follows his son to Paris in search of Violetta.

Alfredo arrives in the middle of a fancy dress party filled with guests dressed as gypsies, matadors and picadors. Soon Violetta walks in on Douphol's arm. To her dismay, Alfredo begins to gamble with the Baron and the stakes are raised every round. Alfredo is on a winning streak when supper is announced.

Violetta returns with Alfredo in her wake. She begs him to stop this foolishness and leave before Douphol's anger leads them into a duel. Alfredo accuses her of caring more for the Baron than for him. As much as it pains her, Violetta keeps her promise to Germont and spurns Alfredo. Her lover's fury knows no bounds and he calls the guests together. To publicly censure her for her disloyalty, he throws his winnings into her face. The crowd wavers between sympathy and disgust. Germont is deeply perturbed. Alfredo repents, while Violetta assures him of her love. But Douphol challenges him to a duel.

ANNINA *(mezzo-soprano)*
GIUSEPPE, VIOLETTA'S SERVANT *(bass)*
SERVANTS AND FRIENDS

281

ACT THREE

Soon after, Violetta is found deadly ill in bed attended by Annina. Dr. Grevil tells her that she will soon recover but confides in Annina that her mistress will probably not last the night. Violetta who has lived so close to life all her years knows that the end is drawing near. She remembers that Germont has informed Alfredo of the agreement between her and his father and alerted her that Alfredo is on his way to be by her side. Alfredo bursts into the room and takes Violetta into his arms.

The doctor returns with Germont, in a last bid to save her, but Violetta knows that life is ebbing and sings a dying farewell. However, that effort costs her dearly and she collapses into the chair again, this time never to regain consciousness. Alfredo hold the lifeless body of his beloved.

Cast:

Tamino *(tenor)*
Three ladies, in the service of the Queen of Night *(soprano, soprano, mezzo-soprano)*
Papageno *(baritone)*
The Queen of Night *(soprano)*
Monostatos *(tenor)*
Pamina *(soprano)*
Three wise boys *(soprano, soprano, mezzo-soprano)*
The Speaker of the Temple *(bass)*
Sarastro *(bass)*
Two priests *(tenor, bass)*
Papagena *(soprano)*
Two men in armour *(tenor, bass)*
Priests, people

Die Zauberflöte

Opera in two acts

Music: Wolfgang Amadeus Mozart
Libretto: Emanuel Schikaneder
First performance: September 30, 1791, Vienna, Austria
Duration: 2 1/2 hours
Setting: Realm of the Queen of the Night and Realm of Sarastro in the Times of Fairytales

ACT ONE

Lost in a forest, Prince Tamino battles with an enormous serpent. When he falls to the ground in a swoon, three ladies appear and spear the snake. Aware that someone has to inform their mistress, the Queen of the Night, that Tamino is in the forest, and unwilling to leave him alone with her companions, the three leave together to bring the news. Tamino rouses from his stupor. He spots a curious-looking individual that is half-man and half-bird, who introduces himself as Papageno, the Queen's bird-catcher. The three ladies who have returned present Tamino with a picture of Pamina, the Queen's daughter, who is imprisoned by the magician Sarastro. Tamino is taken by her beauty and vows that he will go to her rescue. His declaration brings the Queen who promises him Pamina's hand if he can free her.

The Queen departs and the bird-catcher returns. For his quest, Tamino is given a magic flute and Papageno, who is to accompany him, receives a set of magic bells. The three ladies tell them that these two instruments will help them on their journey. Their parting advice to the two is to listen to the guidance of the three wise boys.

In Sarastro's palace, Monostatos is chasing Pamina. Out of breath, the girl faints. Before the Moor can reach her, Papageno, who has become separated from Tamino, stumbles into the room. Monostatos is caught off guard and flees. The bird-catcher recognises Pamina and wakes her gently, telling her that Tamino loves her and has come to rescue her. Tamino is led to a temple by the three wise boys who, before taking their leave, advise him to be silent, patient and persistent. The Speaker of the Temple tells Tamino that he has been deceived - Sarastro is not an evil man but an enlightened sage. He counsels the prince seek wisdom. Tamino picks up the magic flute and starts to play and sing. The sweet tones bring the animals of the wild to him and they lie at Tamino's feet mesmerized.

The bird-catcher and Pamina appear, with Monostatos and his henchmen in hot pursuit. Papageno eludes them and begins a tune on the magic bells. The chimes fill the air and cause Monostatos and his men to dance to another part of the grounds. Papageno and Pamina remain, elated that they have escaped. A trumpet call heralds the arrival of Sarastro. Pamina throws herself at the magician's feet, begging for clemency. Sarastro helps her to the feet and tells her not to worry. The Moor of Pamina's nightmares returns with the man of her dreams. Love blossoms as the young girl and the prince recognise one another.

ACT TWO
Sarastro commands Tamino and Pamina to follow him into the temple, where they will be required to prove the purity of their love. Only then will they be able to outwit the Queen of the Night and thwart her powerful schemes. In a vault within the temple, Tamino and Papageno are being instructed to keep silent, no matter what or whom they encounter on their way. Soon the Queen of the Night's three ladies appear and try to persuade the two to abscond with them. Papageno is dying to speak but Tamino reminds him of the pledge they have made. The three ladies flee when they hear angry voices outside.

Pamina is dreaming of her princely love. Monostatos watches her and is startled by the unexpected materialisation of the princess' mother. The Queen of the Night awakens her daughter and charges her to kill Sarastro. The Queen's directives are overheard by the malicious Moor, who tries to blackmail the innocent girl. However, Sarastro walks by just in time to catch Monostatos harassing Pamina and promptly dismisses him.

Meanwhile, the prince and his companion are undergoing their second test. They are again told to kept quiet. Tamino starts a tune on the flute. The lilting melody carries in the air and soon brings Pamina to his side. Much to her dismay, our hero, ever resolute in his decision to obey the rules set by the priests, does not even notice her. In despair, she moans of his unfeeling behaviour and her lost love. The three wise boys prevent the downcast Pamina from killing herself because she is dejected over Tamino's behaviour. They explain to her that the prince has not forsaken her and that he was bound by an oath of silence. Pamina is thrilled to discover this and with her faith restored, leave with the three boys in search of her one true love.

As Tamino walks to his final ordeal, he is joined by Pamina. The ultimate test of their worth is a trial by fire and water, which they pass through with the help of the magic flute and the love they bear for one another. As they emerge unscathed, the chorus rejoices in a triumphant refrain. Monostatos, the Queen of the Night and the three ladies sneak into the temple to create chaos and confusion. Unprepared for the forces that await them, they are repelled and banished from the temple walls.

GLOSSARY

acciaccatura
a disonant note in a chord, which is released immediately after all the notes in the chord are played, leaving only the main notes in the chord to sound

appoggiatura
a strong disonant grace note, usually a single scale step up or down, used to enhance the melody and bring it a more graceful resolution

aria
an elaborate song for a solo voice, generally with an instrumental accompaniment

baritone
the male voice which lies between the tenor and the bass

baroque (French)
the period from 1600, when the first operas were composed, to the death of Handel in 1759; baroque operas are highly stylized presentations, with elaborate vocal requirements and fanciful plots

bass
the lowest of the male voices

bass-baritone
the male voice with a resonant bass and a strong upper register in the baritone range

baton (French)
a conductor's slender stick used to beat time and cue the entry of a singer or an instrument and indicate loudness and phrasing

bel canto
literally meaning 'beautiful song', it refers to a style of singing that emphasises an even tone, elegant phrasing, and agile technique

billet-doux (French)
a love letter

breeches role
man's role played by a woman

cabaletta
a contradictory or complementary state of mind which may spur the character on stage towards impassioned action, it is either a short aria with a repetitive persistent rhythm; or the concluding section of a long aria or duet that usually has a rapid tempo with increasing excitement

cadenza
a musical passage that contains difficult scales and allows the soloist to display his technical skills as the orchestra joins in only at the initial and closing chords, which usually appears toward the end of a movement or composition or between sections of a movement

cantata
a composition written for voices, with instrumental accompaniment, that is used as a setting for a story to be sung but not acted, and generally has no story line

canzonetta
a short and lyrical operatic song

cavatina
a short piece of music, occasionally instrumental rather than vocal, with a slower tempo and relatively simpler structure than the conventional aria

chest notes
the sound of a singer's voice when he sings at the lower end of his range, often resounding in the chest and usually deep, thick and sometimes rough

chord
a group of two or more notes to be played at the same time

chromatic
a scale pattern which may be used by a singer to embellish a melody line, created by playing all the black and white keys of the piano in sequence

claque (French)
a group of people who are paid to attend a performance and applaud

classical
the period from 1756, which marks the birth of Mozart, to 1830, three years after the death of Beethoven; classical operas were elegant, formal and restrained

coloratura
a description of a soprano, or a style of singing which demands great feats of agility from the singer – fast singing, high singing, trills and embellishments

continuo
the continuous bass line that accompanies the melody, found very often in the music of the baroque period

contralto
the lowest female voice, also known as the alto

contrapuntal
see *counterpoint*

counterpoint
a technique of combining two or more independent musical lines to produce a more harmonious texture

countertenor
a high male voice, generally with a singing range within that of the female contralto or mezzo-soprano, also called the male alto,

crescendo
a musical direction to perform with increasing loudness or a combination of notes that are played or sung in rapid sequence, gradually building to a climax

da capo
Italian for 'from the beginning', it is a direction to repeat a section or whole composition from the beginning

decoration
see *embellishment*

dei ex machina (Latin)
plural of *deus ex machina*

deus ex machina
literally meaning the 'god out of a machine', it is a literary or staging device which refers to the interference of a supernatural being, who has been watching the events unfold from afar and who steps in to salvage a seemingly hopeless situation

diva
a female opera star of great rank and held in high esteem

double mordent
a musical ornament consisting of four notes, a repetition of the principal note and the note below, played sequentially

dramma giocoso
an opera which combines both serious and comic elements

duet
a composition, either with or without musical accompaniment, written for two performers, in which both soloists are given equal importance

embellishment
the addition of extra notes or group of notes to an established melody line which may either enhance the melody or rhythm, or provide the harmony with a richer tone

encore (French)
an additional piece, either one already presented or a reserve piece, that is performed in response to the audience's enthusiastic reception

falsetto
a singing technique employed by any of the male voices to extend the upper end of his normal range in an attempt to imitate a woman's voice, often for comic effect

grace notes
an ornament to be sung or played very quickly just before a main note, whose effect is to give a sharp accent to that note

habanera (Spanish)
a slow Cuban dance, similar to the tango and named for the city of Havana, very popular in Spain during the nineteenth century

heldentenor (German)
a tenor who is able to combine his high notes with a robust lower voice, and is able to sing the long passages that demand great vocal stamina

imbroglio
a confused and chaotic operatic scene, accompanied by a diversity in rhythm and melody

intermezzo
a brief musical interlude, usually of a light-hearted nature, inserted between the acts of an opera

inverted turn
a musical ornament consisting of four notes, starting one note below the principal note, going in sequence to one note above, returning and ending on the principal note

leitmotif (German)
a short, musical phrase or passage used to represent a character, emotion, object, place, idea or even a dominant theme or underlying pattern, which recurs throughout a musical composition

lever (French)
the daily ceremonial dressing of a person of high rank, especially royalty, in the presence of courtiers and other privileged guests, as for the Marschallin in ROSENKAVALIER

libretto
the words of an opera, which may have been written by someone other than the composer of the music

lyric soprano
a high-pitched, sweet voice

maestro
an honorary title or form of address bestowed upon distinguished composers, musicians, or conductors

majordomus (Latin)
the head of all servants pertaining to a large household as in CAPRICCIO

mannerism
a sixteenth-century art style characterized by the distortion of realistic proportions, contorted figures and an avoidance of classical balance

metronome
a mechanical device for keeping a steady beat at various speeds

mezzo
see *mezzo-soprano*

mezzo-soprano
the female voice that lies between the soprano and the contralto

mordent
a musical ornament consisting of two notes, the principal note and the note below played sequentially

Nachschlag (German)
a pair of notes added to the end of a trill or an ornament added to a single note, to be played after that note and showing its time value

obbligato
a musical line or an instrumental part in the accompaniment of a vocal work, which may not be omitted, that compliments the main melody

opera buffa
a comic opera

opera seria
an opera characterized by the stylised treatment of mythological or classical subjects, often with tragic consequences, and its extensive use of arias

operetta
a humourous drama composed of spoken lyrics and popular music

opus (latin)
meaning 'work', a term used, to number in order of composition, musical works by a single composer

oratorio
generally similar to the cantata, it is, however, longer, more elaborate, carries a plot and utilises narrators to explain and connect the events of the story

ornamentation
see *embellishment*

overture
the instrumental introduction, which frequently incorporates the themes of the opera, to a musical drama or oratorio

pitch
the location of a sound on a scale ranging from high to low

prelude (French)
the introductory instrumental composition to an individual act within a musical drama, or any short romantic composition

prima donna (Latin)
the leading female singer in the opera

prima donne
plural of *prima donna*

prompter
a person who provides vocal cues to performers before they are required to sing them

proscenium (Latin)
strictly speaking, the part of the stage between the curtain and the orchestra pit, the term now more generally used to refer to a stage constructed with a formal closure like a curtain

proscenium arch (Latin)
the architectural arch which encloses the curtain

raked stage
a stage which slants upward away from the view of the audience, such that an audience member sitting in the back of the theatre is able to have a clear view of a performer at the back of the stage

range
the entire series of notes, from high to low, that a voice or musical instrument is capable of performing

recitative
a style of singing that is similar to speech, has relatively few changes in pitch and rhythm, and is governed largely by the rhythm of the text

repetiteur (French)
an opera singer's tutor or coach

roccoco
a highly decorative style which is based on disrupted baroque forms and structures

romantic
the period from 1830 and the turn of the 20th century; romantic operas have a strong emphasis on feelings, and composers of this time often sought inspiration in other than musical ideas, such as painting, literature, acts of nature, and nature itself

soprano
the highest of the female voices

sotto voce
a musical whisper, sung in an undertone

staccato
a type of singing or playing that is characterized by notes that are performed quickly, lightly and separated from the notes before and after it

structure
the way elements of a musical composition are put together

surtitles
a translation of the text of the opera which is projected on a screen usually placed above the stage

tempi (Latin)
plural of *tempo*

tempo
the speed at which a passage or composition is to be performed

tenor
the highest of the male voices

tercet
a group of three lines that rhyme with one another or are connected by rhyme with an adjacent triplet or triplets

trill
the most common musical ornament, it refers to two adjacent notes which are repeated rapidly

turn
a musical ornament consisting of four notes, starting one note above the principal note, going in sequence to one note below, returning and ending on the principal note

vibrato
the slight wavering in pitch that occurs when a singer sustains a particular note

BIBLIOGRAPHY

Budden, Julian. **THE OPERAS OF VERDI in three volumes**. 1973-1981. (Cassell)
Blow-by-blow study of the entire output, placed in the context of Italian operatic history - unsurpassed in its detail, unrivalled in authority

Carner, Mosco. **PUCCINI**. 1958 revised 1992. (Duckworth)
Classic full-scale study of the man and his music

Christiansen, Rupert. **PRIMA DONNA: A HISTORY**. 1984 revised 1995. (Pimlico)
Engaging portrait gallery of the great divas, of how they happened and what made them tick - the 'glamorous, dressy, jokey' Kiri Te Kanawa is praised for her consistent loveliness of voice and exceptional self-assurance

Conrad, Peter. **A SONG OF LOVE AND DEATH**. 1987. (Chatto and Windus)
Pungent, virtuoso survey of operatic history by a British-based Tasmanian which incorporates strong, shrewd appraisals of Mozart, Verdi and Strauss

Dean, Winton. **HÄNDEL AND THE OPERA SERIA**. 1970. (Oxford)
An authoritative view of how Händel dealt with different sorts of opera seria from the heroic to the magical

Dean, Winton; and Knapp, John Merrill. **HÄNDEL'S OPERAS: 1704-1726**. 1987. (Oxford)
A more detailed study, treating each opera separately and telling you all you need to know about each work

Fingleton, David. **KIRI: A BIOGRAPHY OF KIRI TE KANAWA**. 1983. (Athenaeum)
A highly readable and enjoyable book containing the facts about Kiri's career up to 1982

Earl of Harewood, The (Ed.). **KOBBE'S COMPLETE OPERA BOOK**. 1987 (10th edition). (Bodley Head)
Most famous of all compendiums of operatic synopses, begun more than a century ago by Gustav Kobbe, but Lord Harewood's updating is what matters

Jacobs, Arthur; and Sadie, Stanley. **THE OPERA GUIDE**. 1964. (Hamish Hamilton)
Reliable study of the mainstream repertoire, in a composer-by-composer format

Kenyon, Nicholas; Walsh, Stephen; and Holden, Amanda (Ed). **THE VIKING OPERA GUIDE**. 1993. (Viking)
Lavish modern guide, presented on a composer-by-composer basis with short, sharp critical studies of each opera, clear synopses, and recommended recordings

Kerman, Joseph. **OPERA AS DRAMA**. 1956 revised 1989 (Faber)
Brilliantly quirky and elitist study of the key works of operatic history, where the argument of the book is based impressively on the belief that 'the composer is the dramatist'

Kimbell, David. **ITALIAN OPERA**. 1991. (Cambridge)
Overview of Italian operatic history, with a good coverage on the early years

Mann, William. **RICHARD STRAUSS: A CRITICAL STUDY OF THE OPERAS**. 1964. (Cassell)
Incorporates substantial, readable essays on the three Strauss operas in Kiri Te Kanawa's repertoire

Mann, William. **THE OPERAS OF MOZART**. 1977. (Cassell)
Expertly comprehensive, warm-hearted, witty study of the works in chronological order, filled with fascinating asides about the man and his times

Phillips-Matz, Mary Jane. **VERDI: A BIOGRAPHY**. 1993. (Oxford)
Massive, up-to-date portraits of Italy's greatest opera composer, containing new information about the man and the way he lived

Solomon, Maynard. **MOZART**. 1995. (Hutchinson)
Best of the modern biographies, incorporating a pungent new interpretation of the young composer's troubled relationship with his father